Chasing
Steinbrenner

Other baseball books from Brassey's, Inc.

Bob Feller: Ace of the Greatest Generation, John Sickels

Deadball Stars of the National League,
The Society for American Baseball Research

The World Series' Most Wanted™: The Top 10 Book of Championship Teams, Broken Dreams, and October Oddities, John Snyder

Getting in the Game: Inside Baseball's Winter Meetings, Josh Lewin

Paths to Glory: How Great Baseball Teams Got That Way,
Mark L. Armour and Daniel R. Levitt

Throwbacks: Old-School Baseball Players in Today's Game,
George Castle

Mickey Mantle: America's Prodigal Son, Tony Castro

Baseball's Most Wanted™ II: The Top 10 Book of More Bad Hops, Screwball Players, and Other Oddities, Floyd Conner

Baseball's Most Wanted™: The Top 10 Book of the National Pastime's Outrageous Offenders, Lucky Bounces, and Other Oddities,
Floyd Conner

Chasing Steinbrenner

Pursuing the Pennant in Boston and Toronto

ROB BRADFORD

BRASSEY'S, INC.
Washington, D.C.

Library of Congress Cataloging-in-Publication Data
Bradford, Rob, 1969-
  Chasing Steinbrenner : pursuing the pennant in Boston and Toronto / Rob Bradford.—1st ed.
    p. cm.
  Includes bibliographical references.
  ISBN 1-57488-861-7 (alk. paper)
  1. Boston Red Sox (Baseball team)—Management. 2. Toronto Blue Jays (Baseball team)—
Management. 3. Epstein, Theo, 1973- 4. Ricciardi, J.P., 1959- I. Title.

  GV875.B62B73 2004
  796.357'64'0974461—dc22

                                                                              2004009613

Printed in the United States of America on acid-free paper that meets the American National Standards Institute Z39-48 Standard.

Brassey's, Inc.
22841 Quicksilver Drive
Dulles, Virginia 20166

First Edition

10 9 8 7 6 5 4 3 2 1

To the people who have made me

—Mom, Dad, and Jen

CONTENTS

ACKNOWLEDGMENTS

Making the seemingly impossible possible isn't a one-person job. This much I have learned.

The relatively long road to completion of this project is littered with folks who have served as guiding lights for someone who sometimes appeared lost in the wilderness that is constructing a book project. My hope is that I can somehow relay my appreciation for some of those folks. As I learned from the teenage boy in Dunedin who slipped J.P. Ricciardi a note of thanks on the final day of spring training without uttering a word, it doesn't take much to let someone know you care.

Unfortunately, words sometimes don't seem to be enough (at least for the deliverer of the message), and that is how I feel when mentioning some of the people who have served as the chief tour guides for this most crooked of roads. Topping that list is John Paul Ricciardi, the former scout who used to go out of his way in the Fenway Park dining room to talk basketball with a fellow high school basketball coach who carried no weight among a room usually full of baseball power. In the cutthroat world of media, scouts, and other executives, there is no more genuine person in any business than J.P. His faith and support throughout the entire project is as inspirational of an act as I could imagine.

Also residing at the pinnacle of my appreciation are the people running the Boston Red Sox. In among one of the most difficult professional scenarios any group of people could ever endure, they showed a level of kindness and acceptance that would be difficult for most to fathom.

As I also came to realize, dealing with the story in front of you is only a fraction of the process. And leading the charge behind the scenes was my literary agent, Barbara Collins Rosenberg, whose expertise, commitment, and belief helped overcome even the most precarious of obstacles. Chris Kahrl, Kevin Cuddihy, Teresa Metcalfe, and Julie Kimmel of Brassey's, Inc., are others whose understanding and belief in the project were an author's best ally. Their tireless work is the foundation upon which the completion of the book has been built.

There were also those who helped me in not stepping on my toes too many times when it came to both putting the actual words on paper, and simply surviving the process. The feedback and support from people like Bob Albright, Phil Stacey, Bob Hohler, Chris Price, John Tomase, Alex Speier, Jackie MacMullan, Dan Shaughnessy, Nick Cafardo, Steve Krasner, Sean McAdam, Wendi Nix, Bob Schron, Mike Muldoon, Jim Fenton, Bill Doyle, and Leslie Epstein were invaluable for a writer who often needed a little constructive criticism to go with a lot of moral support.

The sacrifice of my coworkers in the sports department at the *Lowell Sun* was an act that I am truly appreciative of. To show the kind of professional patience exhibited by Dennis Whitton, Dave Pevear, Barry Scanlon, Chaz Scoggins, Carmine Frongillo, Rick Harrison, Mike Davidson, and Kevin Keane is about as kindhearted and understanding of an act as could be demonstrated in the newspaper business.

The understanding and assistance from both the Blue Jays and Red Sox organizations were both unbelievably helpful and insightful. In Toronto the cooperation of Paul Godfrey, Rob Godfrey, Keith Law, Tony LaCava, Tim McCleary, Bart Given, Mike Shaw, Jay Stenhouse, Ron Sandelli, Brian Butterfield, and the entire Jays organization left me with memories I'll never forget and a new bunch of guys to root for. And in Boston, the acceptance and help of Theo Epstein, John Henry, Josh Byrnes, Jed Hoyer, Ben Cherington, Galen Carr, Glenn Geffner, Megan McClure, Kerri Moore, and the rest of the Sox front office will never be forgotten. Also of great support were many of the subject's families, whose uniqueness and closeness left the most positive of impressions.

Another group who deserve more thanks than I can give are my chief sounding boards, who absorbed more waves of frustration and anxiety than anyone should be subjected to. Kirk Minihane, the world's greatest screenwriting, J.V.-basketball-coaching, marathon runner in the business. First it was dealing with my near-death experience on "Heartbreak Hill," then came tearing me away from the Niagara Falls casino blackjack tables, and finally was reeling in my sometimes-warped view of reality. My mother, Bonnie Bradford, who not only fixed my punctuation, but often fixed my state of mind with the kind of understanding only a mother could give. My dad, Bill Bradford, for continuing to exude the kind of sports passion that rubbed off on me long enough to write a book about it. (That publicity work you did each morning at Dunkin' Donuts didn't hurt, either.) My brother, Eric Bradford, who taught me how to turn on a computer and try to get into back entrances of seedy music establishments. My wife, Jen Bradford, whose undying support and love is undoubtedly the reason I am able to function. My kids, Taylor, Riley, and Colby, whose smiles, hugs, and drool put it all in perspective.

Thanks to all.

The Birth (and Death) of a Season

"If there is no life, there is no death!"

—Ricky Epstein

Leslie Epstein never understood what this meant. As best he could figure, it was simply his brother being his brother, grieving their mother's death in his own intensely spontaneous way. Maybe it would be better if Leslie had never found out the exclamation's true meaning.

On October 16, 2003, Leslie discovered why it hurts to care so much.

The uncovering of his brother's declaration occurred in the most unsettling of venues. Plain and simple, cut and dried— Yankee Stadium gave Leslie the creeps. He and his wife, Ilene, hated the place. They disliked the team that called it home. And they had no particular fondness for Yankees owner George Steinbrenner, the man whose limitless checkbook left the rest of Major

1

League Baseball scrambling for dollar sign–repelling philosophies.

Still, the Epsteins were drawn to the entire package. When your son is the general manager of the Boston Red Sox, a team one Yankee Stadium–win away from the World Series, it's hard to stay away.

A baseball fan all of his life, Leslie didn't have a hard time embracing Theo Epstein's team. But it was one thing to watch a season unfold, and quite another to watch it unfold as the father of the youngest general manager in Major League Baseball history. The whole family repeatedly asked the question: Was every year this indescribably profound, or was it just because their twenty-nine-year-old son's status was thrusting them into the schedule that, as Red Sox manager Grady Little had described, seemed like "not 162 games, but 162 seasons"? Make that 175 seasons.

This team, the Red Sox of 2003, had lived a good life, one hundred and one wins kind of good. Its death . . . that was another matter, entirely.

Leslie watched the ball sail into the left-field stands. The cheering surrounding him and his family didn't register. Tuning out the external elements at the home of the New York Yankees had become a prerequisite.

It didn't matter that the source of the majestic fly ball was Aaron Boone, a player who Boston had been on the verge of keeping away from New York via a late-June three-way trade. (The Cincinnati Reds backed out of the deal, leaving the Seattle Mariners having to watch their new third baseman settle in at The Stadium instead of Safeco Field. Such particulars wouldn't be a priority until days later.)

And recalling that Tim Wakefield, the knuckle-balling stalwart with the longest Red Sox tenure among any of the team's current players, served up the fateful eleventh-inning pitch wasn't important, either. In the big picture, the faces and names were inconsequential. The result of the moment was anything but.

Leslie's son's team had just lost the seventh, and decisive, game of the American League Championship Series on a home run by

Boone, the Yankees were going to the World Series, and the Red Sox were not. Theo's dad now knew what his brother was talking about. Plenty of teams are left dead in the wake of the Major League's richest team, but only a select few can say they went toe-to-toe with the Yankees and their $180 million payroll without flinching.

Emotions started to bubble in Leslie, a season's worth of emotions. This must have been what his son felt on Opening Day when Tampa Bay's Carl Crawford made the unkindest parting of all—a walk-off home run—creating the first half of an unhappy parallel. Except this wasn't one game, this was a season, a full, rich, rewarding, living, breathing season. And now it was gone—dead.

Why did there have to be so much damn life in this season? The thought would linger with Leslie Epstein for days to come.

Two states away, sitting on a black leather couch in the living room of a comfortable, ranch-style home in West Boylston, Massachusetts, was a forty-four-year-old man who also had lived the life—that of chasing the Yankees in the AL East standings.

The death of J.P. Ricciardi's team was considerably different than the Red Sox's passing. In June, the Toronto Blue Jays were behind by a paper-thin margin, a half game away from calling the Yankees their pennant race equal, but by mid-July they were left focusing on the construction of a contender, falling short of the finished product. Their meeting with baseball mortality might have been more drawn out than Boston's, but the pain was still there.

Ricciardi is the supremely energetic general manager of the Blue Jays, but on the night of Game 7 he was joining the rest of the baseball-watching audience, submerged in the role of innocent bystander.

J.P.'s full head of jet-black hair and still-athletic 5-foot-9 frame suggest a man younger than his birth certificate might suggest (one of the reasons he was consistently lumped in with Theo Epstein, a man fourteen years his junior, as baseball's new breed of bosses). Enthusiasm might have also had something to do with it, a notion being supported while watching his forty-two-inch Panasonic.

3

This might not have been his team playing on the screen in front of him, but any separation couldn't diminish the animation that was cutting loose in the Ricciardi household.

Diane Ricciardi, J.P.'s wife of nineteen years, tried to endure the late-night hours to watch the game. After all, the participants in the Game 7 extravaganza weren't simply in-living-color images. The Ricciardis' lives had been tossed to and fro inside the world of professional baseball long enough so that they had relationships with many of those still holding out hope for that 2003 World Series ring. J.P. had always liked Theo (once trying to hire him), and Cash (Yankees general manager Brian Cashman) was a great guy. Rooting wasn't the thing, but watching was.

But in the middle innings with the Red Sox carrying a 4–1 lead and Yankees starting pitcher Roger Clemens already out of the game, Diane went to bed. The couple's two young children, seven-year-old Dante and five-year-old Mariano, had school in the morning and a sleepless night was much tougher to deal with than not knowing the game's final outcome. If it wasn't the Blue Jays, it wasn't important enough to rely on two extra cups of coffee.

But then came a yell of baseball-induced disbelief, which Diane had heard plenty of times before—through the kitchen, down the hall, past the boys' room, and into Mrs. Ricciardi's sleep-induced unconsciousness. J.P. had just witnessed the death of the Red Sox's season.

The Blue Jays' following had grown by leaps and bounds in and around West Boylston, a forty-nine-mile drive from Boston. Staking claim to a Major League general manager as a resident will do that. But the Central Massachusetts, foliage-covered town still resided smack dab in the middle of perhaps the largest stronghold of fandom in all of sport—Red Sox Nation.

West Boylston bordered Worcester; Worcester was a half a Mass Pike drive from Boston, and Boston, of course, was the origin of the eighty-five-year-old championship celebrating fans-in-waiting. That's why, more than a week after the dearly departed 2003 Red Sox season was laid to rest, Ricciardi couldn't escape the talk.

As the days of October slowly dissolved into November, a few rhythms of J.P.'s hot stove league life were constant with every step in and around the hub of the middle of Massachusetts. First, he was probably going to bump into one of his innumerable cousins, an unavoidable occurrence considering he lived just eleven miles away from his childhood home in the blue-collar east side of Worcester. Second, there were the Game 7 questions.

As a Little Leaguer he was once sponsored by Brown Square Civic Club, then Manzi Funeral Home in American Legion ball. But Ricciardi was now the property of Worcester-area baseball fans. J.P. was the man with the answers—at least when it came to the mysteries of the Major Leagues—and when it came to Game 7 New Englanders had plenty of questions. In a world asking "why," he was Shrewsbury Street's baseball therapist.

J.P. was experienced in every aspect of professional baseball, starting his career in the industry as a New York Mets' minor leaguer and culminating in his current position. But that didn't mean he had the solution to the Red Sox's season-ending problem. Ask him about re-signing Greg Myers or Frank Catalanotto, and he could give you an earful. But Boston? What could he say? He knew he felt bad for his friend, Theo, and he certainly admired the Red Sox's resiliency. But what could Ricciardi possibly express that could satisfy these fans' thirst for resolution?

There was an answer to that question: Nothing.

Ricciardi knew that his neighbors and well-wishers were Red Sox fans, and a bit used to being miserable. J.P. didn't need to give them directions to the edge of the cliff, he understood most Red Sox fans already knew the way. The innocent days of running across from the fields of Worcester to Wonder Bar for post–Little League game pizza were over. The Red Sox season had been killed, and this time the kid from 1 Ingleside Avenue was being subpoenaed by Red Sox Nation to testify to whatever inside scoop he had concerning the murder.

What most of the inquisitors didn't know was the real reason why Ricciardi should have been linked to the life that had been

Boston's 2003 season: He could have been the general manager immersed in Yankee Stadium misery on that blustery night.

Where would the Red Sox have ended up if that were the case? Where and when would Epstein be allowed to show the front office skills he exhibited throughout 2003? Who would have been running the show in SkyDome?

Almost two years before, the fates of two cities' baseball landscapes were being formed with one phone call.

*"Today's game is always different
from yesterday's game."*

—Red Smith

IT WAS MOM'S gym day at the Ricciardi house, and J.P. was supposed to watch the kids. But when Diane got home what she found wasn't part of the deal—a husband talking on the phone while Dante and Mariano were bludgeoning each other in the playroom.

"Jay, what's going on?" said Diane in her best disbelieving wife's voice.

"Billy called. Toronto wants to talk," explained J.P.

What the Blue Jays wanted to talk about on this gray fall day in 2001 was their vacant general manager position. Billy was Oakland A's general manager Billy Beane, the man who had befriended Ricciardi twenty-one years before in Little Falls, New York, and who had worked side by side with J.P. in the A's organization for the past decade.

Billy had been a bonus baby, a first-round pick of the New York Mets, while Ricciardi was the ultimate bottom-feeder of the Single-A food chain, an undrafted free agent. Still, the two hit it off instantly, thanks to endless supplies of endorphin-driven sports conversation.

Years after the playing ended and the decision making began,

6

Ricciardi was Beane's right-hand man in Oakland, carrying the title of the team's player personnel director. But titles didn't really do J.P.'s role with the Athletics justice. He was to what Maddox was to Glavine. They were best friends who worked best together.

J.P. trusted Beane like few others. Only once since Little Falls had the two ever raised their voices to one another in anger, and that was to debate the merits of which collegiate quarterback was better, Dan Marino or John Elway. At the time, Billy was eighteen, two years younger than J.P., but even then, they could filter through the unknown well enough to decipher who was going to be better than the best.

It was this camaraderie that made J.P. believe Billy when he said that this Toronto deal would be a good thing to think about. But Beane also brought a fair share of anger to the phone conversation, stemming from the fact that Oakland's owner, Steve Schott, didn't want to give Blue Jays president Paul Godfrey permission to talk to Ricciardi. Despite the exasperation, both knew that time would most likely solve the Schott dilemma.

The request from Toronto may have been news to Ricciardi, but for the rest of the Oakland organization it was old hat. For that, the A's could thank their twenty-eight-year-old assistant general manager, Paul DePodesta. He was at least partly responsible for the call that was making J.P. shirk his afternoon babysitting duties.

DePodesta was a former Division I college football player, although he may not have looked the part. Despite a slender build and a studious look, his ability to run a 4.7-second forty-yard dash had helped him merge into the world of big-time collegiate athletics. When his playing career was done, it didn't hurt that his school colors of maroon and white belonged to academia's symbol of brilliance—Harvard University.

In 1995, "Depo" took the un-Harvard-like postgraduation path, taking a front office job with the Cleveland Indians for the un-Harvard-like postgraduation salary of $800 a month. A year later he was sitting by himself at Fenway Park, collecting advance scouting info on the Yankees, when Oakland's Ricciardi introduced himself. Nobody had given the just-out-of-college scout the time of day . . . nobody but J.P.

Depo's introduction to Ricciardi was one of those unforgettable moments in a career and a lifetime. It would eventually lead Paul into the inner circle of the A's decision makers starting in 1998, while also exemplifying for him the promise of finding like-minded people like J.P. within the cutthroat business of baseball.

As they spent time together, Depo's respect for Ricciardi grew. Any baseball man's utmost desire is to be able to master the art of evaluation, and Paul was no different. That's why being around J.P. was always helpful. The trips with Ricciardi always included lessons, lessons learned through the miles of scouting trips, sifting through hundreds of aspiring professional ballplayers. One subject that always jumped into DePodesta's memory when rehashing his days with J.P.: Barry Zito. The Oakland A's were thinking about making the off-center left-handed pitcher the ninth pick in the 1999 amateur draft.

It was the weekend before the draft, and the A's front office was divided on the subject. Beane and some scouts were heading to Stanford to take a look-see at a pitcher named Kyle Snyder, while Ricciardi and DePodesta boarded the one-hour Southwest Airlines express to Los Angeles to see USC's Zito.

As the Oakland duo took their place among the small horde of scouts on the Los Angeles campus, they were distinguished from the crowd by one trait in particular: they had no radar gun, the otherwise ubiquitous tool of pitching-hungry bounty hunters.

Ricciardi had seen Zito before. He knew that the only thing the radar gun would do was highlight the pitcher's most negative trait—he could only throw a modest eighty-eight miles per hour. What J.P. wanted to see was if the pitcher was still making batters look foolish. He was.

On the flight back, DePodesta was going through his mental checklist when it came to analyzing pitchers: Where was his arm slot? How was his deception? Was his location consistent? They were all important qualities when it came to finding a player worth picking ninth overall in the draft. J.P.'s checklist was dramatically more streamlined: Could he eventually pitch in the Major Leagues? By the time the orange-and-red plane landed in Los Angeles International Airport, the answer had been uttered over and over again—Yes!

Three years later, Barry Zito was being awarded the 2002 American League Cy Young Award. Ultimately, Paul and J.P.'s answer had been correct.

By the time the post-2001 off-season rolled around, DePodesta had distinguished himself as one of the poster boys for the way the low-budget A's went about doing things. He was also getting the word that Toronto wanted to interview him for its GM job.

Depo's initial reaction was outright surprise, considering that the other candidates being interviewed by Godfrey were Dave Dombrowski, John Hart, and Doug Melvin, all men with distinguished track records when it came to running organizations. He flew to Toronto for the Tuesday interview, believing that it was going to be nothing more than an exercise in making a good impression. Expecting a job offer wouldn't have been realistic.

But then Depo started talking, and Godfrey started listening.

The three other interviewees had all proven their worth with past successes. Dombrowski had built the Florida Marlins from their inception to a World Series win in 1997. Hart had helped make the Cleveland Indians a perennial contender throughout the '90s. Melvin had guided the Texas Rangers to numerous pennant races during his tenure.

DePodesta didn't have their pasts, but he did have his future.

Depo told Godfrey of the way Oakland did things on the kind of limited budget Toronto could afford. There would be more emphasis on statistical analysis, on-base percentage, and drafting the certainty of college players. It wasn't what the other candidates had said, but then again, the others hadn't entered the world of winning with an Oakland-size payroll, either.

The Blue Jays may have won World Series championships under the watch of the esteemed general manager, Pat Gillick, in 1992 and '93, but since then the payroll had been climbing and the win total wasn't rising with it. Gillick's replacement, Gord Ash, put together some solid teams in his seven seasons, but none finished higher than the perennial first- and second-place finishes of the Yankees and Red Sox.

As far as Godfrey and Rogers Communications (which had taken over the check-signing duties in 2000) were concerned, it was time to go in another direction, and DePodesta was the man to show them the map.

Depo was supposed to be hearing from Toronto by Monday, six days after his meeting with Godfrey. But he had already made up his mind that Oakland was where he wanted to be. He formulated exactly what he would say in a preemptive phone call to the Blue Jays on Friday. He was getting married in three weeks, he liked living in the Bay Area, and he enjoyed working with Beane. It was nothing against Toronto, especially one of the most likeable team presidents in baseball in Godfrey, but DePodesta just wanted to stay in place for now.

His plan was completely derailed on Thursday. When Depo returned home, Godfrey had already left a message asking Paul to call him. Panic set in. He wasn't ready to give his speech, but he called nonetheless, and what he heard brought back that high school gridiron feeling of taking an ear-hole shot on a pass across the middle—it woke Paul up in a hurry.

The Toronto Blue Jays wanted Depo to be their general manager.

There were more than a few quiet seconds across the line between Godfrey and DePodesta. "Are you floored?" asked the Blue Jays' president. Of course he was. Not only because of the opportunity, but also because Depo had to utilize the rough draft of why he didn't want the job. Now it was Godfrey's chance to be floored.

By this time, Dombrowski was headed for Detroit and Hart seemed a lock for Texas, yet all of the pre-DePodesta candidates hadn't really entered Godfrey's mind when he got the rejection from his first choice. The Blue Jays' president was more concerned with how he could find that same Oakland brand of winning on a budget that Depo had teased him with.

That's where J.P. came in.

"Never surrender opportunity for security."

—Branch Rickey

DIANE DIDN'T KNOW what to make of this phone call that had pulled her husband away from the kids. Maybe it wouldn't matter in the end, anyway, since the A's were still balking at giving J.P. permission to talk with Godfrey. But a week later, Schott succumbed, leaving Mrs. Ricciardi more nervous than her general manager–candidate spouse.

The couple talked, and both decided that interviewing could only be a good thing. If nothing else it would make Oakland value J.P.'s services even more. What it also did was make Diane realize how much she loved West Boylston and leaving the area she grew up in petrified her.

Forget the power, the money, and everything else that accompanied being in charge of a Major League Baseball team. She liked driving her pickup truck down Route 9. She did not want her husband to get this job.

Their lives had taken them to places such as the Mericopa Inn in Mesa, Arizona, and a street in Helena, Montana, fittingly named Last Chance Gulch. But Toronto? Just when Diane thought the family had found its niche, the journey was potentially starting all over again.

J.P. had made his name in the world of scouting, but it was the former Diane DiPalato who first staked the claim to the discovery of her husband.

Her initial report had been on a sixteen-year-old Ricciardi, the popular kid from the school over on Worcester's Grafton Street, a healthy bus ride from Diane's Shrewsbury classroom. It was the summer before Diane would head into eighth grade and she had

11

joined her friend, Lisa Pellagrino, in staking out the scene at the annual city get-together at Foley Stadium.

"Who is that in the white shorts?" Diane asked Lisa, pointing to J.P., who was in the middle of joining one of his endless stream of cousins, Jimmy, in showing off at the extravaganza's football toss event.

Eye contact was made, and the initial scouting report had been filed, albeit only in Diane's head and not to her parental scouting bureau.

It wasn't until later that school year that Diane saw J.P. again, this time thanks to a picture in the *Worcester Telegram and Gazette* of him throwing his slight-yet-sleek body around the basketball court for St. Peter's–Marian High School. The photo led to subsequent scouting assignments, each coming at every one of St. Peter's home hoops games. Finally, the persistence paid off one night, with a mutual friend giving the two of them rides home.

Diane had gotten a read on her subject, now she was ready to close the deal. The couple-to-be arranged a walk to East Park, and then another, and another. Six months of walks later, J.P. officially had a new girlfriend.

High school graduation loomed for Ricciardi, by then a good enough baseball player to get an offer to play at Division II St. Leo's College in Florida, and the duo drifted apart. Diane eventually went on to nearby Clark University in Worcester, while J.P. signed on with the New York Mets. Still, even in the world of the minor leagues, the one-time girlfriend back home hadn't been forgotten.

First came the message passed on from the nearby underage disco in Dalton, Fat Albert's, that Ricciardi had been asking about Diane. And then a letter arrived carrying a Little Falls postmark inquiring about his former girl's availability. The feelings from that first wordless introduction at Foley Stadium had returned, but J.P. hadn't. He was still miles away and the idea of waiting in the unsettling world of professional baseball was not an appetizing option.

The answer to Ricciardi's query: Diane was taken.

Six months later, J.P. finished his 104-game season for Shelby in his second year in the minors and was unceremoniously released. He could do it all, field, run, you name it . . . as long as it didn't include hitting. And now the inability to make connection with the ball at the plate was leading him back to Worcester, where the uncertainty of life without baseball or Diane awaited.

The bad news was that Ricciardi's playing days were over; the good news came when he found out that Diane's relationship with her old boyfriend was too. Two months later, J.P. was sitting in his Honda Civic, proposing to the nineteen-year-old brunette from Worcester's East Side. Two months after that, Ricciardi was hooking on as a minor league coach with the New York Yankees thanks to his former college coach, Jack Gillis, and Diane was canceling a trip to England. He was in Fort Lauderdale, she was in Worcester, and both of their minds resided at an undisclosed venue. A Florida elopement was discussed, but so was the look on J.P.'s mother's face if she would find out.

In 1984 J.P. and Diane officially became the Ricciardis. Life would never be the same, as Diane found out when she discovered herself cleaning an apartment in Oneonta, New York, the day after getting her nails done in preparation for her wedding. Reality had struck in the form of an empty room, a mop, and a husband that was spending the majority of the fledgling marriage on a baseball field.

Diane made do. She worked as a realtor and a saleswoman for Gloria Vanderbilt, tried unsuccessfully to get a library card in Montana, and managed to live in places that would make Worcester seem like Paris. In short, like thousands of baseball wives before her, she managed.

Now, seventeen years and two sons later, they were on the verge of entering into the world of Major League Baseball's elite via this new opportunity in the fourth-largest city in North America—Toronto.

Diane was under a treatment of hair dye at the local salon when her cell phone rang. "Di," said the familiar voice of her husband on the other end, "they offered me the job."

It hadn't taken long for Godfrey to decide Ricciardi was his man; thirty-eight hours to be exact. Some of the decision's ease was due to DePodesta's groundwork, but most of it stemmed from J.P. just being J.P.

There was no in between when it came to Ricciardi's focus, and interviewing for what every scout perceives as the job to end all jobs, a general manager's position, was no different. The early November talk centered around strategy, game plans, managing risk, fiscal responsibility, and reeling in expectations. J.P. told Godfrey he was going to bring in players nobody had ever heard of. Godfrey told J.P. he would stand by him no matter what names were coming his way.

A partnership was being born. Now Ricciardi just had to convince his wife.

Once the offer was made, J.P. and Diane left Dante and Mariano with relatives (happily, there were plenty to choose from), and took a night out at one of their favorite restaurants to talk about their future. After weighing the pros and cons of the position, the couple went home, prayed that they would make the right decision, and proceeded to fall asleep. The next morning, their prayers were answered.

Diane immediately had three quick thoughts pop into her head upon opening her eyes. First, she loved her husband so much that, no matter what, she had to support his decision. Second, her kids had been insulated in Massachusetts their entire young lives and it might be time for them to start seeing more of the world. Finally, the money J.P. would be making, even if it was potentially a short amount of time, could help pay for the education of both Dante and Mariano.

By the time Diane's thoughts were sorted out, it was still only 6 A.M., but she had to wake up her husband. The first words in the Ricciardi household that day were, "J.P., I want you to take the job."

A few days later Diane's biggest concern was not tripping over the television cables taped to the floor at J.P.'s introductory press

14

conference. She didn't, and her husband glided though his big day without a hitch.

The Ricciardis had come a long way from Last Chance Gulch.

"He was right out of central casting."

—Larry Lucchino describing J.P. Ricciardi, New Englander/Toronto GM

SIX MONTHS AFTER hiring his new general manager, Paul Godfrey started to hear the rumors. The Red Sox wanted Ricciardi. It is, after all, nearly impossible to keep a secret in the gossipy world of Major League Baseball. So on one early September afternoon, in the waning days of the 2002 season, the team's president walked down to J.P.'s office for a preemptive strike.

The Blue Jays wanted to redo Ricciardi's three-year contract, thereby eliminating any chance the Red Sox had of swooping in. The answer wasn't what Godfrey had hoped for—let's talk at the end of the season.

The Blue Jays' president went back and forth in trying to pinpoint whether Ricciardi's response should be taken as a positive sign, or if it might be something to worry about. Maybe J.P. just didn't want the distraction during what was becoming a foundation-building nineteen-win month. Or could this be the prelude to the end of a one-year tenure in Toronto?

After a couple of nerve-fraying weeks Godfrey couldn't take it anymore, so he picked up the phone and called his Boston counterpart, Larry Lucchino. Waiting around was not one of the Blue Jays boss's qualities.

"Larry, if you're thinking about coming at J.P., don't," Godfrey told Lucchino, in his stern, unmistakably polite way.

Lucchino admitted that Ricciardi was on his team's general manager wish list, but he was going to talk to team owner, John

Henry, and give Godfrey a call back. Nine days later . . . still no call.

On the tenth day without response from Boston, Godfrey sprang back into action and dialed the number for Henry himself. "I suppose you've already talked to Larry," Godfrey began his conversation. The answer was a bit shocking. "Larry hasn't spoken to me," said Henry. "But if you're not going to give us permission to talk to J.P. then I guess there isn't anything we can do."

While the calls were being made to Boston, Godfrey handed his son, Rob, the unenviable task of drafting Plan B: formulating a list of general manager candidates if Ricciardi's path led to Fenway Park. It was a tremendous amount of work . . . work that Rob hoped could be thrown in the trash a few weeks later.

Unbeknownst to Godfrey were the conversations J.P. and Diane were having regarding their family's future. They had known for some while that the Red Sox were interested, but, as the final weeks of their first season in Toronto were ticking away, they now faced the reality that a decision might have to be made.

Everyone around the Ricciardis believed that the Red Sox were J.P.'s dream job, although no one actually confirmed that with him. Both Diane and J.P. knew the pitfalls of the position. For J.P., he understood that his dream of building an organization from the ground up wouldn't be a realistic scenario in Boston considering the Red Sox fans' propensity for impatience. He also enjoyed working for Godfrey immensely, and coexisting with the more hands-on Lucchino might not create the ideal atmosphere.

Diane also was familiar with the innards of the Red Sox situation, having grown up in the region, immersed in the team's passion. But she had also witnessed what had happened to former general manager Dan Duquette. By the time Duquette left his post with the Red Sox in the spring of '02, he was being portrayed as a heartless, impersonal robot by Boston fans and media. It was a description that seemed odd to Diane, who witnessed the personable side of Duquette on several occasions. The Duke had even gotten her tickets to a Bruce Springsteen show in 1999, and in the world of Mrs. Ricciardi that was about as good a gift as could be given.

If it could happen to Duquette, it could also happen to J.P.

In the end, the couple knew there was one underlying theme that J.P. couldn't ignore, no matter the money, prestige, or proximity to Worcester. He hadn't finished what he started.

So, as the 2002 season's final days unfolded, while Godfrey still awaited his end-of-the-season talk with his general manager, Ricciardi had already made up his mind that Toronto was where he wanted to be. When the last Friday morning of the season arrived, so did J.P. in Godfrey's office with the good news. They agreed that a new deal would be struck the following Monday morning.

True to their word, Godfrey and Ricciardi met in the Blue Jays' offices at 9 A.M. on the day after the conclusion of Toronto's seventy-eight-win season. They talked for three hours, eventually shaking hands on a new five-year contract that would also allow J.P. to spend more time during the season at his home in West Boylston. For the first time in months, Godfrey left work that day without the anxiety of uncertainty. There would be no more GM searches, at least not for another five years.

Yet, Godfrey also knew that he would be hearing from the Red Sox again. It didn't take long. Five hours after sealing the deal with Ricciardi, the Blue Jays president's blue, Blue Jay–emblazoned cell phone started playing Albert Von Tilzer's "Take Me Out to the Ballgame." Godfrey's assistant, Julie, was calling in. "Paul, I have John Henry and Larry Lucchino on the line."

The timing was pure coincidence. The Boston contingent had no idea that Godfrey's handshake with Ricciardi had been made earlier in the day, but had logically chosen the first day outside of the '02 season to make its move on J.P.

Godfrey liked both men, but he was a bit incredulous regarding their persistence. First, he reminded Henry and Lucchino of the Blue Jays' stance that had been echoed to Boston on two separate occasions—Ricciardi was not going to be made available for any interview. Then he dropped the bombshell, that day's contract agreement. The conversation ended, and so had Boston's chase after J.P.

This time, it was the turn of the Red Sox to formulate Plan B.

"Unless you believe, you will not understand."

—Saint Augustine

THE FIRST THING you notice about Theo Epstein is his height. The tape measure might state that he stands at just over six feet, but the manner with which he carries himself suggests otherwise. His slender frame remains perfectly upright, usually placing his head in a position of attention. It is an appearance that can partly be attributed to a keen sense of posture, but seems more due to a round-the-clock focus.

His friends and family noticed it in 2002 more than ever. It had been six years since he left Yale University to work for the Padres, but now he had returned home to punch the clock within two miles of his childhood residence in Brookline.

When Epstein first arrived in California, his position included posting sappy messages on the Padres' Jumbotron and innovating in-game acts such as a fan named "Flag Man." Flag Man's job was to shake the apathy out of Southern California fans. Theo also had to make sure the San Diego Chicken didn't lay an egg when it came to his cheer-eliciting performance. But Theo was twenty-two years old, he had a job in baseball, and all was right with the world.

At twenty-eight, Epstein came home to Boston a new person. His title was assistant general manager for the team he had surrendered his passion for, the Boston Red Sox, and his responsibilities were being taken to a whole new level. The quick-witted sense of humor was still there, but the innocence had vanished. Marriage proposals, Flag Man, and The Chicken were distant memories.

The process of actually getting to his position of power as an assistant general manager with the Red Sox was built on trust and hope. Ricciardi had offered Epstein a spot next to him in the Toronto front office, serving as the Blue Jays' assistant. But Theo had heard the rumors that his boss in San Diego, Lucchino, was headed to Boston with the Henry ownership group, and that he would be taking guys like Epstein with him.

In Epstein's mind, working with J.P. would have been ideal. They shared the same philosophy, ideals, and work ethic. Building a franchise in their mold was an appealing picture. But the chance to go home and work for the Red Sox, well, that was unimaginable. As it turned out, it almost stayed that way.

Lucchino did take flight to Boston, predictably wanting to take both Epstein and Theo's childhood buddy from Brookline, Padres' sales whiz Sam Kennedy, with him. The problem was that John Moores, San Diego's owner, wasn't about to let his former president take the team's future across the country. Even though neither had contracts, permission had to be asked to interview the duo. So it was asked, and it was denied.

Kennedy, like Epstein, had the lifelong ambition to work for his hometown team. Letters upon letters were always sent to Yawkey Way, hoping for some kind of internship or any other avenue into the Red Sox. Kennedy used to sneak out of Brookline High baseball practice to even witness Fenway's emptiness during a college baseball game. Being there was half the fun, a notion that hadn't changed in his professional life.

Now someone was saying that admittance to Fenway was not an option. Walls were punched, e-mails sent, and calls made, but still no change. It looked as though the kids from Brookline would be sleeping in San Diego for a while. It was the same feeling they both had to endure while watching the Oakland A's sweep their Red Sox in the 1988 American League Championship Series . . . only worse.

But then came their personal forty-eight-hour Declaration of Independence.

In the midst of 2002 spring training, Moores finally gave Lucchino permission to talk to Kennedy and Epstein. But there was a catch—the interviews, job offers, and acceptance or denial had to all come in a span of forty-eight hours. It set Kennedy and Epstein off in motion, spending all but twelve of the allotted hours together formulating the best course of action. The plan worked. Toasting their good fortune with champagne in Lucchino's seaside office, they had come full circle in their baseball lives. They were saying good-bye to the left coast, and hello to their roots.

As bizarre and fortunate as the return to Boston was for Epstein, his subsequent days in the team's front office were appreciably more surreal. As the 2002 season progressed, Lucchino's plan started to take shape. Mike Port was a good baseball man, but the Red Sox clearly wanted to go in another direction at general manager. That was why the idea of getting a second chance to work with Ricciardi brought a smile to Epstein's face. But when Godfrey's final message to Henry and Lucchino was sent on the first Monday after the 2002 season, Theo got that sinking feeling that pitching his ideas to some GM he had no connection with might put them on their way to getting lost in the shuffle. He knew what his only hope was—partnering up with Billy Beane.

As much as Epstein enjoyed the idea of working with Beane, the forty-year-old Billy equally looked forward to throwing ideas back and forth with Theo. The Oakland boss also was intrigued by the idea of what he could do with a payroll that stretched more than double what he was working with under the A's ownership.

This time the Red Sox would get the object of their affection, if only for fifteen hours.

Three times a day, Beane and Ricciardi talked throughout the A's general manager's courtship by Boston. Billy didn't need baseball advice, he needed a friend and that's what he had in J.P. They both rattled off the plusses: Becoming the highest-paid GM in baseball ($2 million more than he was making in Oakland), the payroll, the established talent, and the city's passion. They were all avenues J.P. had gone down a month before, and was now revisiting for his best friend's sake.

The phone conversations also covered the negatives, most notably the reality of Beane being the nation's full breadth away from his thirteen-year-old daughter, Casey. Billy understood that this wasn't a short-term change. If he was going to Boston it was going to be for a long stretch.

Back and forth, back and forth, back and . . . "OK, let's do it!" Beane was in the fold, and so was Epstein's sanity.

The handshakes were made in Florida between Beane, Henry, and Lucchino on a Saturday, allowing Billy to fly back to the Bay Area that day to start life's new rotation. Epstein got the call before the Sox's new GM had left the Sunshine State. As far as Theo was concerned, it was the best news of the year.

Unfortunately, by the time Beane reached Oakland, his mind had been swirling for the duration of the five-hour flight. Again a call was made to Epstein, who might have been in Tucson for the general manager's meetings, but whose thoughts were simpatico with his new boss.

The two talked about everything, from the prospects of utilizing the overabundance of academia in the Boston area to upgrade the franchise's way of thinking, to literary references from Epstein's favorite book, *Crime and Punishment*. But as wild a ride as the Russian novel's prime character, Raskolnikov, had in Fyodor Dostoevsky's classic, it paled in comparison for what awaited Theo and Billy in the coming hours.

Beane was a direct descendant of Scottish war hero Gilles Mac-Bean, who killed fourteen men in the Battle of Culloden and whose likeness still overlooks Loch Ness (as well as Billy's desk). Now it was Ricciardi's former minor league teammate who was chopping down the unwanted, in this case Boston's players and payroll. Epstein supplied the organizational information, and Beane analyzed it. What he saw was an obstacle more daunting that the sea of Hanoverian mercenaries his ancestor had stared down hundreds of years before.

By the time Beane finally hung up the phone at three in the morning, a few things had become evident: Boston's farm system was in disarray, the big league team was tied into some unbearably huge contracts, and ownership had mandated a payroll in the opposite direction of where the team had been built to arrive. On top of that, Billy's conversations with another Tucson attendee that day, Paul DePodesta, had produced the likelihood of Oakland taking claim of Red Sox top prospect, Kevin Youkilis, as compensation for Beane's departure.

Then the early morning thoughts really started kicking in for Beane. Did he really want to be that far from Casey? Could he spend the time in his office that would be demanded by the Red Sox Nation? An arrangement had been made with Henry and Lucchino to spend some of the season running the team from an office in Newport Beach, California, but deep down Billy knew that probably wouldn't fly in the life-and-death world of Boston's professional baseball team, especially if losses started mounting up higher than wins.

Epstein awoke early Sunday morning, fully expecting to pick up his stream of consciousness with Beane. But 9 A.M. had come and gone and his phone still hadn't rung. Finally, at 9:30, in the middle of an arbitration meeting, Billy called. "Theo, we've got to talk." Epstein stepped out of the room and started to listen. Three hours later he had come to grips with the agonizing reality—the Red Sox were still without a general manager.

Epstein's anxiety bordered on feverish. Not only were the Red Sox running rudderless through the most important weeks of the off-season, but the prospects of digging up whomever Boston might get to guide the franchise's ship weren't all that comforting, either. Theo wanted to believe in his would-be boss, a notion that made the prospect of hiring Ricciardi or Beane so intellectually compelling. Now, with the change of direction, Epstein was being forced to contemplate an unthinkable notion in the eyes of his friends and family—leaving Boston and his Red Sox.

*"Sometimes you've just got to say
'What the fuck.'"*

—Tom Cruise (Joel Goodson) in the movie *Risky Business*

JOHN HENRY KNEW he wanted Theo Epstein to be his general manager; it was just that the Red Sox owner hadn't come to grips as to if that time should be sooner rather than later.

So one night, as the day of decision approached, Henry made a late-night phone call to Epstein for a heart-to-heart. The likable, soft-spoken commodities trader cared for his young executive too much to put Theo in an uncomfortable position. Henry's goal was to upgrade the Red Sox, but not downgrade Epstein's way of life. The conversation, if nothing else, gave both men something to think about before the next day's sunrise.

Epstein's conclusion was that there were going to be good breaks and bad breaks no matter what the timing. The best two guys for the job (J.P. and Billy) had already turned it down and that, in the words of Joel Goodson, sometimes you've got to say 'What the fuck!'

So on a sunny November 24 afternoon, while sitting in his office watching the New England Patriots' game against the Minnesota Vikings, Epstein got the call from one of his mentors from San Diego, Lucchino. He wanted Theo to walk down the hall, enter the team president's office and be offered the position of general manager of the Boston Red Sox. Contracts were drawn up, handshakes were exchanged, and a press conference was scheduled for the very next day.

There was a lot to do, and not a lot of time to do it in. Members of the Red Sox staff were called, as were friends and family. Also on the docket was informing some players of the move— Wakefield was gotten ahold of, while messages were left for Pedro Martinez, Nomar Garciaparra, and others. The problem was that as the day's hours wound down, nerves were fraying. It was the night before his first press conference and Theo didn't know what his directive was going to entail.

Coping with the responsibilities of professional baseball was easy for Epstein. Doing it with a microphone and a mass of media in front of him was unknown.

When the actual event finally came around, Epstein felt appreciably better about his state of mind. The morning allowed for drawing up some notes, providing for some mental reassurance that he did, in fact, have a grasp on what were otherwise uncharted waters. As preparation goes, it was about as much that could be mustered up for the afternoon's event.

Finally, the moment arrived. As Lucchino addressed the crowd, getting ready to introduce his new GM, each of those most intimately affected by the hiring reflected on the moment. For Epstein, everything would be fine after the first few sentences had been uttered. Henry's trepidation revolved less around Theo's ability to handle the job, and more concerning his employee's acumen in the intensity of a press conference. A few moments into Epstein's speech, anyone's worries were dismissed.

Then there was Paul.

One person who couldn't be present for Theo's press conference was his twin brother. While the trappings of becoming the Red Sox general manager may be too numerous to comprehend, one of the pitfalls of working as a Brookline High School guidance counselor is not being able to attend your brother's history-making coronation.

Following the event meant finding good radio reception at Brookline High, just minutes away from Fenway Park. The permanent smile on the attentive Paul's face was hardly a surprise, but what did astonish the listener was the sounds that came out of the speakers. It sounded like the tone of his brother's voice, but the cadence, annunciation, and pace couldn't have belonged to the kid he grew up with. It was just starting to sink in—Theo was the general manager of the Boston Red Sox.

"Have no friends not equal to yourself."

—Confucius

ONE MINUTE SEPARATED Theo and Paul Epstein's entrance into the world. On December 29, 1973, the two made their appearance together, and more than twenty-nine years later, the dynamic hadn't changed. More often than not the Brothers Epstein are within walking distance of one another, whether in the halls of Fenway or Brookline High.

There were certainly forces that allowed for a separation, such as the Brookline Middle School's policy of not allowing twins to share the same homeroom teacher. And when Theo took his seven-year sojourn to San Diego, the duo's disdain for lengthy phone conversations complicated things.

Still, the bond formed in and around Parkman Street could never be permanently swayed. Miles could never diminish the memories.

Traditional copyright laws might not have applied, but Theo and Paul were pretty sure nobody else could stake claim to the particulars of their youth. Take such not-ready-for-prime-time sports as "Tennyball" and "Gutterball," for example. Tennis rackets were used in the place of baseball bats, the back of the neighboring Holiday Inn was their personal "Blue Monster" outfield wall, and the two end-of-the-street gutters made for a perfect goal, at least until one of them had swallowed a container of Leslie Epstein's tennis balls.

Even the traditional prepubescent sporting fare, such as Wiffle Ball, was branded with the Epsteins' unique trademark. While at least two participants played (usually including Sam Kennedy), an extra body was always needed to use the family's video camera to document the activity. Even in the early days of the 1980s, the cutting edge of scouting didn't escape the boys in the back alleys of Brookline.

The family's propensity to dive into athletic endeavors, no matter what the venue, didn't always turn out with a smile and a pat on the back. One of the sporting endeavors that went awry came when the Epstein parents gave the twins one pair of boxing gloves. The impetus of the gift came from the memory of Leslie's uncle Julius and his days as the NCAA champion boxer while at Penn State University. Needless to say, Julius never had to endure the one-mitten, one-boxing-glove style the boys invented within the ring that was the family's living room. Good clean fun got a little messy.

The complement to the controlled chaos of Parkman Street was the far more organized postcardlike youth sports teams the brothers played on. There was youth soccer and youth baseball. As a baseball player, Paul was a good soccer guy, while Theo could hold his own in both, albeit not in spectacular fashion. Individual achievements aside, the duo did team up for a championship.

Seventh-grade, Pony League Baseball, city champions, all while playing for the . . . Yankees. Ultimately, winning was the only thing that made wearing the uniform bearable for the Epstein boys, that and being able to hear the voice of longtime Sox public address announcer, Sherm Feller, from nearby Fenway Park.

By the time high school introduced itself, Theo and Paul no longer were subject to Brookline's "twins separation" rule, bringing the duo together in, and outside, the realm of academia. Judging by the end results, the interaction only helped: Theo was admitted early to Yale University to pursue American Studies, while Paul chose Wesleyan over Penn for the chance to play soccer.

Soccer had also jumped to the fore of Theo's athletic achievement, as he joined his brother to form a pair known to the outside world as "The Goggle Twins of Brookline": both suffered eye injuries among their earlier soccer days, forcing them both to wear awkward-looking eyewear. In their senior season, Brookline finally reached the Massachusetts State Tournament, where the Warriors were bounced in the first round. It marked a permanent transition for Theo, from the soccer fields to whatever kind of form baseball could present itself.

Posting fair enough batting averages as a junior varsity player before spending his junior and senior seasons playing behind Kennedy in Brookline High's middle infield, Epstein's baseball existence took a dramatic turn at Yale. Playing at Brookline's home field, the Armory, less than one mile from Fenway Park had been a blast, and so would have been carrying the good times over to Yale Field in New Haven. However, Epstein's baseball talents resided somewhere beyond the diamond. It was just a matter of who was going to find them.

By the time Theo started his second introduction to baseball, via an internship with the Baltimore Orioles, Paul was beginning his transformation from an aspiring architect to a counselor of the future—kids. In the brothers' minds, both professions were pretty cool, although by the time Theo reached San Diego, Paul couldn't quite fathom the excitement on the other side of those cell phone calls from Rancho Cucamonga.

Four years later, Paul sat in Yankee Stadium watching the Sox, only one game away from seeing Theo earn a trip to the World Series as the general manager of the Boston Red Sox. It just didn't get any cooler than that.

But then came the Boone-doggle, a home run that left the brothers' father overcome with emotions, and Paul heading for the exits before the ball even touched down in the left-field stands. That wasn't cool. Not at all.

Paul got in his car and rode straight back to Brookline with the memories of a season and its murderous final game hurrying along the mile markers. There were plenty of stops at the Mobil stations littering the Merritt Turnpike, and at every one could be found equally catatonic Red Sox fans, driving through the night, hoping that reality might change once the state line was crossed.

Just like Leslie, J.P., and Theo, they had all lived the life, albeit from entirely different angles. If nothing else, a lesson had been reinforced—there was nothing ordinary about spending a season in baseball's most dynamic division, the American League East.

From Cuba to Beaumont and Back

"Sport is imposing order on what was chaos."

—Anthony Starr

Jed Hoyer and Galen Carr thought they knew what was coming. As it turned out, they had no idea.

The pair of twentysomethings had the face of the new Red Sox front office, both physically and historically. They still carried the athleticism that was officially left behind just a few years before in college, as well as the relative outsider's view of pro baseball, having both ventured into the private sector upon graduation.

Truth be told, besides the four or five inches Carr had on Hoyer, there wasn't much that separated their dossiers. Both grew up as Red Sox fans in New Hampshire, Hoyer a Plymouth kid, while Carr claimed Walpole as his hometown. Each excelled at baseball in college; Hoyer culminating his career at Wesleyan with a two-hit day against future big-leaguer Jarrod Washburn in the

Division III World Series title game, and Carr anchoring the Colby College pitching staff.

They also both utilized their familiarity with another New Hampshire native, Boston's twenty-eight-year-old, newly named farm director, Meriden's Ben Cherington, to break into the world of the Red Sox. Letter after letter, followed by repeated phone calls, finally put Hoyer and Carr in their respective cubicles in the sea of youthful dreamers that now stocked the Sox's offices.

The 2003 season, however, was going to be different from their initial introduction into Major League Baseball. Hoyer had moved into an actual office (shared by Assistant General Manager Josh Byrnes) while being promoted to baseball operations assistant. Carr also had four walls and a door, and was charged with the task of breaking down the team's video and statistical data.

The Red Sox were going with energy-generated smarts over experience, and because of it Hoyer and Carr were getting to accompany another neophyte to his professional position, Red Sox general manager Theo Epstein, on an all-expense-paid trip to spring training. In almost three months of firsts, this would be another.

The day of their flight to Boston's spring training home in Fort Myers, Florida, February 12, Carr and Epstein were running late, leaving Hoyer feeling a bit helpless at Logan Airport's Delta Airlines terminal. By this time, airports weren't easily navigated without Epstein being recognized; a dilemma that had been reinforced to his parents when they endured a January trip through baggage claim with their son shrouding himself in a hooded sweatshirt.

This morning there was no time for precautions. Hoyer was already waiting helplessly for his travelmates, who finally showed up, only to have Carr derailed by an individual security screening. It was then that they truly found out that some things were about to change.

"Are you with the Epstein and Hoyer party going to Atlanta?" a gate attendant surprisingly asked Carr. Once the "yes" answer was given, the former Division III college pitcher was ushered all the way to his seat. Not to just the gate, but to his seat. And the treatment didn't stop there. The flight attendants wanted to offer the group two empty first-class seats.

In the eyes of Delta Airlines, the trio of young professionals represented the royalty that was the Boston Red Sox. Carr may have thought he was hot stuff when catching a foul ball off the bat of Toronto's Kelly Gruber just before the third baseman's first big-league hit; Gruber's father had even asked the then-seven-year-old for his autograph. But this was a chance to live on the other side of the curtain, the life of first class.

It was also on the plane that another reality struck Hoyer and Carr: Under Epstein, everyone was playing equal parts in the equation. The message to the airline was, "Thanks, but no thanks." If there weren't enough seats for all three, then it wasn't meant to be. A theme for a front office, and a season, had been set.

The group landed in Fort Myers burdened with three hours of anticipation, and a lifetime of landmarks to mark the moment. One coincidence that didn't go unnoticed was the passing of former Red Sox general manager Haywood Sullivan just hours before their plane had touched down. Sullivan's history with the Red Sox had stretched from player to team executive. As a younger man, Sullivan had been immortalized on the cover of the *Saturday Evening Post* by legendary artist Norman Rockwell. Later in life, as Boston's general manager, the Georgia native was remembered as the man who failed to offer team stars Fred Lynn and Carlton Fisk contracts before a December 20 deadline, rendering Fisk a free agent.

Sullivan had his legacy, and by the time Epstein arrived at his Fort Myers aquamarine-colored condo, he had already started to formulate his own. Putting the flooded floors of his spring training residence (someone had left the washing machine on too long) out of his memory would be easy enough in time, but forgetting his two bouts of off-season international intrigue might be a bit more difficult to dismiss.

"If it weren't for baseball, many kids wouldn't know what a millionaire looked like."

—Phyllis Diller

THERE WAS NO FACE affixed to his name, just a title: The Missing Piece to the Eighty-Five-Year-Old, Seemingly Unsolvable World Championship Puzzle.

This was how the fans of the Boston Red Sox viewed Jose Contreras. If the Sox got Contreras, they had started to believe, all of their problems would be solved. But who was Contreras? Talk-show caller Joe from Quincy could pick out the New England Patriots' special teams coach before he might identify his favorite baseball team's savior. It was blind faith, and Red Sox fans had become really good at it.

The general population of Red Sox Nation did know this much: Contreras was from Cuba, the scouts liked him, and so did the Yankees. To the fans, just that limited bit of information was the hot stove league equivalent of watching the pitcher strike out twenty-seven hitters in a row before 35,000 sets of eyes at Fenway Park.

Perhaps the innocence was a good thing. If the people of Boston knew the full story behind Contreras, then they might just start telling visitors that the "Freedom Trail" wasn't a Revolutionary War landmark, but rather the path for all Cuban pitchers with ninety-seven-mile-per-hour heat and a pinch-me-when-it-has-landed forkball who want to make The Fens their home.

But there were some Bostonians who realized why there was such promise in putting Contreras in between Pedro Martinez and Derek Lowe in the team's rotation, and most of them resided in the offices at 4 Yawkey Way. The Red Sox front office, like the rest of Major League Baseball, knew just about everything there was to know about Contreras, thanks to the brief glimpses Cuban president Fidel Castro would give the world of his nation's premier athlete in international competition. It's not easy to see too far

31

into the Communist shadow cast over the Cuban players, but in Contreras's case some numbers gave enough of an introduction.

The thirty-one-year-old had pitched in the 1999 Pan-American Games, the 2000 Olympics, and 2001 World Cup, finishing the three tournaments with a 7–0 record, a 0.59 ERA, and sixty-six strikeouts in sixty-one innings. In the Pan-Am Games against the United States, Contreras had struck out thirteen American batters in eight innings pitching on one day's rest en route to a 5–1 Cuban victory. And just for good measure, the performance came on the same day as that which marked the beginning of Castro's revolution forty-six years before. For this sort of drama, the nation's ace ultimately got what might have been an oppressed citizen's ultimate prize—a blue Peugeot 400C sedan automobile.

Castro nicknamed Contreras "El Titan de Bronce" (The Titan of Bronze) after the most famous general in Cuba's war of independence against Spain, Antonio Maceo. There was no doubting that, among athletes, Fidel had a short list of his most beloved, and Jose was at the top of the list.

On the first day of October 2002, it was Major League Baseball's turn to play favorites.

Perhaps if it weren't for Castro's admiration of Contreras, teams like the Red Sox would still be viewing the pitcher as the unattainable supermodel Joe Everyman dreams about but knows he will never have. The first proof of this came when Jose's prized car broke down.

The repairs to the vehicle were going to cost $453, an exorbitant amount of money for virtually any Cuban without the first name of Fidel and the last name of Castro. Contreras, who was making $275 a year, turned to the Cuban Sports Federation for help, but there was none forthcoming. The wheels then started turning, not on the Peugeot, but in Jose's head. This was the final straw.

Contreras's frustration spilled over to the mechanic who was charging him to fix the car. He told the man he wasn't coming back. As vague as the statement might have seemed, in the world of always looking over your shoulder, it might have been too much. The next day, Jose was fighting back tears while saying good-bye to his wife of fifteen years, Myriam, and their two daughters. As far as they knew, he was simply taking off from Jose Marti Airport for another baseball tournament. He knew otherwise.

The Cuban national team headed to Santillo, Mexico, to play in the America Series Tournament. The morning after a relatively easy 6–0 win over the Dominican Republic, Contreras told his coaches that he would prefer to stay behind at the Hotel Camino Real because of a pain in his hip. The request was accepted for two reasons. First, Cuba was playing a weak Guatemala team, so he wouldn't be needed, but he was also Castro's poster child for the virtues of Cuban baseball—a superstar of the world who had repeatedly said he had already turned down an offer of $50 million to defect.

Except that this time, Contreras actually was going to switch sides.

He called Jaime Torres, an agent who had told Contreras years back that if defection was ever an option, Jose should contact him and arrangements would be set. The words were, "Lo voy a hacer!" the Spanish version of "I am going to do it!" never meant more to the world of professional baseball. So a car arrived, Jose jumped in, and he was quickly driven to the airport. There he met up with Torres, who had a surprise guest with him, longtime Cuban coach Miguel Valdes and his nineteen-year-old son, Miguel Jr.

Contreras's first reaction was that he might have been set up, since Valdes's affiliation with the Cuban team had stretched more than thirty years and included thirteen world championships and two Olympic Gold Medals. Contreras had entered the world of defection just ten years after giving up his dream of becoming a veterinarian, not long enough to be fully classified as a lifelong Castro loyalist. Valdes, on the other hand, was an institution within Cuban baseball circles, one who surely wouldn't partake in the ultimate risk of defection.

But like Contreras, Valdes had also been pushed too far.

The four men successfully boarded the plane for Tijuana, where a car took them for the short ride to the United States border. If they had been discovered before reaching the gateway to California, the Cubans would have been detained by the Mexican authorities and returned to Cuba under the countries' repatriation agreement. Forget pitching for the pride of an entire country. Forget getting calls in the dugout after every inning of a 2000 Olympic game from Castro. Pressure for Jose Contreras suddenly had a new definition.

When the border was reached, United States customs agents immediately took the three Cubans into custody. This was a mere formality, as was evidenced the next morning when the group was released into Torres's custody. They had run the gauntlet without getting caught. On one hand, the accomplishment elicited a feeling of overriding elation, while in other respects it generated a slap-in-the-face reality. Contreras still hadn't told Myriam, the couple's children, his sixty-six-year-old mother, Modesta, and most frightening, the family's eighty-one-year-old patriarch, Florentino, a man who had sung the praises of Castro's revolution. This wasn't exactly on par with getting home after curfew, as Jose's reluctance to call his parents' hometown of Las Martinas might suggest.

Nine days into his new life in the United States, Jose finally worked up the courage to call Myriam, a smooth-skinned beauty who had married her husband at age fifteen. It would be the first of a stream of calls from Contreras, whose only connection to his family now hinged on the Nokia cell phone residing in the family's two-bedroom apartment in the Cuban city of Pinar del Rio. The posters of the pitcher may have been stripped from the streets and meeting places of his former nation, but his face still littered the walls surrounding Myriam and her two daughters.

Contreras finally called his father, although the communication would have to be placed through a neighbor across the field from his parents' home (they did not have a phone). Florentino knew baseball, having played on a team sponsored by the sugar mills, and he knew his son. Perhaps that is why the man who had raised Jose was surprisingly understanding upon receiving the call. Jose was still Jose, and that would never change.

What would be altered was Contreras's everyday existence. And the Red Sox were hoping that at least a portion of that metamorphosis could take place inside the gates of Fenway Park.

"Do not hire a man who does your work for money, but him who does it for love of it."

—Henry David Thoreau

LIKE FLORENTINO CONTRERAS, Luis Eljaua knew baseball, and he thought he knew Jose.

Eljaua, a man with a football fullback's low-to-the-ground build and straight-ahead approach, grew up playing baseball in high school and then college in Miami. He was a middle infielder who was good enough to join future Major Leaguers Alex Fernandez, Jorge Fabregas, and Ricky Gutierrez in playing a key role in bringing Monsignor Pace High School to two straight Florida high school championship games. But he didn't run well, and lacked the power to make up for his limited legs. The scouts stayed away, leaving Eljaua without a minor league contract and with an uncertain future.

So the son of Cuban immigrants made the logical decision: If you can't beat them, join them.

Al Avila, Eljaua's former college coach at St. Thomas University, had gotten a job with the Florida Marlins and recommended his former player for a position as a bilingual scout in South Florida. Luis spoke Spanish before he uttered a word of English, and he knew the territory's playing fields intimately, so the fit was natural. A career had begun.

By the time Marlins owner John Henry officially joined a group in paying $700 million to own the Boston Red Sox in February 2002, Eljaua had ascended to the position of director of

Latin American scouting. But Henry was raiding the Marlins' cupboard, and one of the pieces he was going to take with him was Eljaua, who would be Boston's man in charge of all of the team's international scouting. It was an honor, but also a transition considering the entire world was now under his umbrella. He had been to Japan just once, helping the Marlins seal the sale of pitcher Hector Almonte, but he never knew the feeling of working in an unfamiliar language and culture.

Chasing down Contreras, however, was anything but foreign to Eljaua.

Like most other Major League representatives, Luis wasn't able to get close to Contreras during his outings with the Cuban National Team, but with Jose, seeing has always been believing. Eljaua's first eyeful of Castro's Titan of Bronze came at an international tournament in Millington, Tennessee, in 1995. "Wow" was the operative word that day, and would be for the twelve more times the then-Marlins scout viewed Contreras until his defection day.

The world may have been introduced to Contreras in his eight shutout innings against the Baltimore Orioles in an exhibition game at Havana's 45,000-seat El Stadio, but that was simply a footnote for Eljaua, whose familiarity with Jose couldn't be thwarted by the ninety-seven miles separating Cuba from Key West. And now, with nothing dividing Luis from Contreras except his agent, the Red Sox representative was going to try and get to know this figure he had been chasing. They were going to be friends, and just maybe they could be coworkers.

The first step came just weeks after the journey from Tijuana, with Eljaua meeting up with Team Contreras in Miami's La Carreta Restaurant. The evening didn't include negotiations, since that still wasn't allowed while Major League Baseball decided how to classify Contreras's free agent status. There was just talk of Luis's and Jose's common interests—baseball and Cuban-born parents. The strangers quickly became like brothers, making the three-hour meal feel like the most informal of fast-food experiences. The first step had been made, and a relationship was being built.

Contreras was humble and personable in his meeting with Eljaua, easily rattling off knowledge of the big leagues with the aplomb of a teenage baseball card nut. It was a familiarity aided by knowing some of Cuba's previous sixty or so defectors, a group that began with Rene Arocha in 1991 and had peaked in 1999 with the $14.5 million contract signed by the country's third-best pitcher—behind Contreras and Pedro Luis Lazo—Danys Baez. If Contreras was nervous about his fate in the majors, he didn't show it, either in his workouts on the fields of Miami or at any of the subsequent dinner meetings with Eljaua.

The comfort level between the two was high, which was the first necessity. If the Red Sox were going to be throwing the amount of money at Contreras that they thought they might be, it was Eljaua's job to find out exactly what they would be getting in return. He needed to find out what made Cuba's greatest pitcher tick.

Boston's next step came in early November, when Eljaua brought Contreras, Torres, Valdes, and his son, along with former Red Sox great and fellow Cuban Luis Tiant, to John Henry's home in Boca Raton. Most Cubans couldn't have imagined such a palatial estate such as the one Contreras was being introduced to courtesy of the Red Sox owner. But there is one, and perhaps only one, place on the island nation that could compare, and Jose had been there—Fidel Castro's palace. When the Cuban teams would win international tournaments, the players wouldn't even get the chance to go home. It was straight to Castro's palace, just for a taste of what could never be anybody's but Fidel's.

Henry's place was different, just as big, but perhaps even more modern. It was the hosts, however, who really separated the two experiences for Contreras—Castro, the fear-inducing dictator who oozed bravado, and Henry, as soft-spoken and gentle a man as one could find in the world of big business.

For two hours Henry did his best to make Jose feel welcome, while trying to get a read on this man into whom he was potentially pouring millions of dollars. The two were alike in the sense that both erred on the side of modesty and a quiet nature. The only obstacle standing in the way of a fast friendship was the inability to speak one another's language. But thanks to Eljaua and Torres, bridges were built, and a rapport was born.

Eljaua knew that familiarity was the Red Sox's ally when it came to Contreras, and further dinner meetings were paving the road to the desired familiarity. Even employees not yet hired by Boston were contributing to the general food-on-the-table, good-feelings-in-the-air cause. The plan seemed to be coming together for the Red Sox, thanks in part to the Pittsburgh Pirates' Latin American pitching coordinator.

Marta Rojas is a great cook. Fantastic cook. It was just that the fifteen or so people her and her husband, Euclides, were expecting for dinner in their Miami home on the November night were a bit much to prepare for. So a Cuban restaurant was enlisted to cater their affair. Cuban food isn't hard to find on the edge of the Everglades.

The Rojas family knew most of their guests—Rene Arocha, Danys Baez, Orlando Hernandez, and a room full of other Cuban baseball-playing refugees. There was one visitor, however, that Euky had met just in passing in his days of pitching for the Cuban national team—Jose Contreras.

The theme for the get-together was "Welcome to Freedom," and nobody embodied the slogan better than Contreras. Jose knew many of his fellow dinner visitors, especially the man they call "El Duque," but it was Euky whom he truly wanted to get to know better. It was, after all, Rojas's story and hospitality that exemplified the story of all of the dinner guests. In Contreras's eyes, he was being hosted by a hero.

Rojas was a savior for his team, for his friends, and for his family. While playing for Havana in the Cuban League, he had saved more than ninety games, including setting a league record in 1994. He was a guy who could pitch all day, every day, sometimes going the final four innings to close out a game. But, then again, when you're playing in Cuba, choices such as when and where you pitch aren't usually a luxury.

Rojas's good-natured, selfless demeanor wasn't lost on his

teammates, either. After Arocha became the first baseball-playing defector in July 1991, it was only Euky who chose not to ignore the nation's new embarrassment, collecting his friend's bags from the floor of the airport terminal to give to Arocha's family. Three rounds of questioning by the Cuban authorities later, and Rojas was officially in the authorities' crosshairs.

Rojas's worries concerning who he might find looking over his shoulder escalated when it was learned that an investigation was forthcoming regarding his involvement in Democratic Solidarity, an anti-Castro organization. That's when the player who had been part of the Cuban national team's bullpen since 1987 decided that floating on four empty fifty-five-gallon drums might not be such a bad thing. So at 11 P.M. on August 17, 1994, Euky, his wife, and their two-and-a-half-year-old son joined thirteen other dreamers in plunging a fifteen-foot raft into Havana's More Castle for a five-day ride that would take them sixty-seven miles out to sea.

The first night was the toughest—there was a big surf, and even bigger anxiety. Just 40 percent of the Cubans who attempt to make the voyage to freedom make it, and trying to accomplish the feat with a wife and a son suffering from a respiratory disorder surely dropped those odds substantially. But Rojas knew what the past and present had delivered for them in Cuba, and the uncertainty of a future outside of that oppression seemed far more appetizing.

Then Euky saw those numbers—721—and he knew the decision to weather the waves, the wind, and Castro's wrath was justified. The sight of the digits on the side of a United States Coast Guard vessel was destiny's way of giving Rojas a big pat on the back.

It wouldn't be until six months of internment in the squalor of the base at United States–controlled Guantanamo Bay (and an emergency appendectomy) that Euky tasted the fruits of his convictions. Nine years later, Rojas was living the life he had dreamed of, a life in professional baseball and a life without fears. Like the other Cubans partaking in the November feast, Rojas had made it. It was time to celebrate the freedom Contreras had only just begun to comprehend.

What Contreras didn't realize was that one of his chief suitors, the Red Sox, were interested in having Rojas tackle their bullpen coaching position. The influx of Marlins people within the Boston organization knew the even-keeled, knowledgeable approach Euky possessed and saw him as a good fit. The fact that Contreras looked up to him didn't hurt, either.

When the job offer came, Rojas was skeptical. He didn't want advancement simply because of his association with Contreras, a fact made clear when meeting with Sox manager Grady Little and pitching coach Tony Cloninger in a get-to-know-you dinner in North Carolina. His fears were placated. Sure, Boston looked at Euky's relationship with the object of their desire as a plus, but the biggest drawing card was the entire package Rojas maintained. He was the coach they wanted in the Fenway Park bullpen.

By the time early December rolled in, Boston had pieced together its battle plan regarding Contreras and was in position to execute it. Eljaua laid the groundwork, Henry analyzed the investment, Rojas was established as an all-important support system, and now it was simply time to spring into action.

"There are no secrets better kept than the secrets that everybody guesses."

—George Bernard Shaw

ALL THE RED SOX were left waiting for was the decision by Major League Baseball regarding what to do with Conteras's free agent status. In order not to be subjected to the June Amateur Draft, the pitcher had to take up residency in another country other than the United States. First, Torres suggested Mexico for his client's new home. "No way," responded the higher-ups at MLB, who deemed the neighboring country just too convenient.

So where was it going to be? Panama? The Dominican Republic? The word finally came down—"Gentlemen, get your plane tickets for Nicaragua."

In the meantime, Epstein, Eljaua, and the rest of Team Red Sox were doing everything short of laying out the dollars and cents in front of Contreras. While at the Grand Ole Opry Hotel in Nashville, the Red Sox contingent took time off from the courtship of other free-agent possibilities (Jeff Kent, Edgardo Alfonzo) to meet with the agent. The underlying theme of the get-together wasn't anything fancy, just simply "We will see you in Managua"—Nicaragua's capital.

They wouldn't be alone.

By the time Contreras was officially declared a free agent by the commissioner's office on December 18, Eljaua had been in Managua for three full days. He still wasn't able to talk money with Torres or Contreras, but that didn't deter him from trying to build on Boston's already well-constructed plan.

Eljaua arrived at the Hotel Campo Real, a less-than-extravagant lodging near the Managua airport, knowing Contreras was staying at the same address. Luis proceeded to discover that his room, No. 3, was conveniently next to Torres's room No. 2 and near Contreras's room No. 1. There were only about fifteen rooms in the ranch-style, yellow-and-green-dominated hotel, so the placement wasn't cosmically accidental by any means. But the rooms' locale did give Eljaua an idea that would undoubtedly aid Boston's master plan.

The morning after touching down in Managua, Eljaua went to Georgina Lacayo, the hotel manager, and asked if any other teams had been represented yet in the complex. The answer was no, not yet. Luis knew the Yankees were coming any day now, along with at least a smattering of other organizations, and trying to maneuver through the halls of a crowded hotel might be a distraction.

"How many rooms do you have available?" Eljaua asked Lacayo. "Eleven," was the answer. "I'll take them all," the determined Red Sox employee responded.

For less than $1,000, Boston not only earned the right to exclusively call Contreras a neighbor throughout the precious few days, but the maneuver also allowed the Red Sox to know who was coming, who was going, and when they were doing it. Everyone realized the bidding for the pitcher was going to be a horse race, so getting out of the gate fastest was the highest priority.

As the days passed, with Contreras continuing to work out with the San Fernando team in Masaya, a town thirty kilometers west of Managua, Eljaua slowly got company. Especially notable was the presence of Seattle general manager Pat Gillick and Yankees' scouting director Gordon Blakely. New York general manager Brian Cashman had left the Contreras affair in the hands of Blakely and his scouts, a move that might have been all the more trusting considering what was at stake.

Cashman is a likable sort, partly because of his matter-of-fact, down-to-earth demeanor, and also due to the perception of what he has to endure while working under the thumb of the infamously spontaneous George Steinbrenner. Cashman had reached the position of general manager at just thirty years of age in 1998, capping a rise through the organization that had started with an internship in 1989.

Cash's first contract as GM had been for just one year, and was sealed with a handshake. Nearly five years later, he was wearing three world championship rings.

When Epstein first got his general manager job, the genial, thirty-five-year-old Cashman called to congratulate his colleague and offer the only piece of advice that he thought worthy of giving: Don't forget to use the power of "no comment" when it comes to dealing with the people with the notepads. Former New York GM Gene Michael had passed the warning on to Cashman and now, AL East rival or not, it was going to be passed along to Epstein.

The cordiality of the relationship between Cash and Theo remained, but a competitive dynamic kicked up in a hurry. It started forming at the winter meetings, when the two bumped into one another, when Contreras was just starting to consume each general manager's attention.

"You know George isn't going to let you get Contreras," said

Cashman, half-joking, but fully understanding that nothing could be more based in reality.

"I guess it's going to get pretty expensive then," retorted Epstein, fighting back the same competitive fire that had consumed him from the days in Brookline, except the opponent had now changed: Playing the rival role of twin brother Paul Epstein was George Steinbrenner.

Another curve in the road to Contreras came in the days leading up to the December 22 starting point for negotiations for the Cuban pitcher. The Atlanta Braves made an offer to the Yankees and Red Sox—would they be interested in pitcher Kevin Millwood? It was as if the baseball gods had decided to test both Epstein and Cashman's resolve.

Millwood was any big league starting rotation's dream—a pitcher who had pitched more than 200 innings in three of the last four seasons while maintaining a career ERA under 4.00. The problem was that he was most likely going to make almost $10 million in 2003.

For both teams, it was going to have to be either Millwood or Contreras.

All it was going to take for Boston to put one of the best pitchers in the National League in between the far-from-ordinary talents of Pedro Martinez and Derek Lowe was to send a left-handed pitcher named Casey Fossum to Atlanta.

Fossum represented a part of the Red Sox's future, as well as the unexplained physics of baseball. The left-hander was a slight six feet tall, and his frame elicited constant tugs at the league's thinnest of waistbands. As one baseball executive said when watching him pitch, "It looks like he had liposuction and forgot to say when." But whatever numbers were lacking on the scale were more than made up for on the radar guns. Fossum threw hard, and the Braves wanted that heat to come south.

The overtures relayed by Atlanta, however, couldn't sway Epstein. Fossum was too good, young, and cheap to let go and by all accounts, Contreras was going to be even better than Millwood. Besides, the Cuban said he wanted to be a Red Sox, so why stray from the path to what was supposed to be mankind's best 1-2-3 starting combination?

The problem was that the Yankees were politely declining Atlanta's offer for much the same reason as Boston was. Cashman's scouts told him that Contreras wanted to be a Yankee, so the decision was made that a Yankee he would be.

Unless he mistakenly thought he could play for both teams, Contreras had plunged into the world of capitalism headfirst by partaking in baseball agents' favorite game—playing the Red Sox and Yankees against one another to drive up the price.

Two days after being rebuffed by both the Red Sox and Yankees, Atlanta made its trade, shipping Millwood to Philadelphia for minor league catcher Johnny Estrada. Epstein then got another phone call, but this time it was from Eljaua.

Luis was starting to see interest pick up around Contreras, and there were rumors that Cashman was on his way, raising the stakes exponentially. Torres also made it clear that a decision was going to be made quickly, in part because the agent's kids were expecting his presence in the family's Florida home on Christmas morning. Eljaua believed Epstein was needed in Managua.

Theo had no qualms about making the trip, knowing it might well be a necessity. What he hadn't planned for was having to update his passport on a Saturday, a task that cropped up as soon as he started to pack his bags. The Red Sox had prepared for every eventuality . . . except this one.

Improvisation was now on deck.

A plan was hatched where Boston's traveling secretary would arrange a flight to Miami that went through Washington, D.C. Once in the nation's capital, Epstein would use his two-hour layover to use a connection of team president Larry Lucchino for a rare weekend passport renewal. A quick trip to Miami, followed by two and a half hours in the air to Managua, and Epstein's excellent adventure was set. As a result, in a month full of days like nothing he had ever seen, Epstein would put December 21 at the top of his head-shakers. It was, as he later said, like a movie . . . from a damn good script.

Epstein had never been to Nicaragua before, although he imagined it couldn't be much different than some of those small Mexican towns he had ventured into while working in San Diego. The surroundings did look similar, and the weather upon landing was a welcome seventy-eight degrees, but when that first chicken ran through the hotel lobby, Theo knew this was more than a slightly different world.

Thoughts of the surroundings, however, didn't have much room in Epstein's head. Neither did reflection that he had been on the job less than a month, and he was a week shy of his twenty-ninth birthday. After all, it had been twenty-four years before to the day that a group of NASA engineers with the average age of twenty-six years old had guided the Apollo 8 spacecraft around the moon. So, certainly in Epstein's eyes, guiding a Cuban pitcher around the Yankees and into Boston shouldn't be too daunting.

At midnight on the morning leading into December 22, just a few hours after Epstein had arrived, the Red Sox made their initial offer to Contreras. They felt good about it, although the feelings were tempered somewhat just knowing the Yankees were waiting around the corner with a checkbook that was prepared to yield up to $8 million per season.

Later that day, Epstein ran into Gillick. The Seattle general manager was leaving town without his Cuban pitcher. Theo wasn't surprised to see the man who had built two world championship teams in Toronto. He always tended to be where the action was. But this time the action was just a bit too rich for his organization's blood. The Mariners weren't a poor team, carrying an $82 million payroll, but trying to keep up with the Yankees in Managua had suddenly become much less viable.

The word came down that Contreras was going to make his decision that night. Most of the meetings had been solely with Torres, but now, in the final stages, the pitcher joined the discussions. Boston had already gone over its planned offer, but for this pitcher, the subject of an elaborate two-month chase, that was OK in the eyes of Sox ownership. At $27 million over four years, Contreras appeared to be a wise investment.

As Epstein and Eljaua sat out on the hotel's patio restaurant, just thirty yards from where Torres was about to engage with Yankees' officials for the last time, Contreras walked by. "It looks good," was the message a smiling Jose passed on to the Boston duo. Looks good! Both Theo and Luis had learned of ninth-inning heartbreak, but when the object of your attention comes over and says, "Looks good," then the feeling becomes the same as if an All-Star closer was coming out of the bullpen to protect a three-run lead.

Two hours later, the Yankees completed their comeback.

Cashman never did make the trip, relying solely on his scouts while staying back in New York. When he heard Epstein had boarded a plane for Managua, he almost went, but he remained true to his own conviction that his people were steering the Yankees in the right direction. So while the Boston representatives sat an easy field goal's distance away from the negotiations, Cashman stayed close via phone calls placed every half hour or so.

So by the time Torres made the walk from Room No. 2 to Epstein and Eljaua's table at 12:30 in the morning of December 23, Cashman was sitting comfortably in his home having already been informed of the result regarding the bidding war. The Yankees had won with a bid of $32 million over four years. Contreras may have truly wanted to be a Red Sox, but not for $5 million less than what his other favorite team was offering. To rub salt in the wound, just days before New York had laid out a three-year, $21 million deal for Japanese outfielder Hideki Matsui.

Every time the Yankees' $150 million-plus payroll rose, the hearts of the Red Sox sunk just a little bit more. The realities of competing in the American League East reality had gotten that much more intractable.

The next morning, Eljaua got a knock on his door. It was Contreras. The pitcher was a huge man, and his face reflected both the size of his stature and of his inner struggle. To see the tears falling down his face upon saying good-bye to the man he befriended two months before just didn't quite seem natural. Neither did the fact that he was going to be finally pitching in *las liguas majores* for a team other than the Red Sox.

The plane ride back to the States flat-out sucked for Epstein.

Contreras's second defection, this time to a Yankees organization Larry Lucchino had deemed "The Evil Empire" in the post-Nicaragua backbiting, was like the biggest lump of Christmas coal that anyone could imagine. Epstein's return voyage on Christmas Eve was filled with questions of where it had all gone wrong. It was going to take more than just a couple of hours in a window seat to find the answers.

In the days to come, Epstein heard it all: Contreras was offended by the Red Sox's purchase of all the hotel rooms (it was a freedom thing); former Yankee Orlando "El Duque" Hernandez had gotten to his friend, singing the praises of living the big league life in pinstripes. But, when it was all said and done, the Boston general manager would accept only one explanation—Contreras was smarter than both sides involved. He had played one team against the other and come up with a deal above and beyond what anybody thought would be struck in Managua. The fledgling capitalist had immersed himself into a new way of life and emerged smelling like million-dollar roses.

The psychological corner from the setback in Managua turned slowly, but it did turn. On December 29, five days after leaving the scene of what the Red Sox classified as another Steinbrenner-bankroll-induced crime, Epstein started receiving some solace. It was his and Paul's twenty-ninth birthdays, a notable occasion if for nothing else that it got Theo closer to thirty and further away from the repetitive boy-meets-general-managing-job references in the media. The daylight hours also presented another gift for the GM—the Red Sox officially signed a player away from the Yankees.

The free agent defection of relief pitcher Ramiro Mendoza from New York to Boston might not have left a ripple on Steinbrenner's usually furrowed brow, but for the Red Sox it was a step toward steering their off-season journey back on the right path. It is one of the beauties of baseball—there is no time to stew. If a hitter goes 0-for-4, there is usually another four at-bats waiting the next day. If a pitcher surrenders a confidence-crippling home run, vindication is only a five-day waiting period (at the most) away. If a team loses out on a one-of-a-kind Cuban flamethrower to its archrival, there's always another player, or two, or three, just around the free agency corner.

Boston might have struck out down south, but the Far East was waiting, and so was a man named Kevin Millar.

"Change your thoughts and you change your world."

—Norman Vincent Peale

THEY SAT AT THE table blinded by their belief.

The Millars could have very easily been distracted by their surroundings—the room at the ritzy W Hotel in the heart of New York City and the highfalutin executives that filled out the fancy swivel chairs. If they took themselves out of their own skin for a moment and gazed upon the afternoon meeting then it would have been as believable as an Oliver Stone cinematic conspiracy theory.

But even with all the unfamiliarity, the Millars' focus could not be swayed. Kevin Millar did not want to go to Japan, plain and simple.

Just the mere notion that Millar, a thirty-one-year-old who puts the "out" and "going" in outgoing, was being courted by any team outside the world of the independent leagues that he had left behind just ten years before, was baffling. It wasn't as if the right-handed pull-hitter hadn't entrenched himself in the world of the majors. There was no arguing that he had become a very good Major League player. It was just that Kevin had always been the chaser, not the object of the chase.

The Dragons, however, didn't care where Millar had come

from. All they cared about was where he was going . . . especially if it was anywhere but the Land of the Rising Sun.

The Chunichi representatives sat glowering across the table from Kevin, his wife, Jeana, his father, Chuck, and his agents, Sam and Seth Levinson. The group of Dragons officials had come from Japan to reiterate the terms of the agreement Millar had originally agreed to on January 8: He would earn $6.2 million to play for the Japanese Central League team for the next two seasons.

For Millar, a player who had begun his professional career making $320 every two weeks, the deal with Japan had been a jackpot. The season before, his fourth in the majors, Kevin hauled in $900,000 for hitting .306 and sixteen home runs. But now he was begging out of this career deal, spending more than $10,000 just so that his wife and dad could join him in trying to seal his immediate employment in the United States.

Nothing has ever come easily for Kevin, and this was no different, except this time the fight had potentially life-altering ramifications. The meeting was the kind of moment Chuck had trained his son for. The family had a buzzword for peak performance in times of extraordinary pressure—"It!"

"It!" was a state of mind. Remembering to prepare, work hard, and be ready for anything before finally letting the moment transpire under the influence of nothing more than relaxation. "It!" was about allowing your instincts to take over.

Chuck had learned the power of "It!" in the most unusual of venues—the bowling alleys of Southern California. His mother, Greta, had been a bowling instructor in the 1950s and had taught her son well enough to the point that he could eventually use the sport for his financial gain. He had always worried that his love of sports would leave him helpless in the professional world, but thanks to his mom's lessons and the pro bowling circuit called the Potbean League, for one year Chuck had his outlet.

They called it "bowling for hamburgers," but so many times it was a lot more. Winning a match could mean anything from $20 to $500. Chuck made more in his job as a lab technician, but the lessons learned in going up against the likes of Dave Hawthorne and Manny Manchester were priceless. In a nutshell, the message was that if you try too hard to knock down that 10 pin it's usually not going to happen. Just throw the ball and don't give a shit. This was remembering "It!"

Now, with these strangers from a strange land putting the heat on, Kevin was being reminded of the family's mantra. "It!" was tattooed on his arm, and it may just have well have been hard-wired into his brain.

Midway through the group's second meeting, it was Chuck who almost allowed his son's preparation and pre–get-together focus to slide into oblivion.

Kevin's dad initially appeared to be on his game, telling the Chunichi folks that with the impending military action in Iraq he wanted his entire family to be stateside. Chuck still had two sons in elementary school and didn't want them worrying about their big brother's safety overseas.

Team Chunichi said no problem, the team would put the kids up in one of the area's best schools and hire a security detail to protect them. And if that wasn't enough, the Dragons offered Chuck $1 million and a house. That's when the kicking started.

Kevin saw the look on his dad's face, and didn't like what he saw. The son started booting his father under the table, leading the pair to take an impromptu bathroom break. Once in the restroom the Millars just broke into laughter. Chuck was a lab technician who would commonly work two shifts a day, but he was on the verge of turning his back on $1 million and a free house. It seemed far too improbable.

If there weren't going to be laughs, there would be tears . . . some tears of frustration, but a few more tears of joy. The kid who didn't even hit cleanup for his youth baseball team was now telling his dad to politely dismiss more zeroes on one check than either had thought they would see in a lifetime.

The Millars had come a long way, with a hotel bathroom suddenly serving as the journey's most memorable checkpoint.

*"Life is like a baseball game. When you
think a fastball is coming, You gotta be ready
to hit the curve."*

—Jaja Q

SOMETHING JUST CLICKED with Kevin and the sport of baseball. Maybe it was because both, the kid and the game, had become
Chuck Millar's all-consuming passion.

Chuck and his wife, Judy, had had Kevin while the family was
still based at Fort Ord in California during Chuck's stint as an
army medic. Even with his military duties, Chuck could always
find a baseball game. And if there wasn't a game to be had, then
swinging his yellow, plastic Wiffle Ball bat would have to suffice.

By the time Kevin turned two, he had drawn a bead on his
dad's bat. He wanted to give it a try, an urge Chuck wasn't about
to discourage. So, with the toddler holding the three-foot-long
plastic stick, Chuck gently tossed a white plastic ball toward the
bat. The ball's journey was just a few inches so the chances of the
two-year-old not making contact were slim. It was when the ball
did miss the bat that the father knew his son's infatuation for the
sport might be even more intense than his own passion (a notion
Chuck previously had never thought possible).

Every time young Kevin didn't make contact, no matter how
hard or soft the ball was tossed from Chuck, the miss elicited a
wave of crying from the batter. It was just two years into his life,
and Kevin Millar already hated striking out more than anything.

Kevin's destiny to live and breathe baseball never missed a
beat. There were the baseball cards, the trophies, the sleeping with
his bat and batting gloves, and the constant simulation of hitting
the game-winning home run while staring in his bedroom's mirror. It was a love that Chuck nurtured, which became uncom-
monly evident when the father first bought a $3,000 Wiffle Ball
pitching machine, and then put up three mercury vapor lights in
the backyard of the family's Newhall, California, home to illumi-
nate night Wiffle Ball.

Kevin was thirteen years old and Chuck was thirty-two. They both decided to take an entire summer off for a reason perhaps rationalized only by their own interest—they wanted to play Wiffle Ball all day and all night, every day and every night. Thirty years after a man named David Mullany had invented the perforated-plastic ball game, a Southern California father and son were taking the baseball hybrid to a whole new level.

The younger Millar's baseball-playing progression continued after high school, going from Los Angeles City College to Lamar University in the 115,000-person city of Beaumont, Texas. It was in the Lone Star State that people started taking notice of Kevin, both because of the skills he had nurtured under those gargantuan floodlights and the personality that made every day on a baseball field seem uniquely special. There were moments like Kevin running out to his spot at third base backward, shooting imaginary pistols at his teammates in the dugout, only to trip over the pitcher's mound. Or the time an errant golf ball had broken his tooth in pregame warm-ups, leading Millar to play with the bottom half of the tooth crudely fastened back onto the top half, making for easily the game's most hideous smile.

Millar was establishing himself as a baseball team's necessity—someone who could keep the game fun with the always-welcome combination of jokes and three-run homers. In his junior season at Vincent-Beck Stadium, a park prone to pitcher-friendly gusts of wind, Kevin hit thirteen home runs, three shy of the school record. With the combination of Newhall's favorite Wiffle Ball–playing third baseman and future Major Leaguer Bruce Aven, the Cardinals played the nation's best and beat the nation's best. It was against one of those elite programs, UCLA, that Millar made his final out as a collegian, grounding into a game-ending double play.

Chuck couldn't help but wonder: Was this the last time his son would play organized baseball? The moment was definitely a tear-jerker. Kevin wasn't the scouts' type of guy, possessing only the sixth of a player's five tools—desire. He couldn't run fast, there were holes in his swing, his throwing arm wasn't anything special, and fielding was anything but his forte. Yes, this might have been the spot where organized baseball and the Millars parted company. It was a notion that only got stronger when the draft came and went without Kevin's name being called, for the second year in a row. A twelve-pack of beer later, and a potential future without baseball had officially sunk in.

Fortunately, Kevin had people in his corner, one being his former coach from LACC, Dan Cowgill. Cowgill arranged for a try-out with baseball's graveyard for never-will-bes and never-will-be-agains, the then–newly formed Independent League St. Paul Saints. Millar made it. No matter about the team or the level of ball, he had accomplished the unthinkable, playing in organized baseball for money ($700 a month, to be exact).

A summer at the 5,069-seat Municipal Stadium might not have been a welcome experience for some players, but it was baseball nirvana for Millar. One of the team's owners was actor Bill Murray, who would often stop by and take the team out for dinner. Kevin was playing, and playing fairly well, hitting .260 with five homers in 227 at-bats. And he even was afforded yet another mentor for his often-crooked baseball journey—a roommate named Leon Durham, veteran of 1,067 games of Major League experience.

Millar continued to leave impressions, the same kind littered on the fields of his collegiate playing days. Fortunately for Kevin, one of those fields he had marked with base hits was Southwest Louisiana State's home field, where the son of Florida Marlins' scout Gary Hughes had taken notice. The elder Hughes was looking to fill some roster spots, so the son let him know of the Newhall Wiffle Ball whiz. A few months later, Millar was a member of a real, live Major League organization. The Midwest League's Kane County franchise would be the next bit of professional paradise.

Millar didn't disappoint the Hughes's faith, hitting .302 in 477 at-bats, before heading to Brevard County of the Florida State League the next season. It was that leap, however, that was perhaps

Kevin's bumpiest transition. For the first time in his life, baseball would cease to be fun.

Heading into the time of year for spring training in 1995, the Major League Baseball players were still in the middle of a strike that had begun on August 12 the season before. The owners' solution was to form teams of "replacement" players, made up primarily of the non-prospect members of each organization's minor league system. Millar, an undrafted twenty-three-year-old who had been playing in the independent leagues two years earlier, fit the roster-filling bill for the Marlins.

Millar knew the risk: to be potentially ostracized by the striking Major Leaguers and their union for crossing the picket line. He also knew the reward, a non-guaranteed contract totaling $115,000 and at least $20,000 termination pay once the striking players returned. Also in the package was a chance to take the "non" out of "non-prospect."

When in doubt, call Dad.

Chuck had never been in a union, but he had shared a dream with his son of playing at the highest level of professional baseball. It just so happened that in the spring of 1995, Kevin was getting a chance to live the dream, albeit via a slightly tainted scenario. So when the son asked the father what he thought was the best course of action, the answer was simple. "What harm could it do?" asked Chuck.

Kevin had told his father about the money and the perception he believed was being relayed by the Marlins, that if he didn't join the team's other thirty-one replacement players, there would be no future for him in the Florida organization. From Chuck's perspective, the salary bump would also make up for any cash Millar had missed out on by not being drafted, and the risk of being out of favor with the Marlins wasn't worth not playing.

As it turned out, it wasn't the Marlins who Millar should have been worried about.

Kevin played throughout the five weeks of uncertainty, the big leaguers eventually came back, and suddenly the Millars realized that maybe it wasn't the right decision after all. As with many of the players who, for one reason or another, chose to appease the owners and take the money, Kevin was shunned by many of the returnees. He was one of the most likable guys ever to grace a clubhouse, but once any team meeting began that involved players belonging to the MLB Players Association, Millar was forced to head outside to take some of the loneliest batting practice of his life. Clubhouse fights and lonesome batting cages were not supposed to be part of the dream.

Fortunately for Kevin, time and a few hits would heal quite of few of Millar's wounds.

The inkling that Millar's journey from backyard Wiffle Ball champ to Major Leaguer might be a reality came in 1997. As a member of the Marlins' Double A team in Portland, Maine, he had hit .342 with thirty-two home runs and 131 RBI. Kevin was named the best player in all of Double A, and suddenly the tag of "prospect" was finally finding its way to an attachment with his name. Then–Sea Dogs' manager Carlos Tosca still remembers the moment he and Florida's then–farm director John Boles sat in the offices of Hadlock Field, and agreed that the positionless power hitter had been transformed from minor league roster-filler to Major League prospect.

It wasn't an easy admission for the Marlins' brass to make. Before '97, the reports dismissed Millar's chances, thanks to a propensity to chase sliders. But then the sliders started to either be guided out of the strike zone, or hammered into the outfield. A transformation had been made.

Millar finally made it to the majors in 1998, stepping to the plate against Arizona and its pitcher Jeff Suppan. It was the climax of a harrowing climb through baseball career minefields, stepping to the plate against a real big-league pitcher, while wearing a real big-league uniform and playing in a real big-league park. Suppan got the sign, wound up and delivered a ninety-mile-an-hour fastball toward the twenty-six year old. Millar swung hard. Too hard.

The force of Kevin's swing had fractured the hamate bone of his left wrist. Millar was in store for another first—a stint on a

Major League team's disabled list. Welcome mats were never part of his baseball-playing repertoire, anyway.

After healing up, Millar held his own with the Marlins, peaking in 2001 with a .314 batting average with twenty homers in a healthy 144 games. He had not only earned the respect of the Marlins, but had also drawn attention from the league's upper echelon of decision makers. One of those who put Kevin on his radar was Theo Epstein.

Theo brought Millar to the attention of his boss, San Diego general manager Kevin Towers. "Can he play catcher?" was Towers's first reaction. The response wasn't far-fetched considering it was a query that just about every coach, including Tosca, had asked in the hope of having Millar's bat in the lineup without the liability of what was perceived as a suspect glove in the outfield or at first base.

Catching wasn't an option, but hitting has a way of always finding a home on a roster. Starting in the summer of 2002, Boston was trying to steer Millar and his bat's relocation program all the way to Fenway Park.

The quest began at the '02 trading deadline, when the Red Sox started their inquiries regarding the Beaumont Basher. The Marlins, however, had become enamored of their former minor league roster-filler, and asked for two top-of-the-line prospects—infielder Freddy Sanchez and pitcher Seung Song—in exchange for Millar. That wasn't going to happen, so Boston turned to a pursuit of outfielder Cliff Floyd for their in-season lineup enhancement.

Millar's name came up between the teams again in the off-season. The Marlins got closer to making a deal reality—requesting $1 million and a former No. 1 pick, lefty pitcher Phil Dumatrait—but still no dice.

Time was ticking for a decision on Millar, because if Florida didn't offer the outfielder arbitration by December 20, he would become free to the world of Major League Baseball. That's when a third party stepped in. There was a Japanese team interested in having the Wiffle Ball whiz become one of their roster's three "gaijin" (foreign) players.

Arbitration was offered. Millar tentatively stayed a Marlin and then started flying all over the place. The Chunichi Dragons were telling the Marlins they had a major interest in Millar. Florida was passing the message on to the player that it was in his best interest to go to Japan, because interest in the United States was limited. And the Red Sox were being left out of the loop, or so at least the Dragons thought.

John Lin was a Chunichi representative whose responsibility included dealing with matters in the Major Leagues. Jon Deeble had a similar job with the Red Sox, serving as the chief scout for the entire Pacific Rim. Deeble, an Australian with an air about him that suggested a beach must not be far away, was summoned by Boston to talk to Lin about the possibility of shipping a player, Benny Agbayani, over to Japan.

Deeble also got the word from Epstein that, while he was in, he should see what Lin knew about Millar. Whatever secret Chunichi and Florida thought they shared was out in the open now.

Calling from a Sydney hotel room, Deeble first asked about Agbayani. Lin said he knew nothing. Then the Boston scout inquired about Millar. Again, Lin claimed to not have any knowledge of the situation.

"How come every time I talk to you, you don't know anything?" Deeble heatedly asked Lin. Moments later, curse words were exchanged and phones were slammed down. A few days later, on January 8, the Marlins announced they were selling Millar to the Dragons for $1.2 million.

In order for a player to be sold to Japan, the Major League team must first pass him through waivers. It's a process that had been previously considered a formality, since usually the player heading overseas isn't that desirable to begin with, and the teams in the majors don't want to disrupt what has become a lucrative partnership by staking a claim. It is the rarest of items within the baseball industry—a gentleman's agreement.

Because of the assumption that twenty-nine teams were going to leave the waiver wire alone, Millar was ready to sign his dream contract to play in the Nagoya Dome (described by some as nine-tenths mall and one-tenth baseball stadium). The undrafted, minor league roster-filler was going to make $6.2 million over two years. That was until Millar got a call from his agent, Sam Levinson, while snacking at a Cracker Barrel.

The Red Sox had read the rulebook, and saw nothing preventing a claim on Millar. So they proceeded to make the majors' most controversial, feather-ruffling maneuver of the off-season. Much to Millar's surprise, someone in the boundaries of the United States actually did have an interest in his services. It was a fact that was first echoed in the Levinson phone call, and then reiterated moments later when Epstein rang up the object of his waiver claim.

Larry Beinfest, the Marlins' general manager who had tried to hire Epstein the year before to become his assistant GM, was pissed. He wasn't alone. Some around the majors were dumbfounded that a team, never mind one run by the newest member to the general-managing fraternity, would break this unwritten rule. Most of their concerns revolved around the possibility that the once-profitable relations with Japan were now being thrown out the window.

The Beaumont Basher was stirring things up.

Epstein made a few calls to feel out the community's sentiment. He also did something he hadn't done before, and may never do again—he dialed his father for advice on a baseball matter. "Sometimes," Leslie Epstein told his son, "you've got to have ice in your heart." It wasn't going to be easy, but the Red Sox and Millar were officially bracing themselves for a five-month journey to go anywhere but Japan.

Millar didn't speak to Epstein for more than a month, letting the process run its naturally unnatural course. During that time, it was Levinson's job to keep drilling the message into the folks from Chunichi, that his client had changed his mind, hadn't signed a formal contract, and didn't want to leave the United States. That sort of technicality wasn't going to stop the Dragons.

Beaumont, Texas, was about to get a new visitor—John Lin.

*"It just proves how good Millar is, and all this
makes good headlines."*

—Dragons' president Junnosuke Nishikawa

LIN WAS SENT TO Texas by the Dragons, and was basically
charged with the mission to not let Millar out of his sight or mind.
The intensity of the Japanese team's feelings on the matter was
wearing on their representative in the United States. Lin was
everywhere, and his desperation all-consuming. The Dragons'
representative's intensity brought up suggestions that he might
commit suicide if he couldn't bring Kevin back to Nagoya. He
even asked the Millars for bank account numbers, Kevin's or his
dad's, to put chunks of Chunichi money into (again, Chuck was
tempted).

The pressure, and the presence of Lin, was getting unbearable
for Millar. On top of his future's uncertainties, he had also heard
outlandish rumors that the Japanese mafia might be involved. Then
there was the time he returned from a workout to find sixty-seven
messages on his answering machine. "Why me," he thought. Millar didn't have anything against anybody. He just wanted to play
in Boston, not Nagoya.

Hadn't Japanese outfielder Norihiro Nakamura done the same
thing when he agreed to a contract with the New York Mets a
month earlier, only to back out at the last moment? The whole
thing was out of hand. Millar had to get away.

So while Lin was joined in Beaumont by more Chunichi reps,
and Levinson continued to grease whatever wheels he could, and
Major League Baseball tried to figure out what to do, Millar
headed to Las Vegas.

Finally, Kevin could go back to being Kevin—carefree without
caring how he was going to fit into a lineup behind Kazuyoshi Tat-
sunami. Thanks to a high-roller friend, a lawyer who Millar met
through his Harley-Davidson motorcycle dealings, he hopped
aboard a Lear jet and wasted away the hours until decision day by

59

stacking his buddy's chips (and there were a lot of them). After the casino came an impromptu trip to South Dakota, where the posse decided to do a little pheasant hunting. The game of keeping away from Beaumont produced a unique combination of events. "Dad," Millar said to Chuck through his cell phone, "you're not going to believe this, but right now I'm riding down a dirt road in South Dakota with a million dollars of cash on my lap!"

Back in Boston, there was no getting away. There wasn't much of anything the Red Sox could do, since Major League Baseball had told them to stay in the shadows while an agreement was mediated with Chunichi. And whatever information Epstein did receive from MLB, it wasn't for public consumption in and around the Sox offices.

And, thus, the "Millar-O-Meter" was born.

Epstein would enter the office, the subsequent "How's it going?" would come from somewhere inside baseball operations and the general manager would inform the masses using up and down hand gestures. When it came to cracking this case, nothing was coming easy.

The ordeal continued. Millar had gone to Vegas, taken his family to New York for the face-to-face with the Chunichi people, taken some time in California, and finally returned to Beaumont to continue the waiting. The only certainty was that every morning was going to be full of questions, and the closest answers could only be found by riding around on his Harley-Davidson.

Finally, in the waning hours of Valentine's Day, Millar heard the unfamiliar voice of Epstein. "You're a Boston Red Sox," his new boss said. Five hours later the Beaumont Basher had loaded up his stuff and his wife into his black Cadillac Escalade, put a healthy pinch of Copenhagen chewing tobacco between tooth and gum, and was headed straight for the Red Sox's minor league complex in Fort Myers. The driving time was sixteen hours, but it was well worth it after enduring five weeks of trying to dodge Chunichi's embrace.

One of the first people Millar saw upon venturing out onto the expansive fields where Boston began spring training was Epstein.

They had never met, and had talked only a couple of times, but that didn't mean a hug wasn't in store. "I'm the invisible player, you're the invisible general manager, and now we're together," said the exhausted but elated Beaumont Basher. It was, as Millar later said, like they had known each other their whole lives.

The wildest off-season a twenty-nine-year-old general manager could ever experience was officially over with. Nobody said that trying to win a World Series was going to be easy.

CHAPTER 3

Postcards from a Picnic Table

"That is why this game is so screwed up."

—J.P. Ricciardi

The topic of the 2002 Major League Baseball amateur draft had hit a sore point with J.P. Ricciardi. The Toronto Blue Jays' general manager just couldn't fathom that a high school baseball player could have turned down a $4 million signing bonus, as his lunchmates had informed him. As Ricciardi later reinforced, "That's $4 million in the bank, no matter what happens to him."

Unfortunately for organizations like Toronto, disbelief had become all too commonplace in the current world of Major League Baseball. The Blue Jays were coming off a year in which they lost $35 million, finished with a 78–84 record, drew two million fewer fans than ten years before, and were in such a long-term rebuilding process that their general manager had to pass along a most unappetizing message for the second straight spring. It was a directive much more difficult to swallow than the meatloaf being dished out thirty feet away. "We know we're not going to win the World Series this year," Ricciardi said bluntly.

It was just three days into spring training, and the Blue Jays' reality hadn't gone anywhere.

The time and place of the Ricciardi-led conversation wasn't important. It could have happened anywhere at any time, not just on a picnic table in the Blue Jays' spring training complex in Dunedin, Florida. But on February 18, 2003, at 12:34 P.M., the day's issues paved the way for a transcendent baseball experience, complete with the minimal fanfare afforded to other splinter-filled, open-air luncheons before it.

The meal involved a group of six men who were in the process of unself-consciously defining the new generation of Major League Baseball. But first, even before talk of potential millionaire high schoolers, came the baked goods.

"This is really good," said seventy-five-year-old John Ricciardi, one of ten children who had experienced life as a professional baseball player, a member of the armed services during the Korean War, and part of the Fire Alarm Unit in Worcester, but up until now, had never taken a bite of cornbread. "I just thought . . . corn . . . how good could it be?"

Joining in Ricciardi's culinary discovery was his son, J.P. One look at the younger Ricciardi, and there was no mistaking that he was his father's son.

J.P.'s face was carved almost identically to John's original map of Italy. Both men possessed the same slim, athletic features that had once allowed for short minor league baseball careers, John with the Red Sox and J.P. as the property of the New York Mets. The pair of just-under-six-foot frames were capped by serious dark eyes and thick black eyebrows. Despite their ages, both men fit into the spring's sea of athleticism seamlessly.

One of the perks of being atop of the Blue Jays' chain of command had been J.P.'s ability to allow his father free rein of Toronto's minor league facility. The elder Ricciardi was used to the Florida winters, having followed J.P.'s exploits religiously while the former infielder played his college ball in nearby Saint Leo,

Florida. Still, it was a safe bet that John's previous tenure in the Sunshine State was nothing like his current existence in the out-of-the-way, 36,000-person town of Dunedin.

John Ricciardi roamed the fields of the newly refurbished Englebert Complex with the same aura and intensity of any of the Blue Jays coaches. J.P. was going to keep his dad involved because, No. 1, he was his dad, and No. 2, he knew his dad was a baseball guy. If John was cold, he was going to get a Blue Jays warm-up jacket. If John was hungry, he was going to get cornbread.

J.P.'s everyman generosity had been documented well before his father donned his first Blue Jays hat. In 1999, a kid by the name of Theo Epstein had been put at ease by the then-director of player personnel for the Oakland A's. Epstein, a jack-of-all-trades employee for the San Diego Padres, had been roaming around the league's winter meetings in Anaheim, not eliciting any kind of attention. It seemed as though nobody was going to take the time to talk to the innocuous twenty-five-year-old—except Ricciardi. The Oakland A's scouting whiz branched away from the meeting's heavyweights, went over to the unassuming Padres employee and started comparing notes concerning their shared home state of Massachusetts. Neither could have possibly imagined that four years later they would be sitting behind home plate at an early March spring training game between the Blue Jays and Boston Red Sox, overseeing the organizations that they were now respectively in charge of.

John Ricciardi, like Epstein before him, was going to get much more than he had bargained for. Thanks to J.P, Toronto assistant general manager Tim McCleary, the team's traveling secretary Bart Given, Blue Jays' vice president of communications Rob Godfrey, and scout Andrew Tinnish, John was receiving a free lunch AND a peek into Major League Baseball, circa 2003.

Usually, when describing baseball spring trainings, integrating irony into the setting is about as common as a fleet of Yugos in a "For Millionaires Only" players parking lot. There was, however, no other way to label the senior Ricciardi's introduction to his new favorite side dish. For one half hour, "beginnings" was the accidental theme in a meeting that morphed from "benign" into "definitive."

"Good job, buddy!"

—Andrew Tinnish, Toronto Blue Jays' scout

TINNISH, A LATE ARRIVAL to the midday meal, patted McCleary on the back as he offered the congratulatory greeting. There was no explanation needed for the kind words since everyone at the table already knew the source of the kudos. The Jays' assistant GM had spearheaded the charge that had gotten Toronto outfielder Shannon Stewart signed to a one-year, $6.2 million contract earlier in the day. The agreement avoided a pending arbitration hearing between the sides, at which a three-person panel would be deciding if Stewart was worth the $7.5 million he was asking, or the figure of $5.5 million Toronto had submitted.

McCleary is a thirty-eight-year-old Queens, New York, native who had been with Toronto for the past eight years, but he still lets his New York accent slip out about every fifth word. He humbly thanked his coworker. Tinnish was just a first-year scout, roaming Florida for the last few months, but his compliment carried plenty of weight this time around. It showed that, from top to bottom, the entire Toronto organization had acknowledged McCleary's subtle victory, and was ready to give a not-so-subtle tip of the hat.

Simply put, the Stewart case was a must-win for Toronto. The figure of $7.5 million made the Jays' front office squeamish, a feeling that most likely wouldn't go away by settling for the halfway point of $6.5 million.

Stewart certainly had his merits. At twenty-nine years old, he had been playing in Toronto for the past five years and sixty-three days, the second-longest tenure of any current Blue Jay. His strengths were an offensive blend, which included both speed and power. He had totaled sixty-six home runs, 321 runs batted in, and 162 stolen bases in 784 Major League games, all numbers befitting a valuable bat in any team's lineup.

If the day of arbitration had arrived, it was then the job of Ricciardi, McCleary, Keith Law (another assistant to the Toronto GM), and one of the team's attorneys, Harry Zinn, to make the case that Stewart and his agent, Jeff Moorad, had overrated the player's value. As Ricciardi told the Toronto media earlier in the day, the Blue Jays were ready to present a case that was as extensive as "The Monroe Doctrine." ("Although I'd rather have the Marilyn Monroe Doctrine than the James Monroe Doctrine," the GM would later say.)

The reality? While the meat and potatoes of James Monroe's December 2, 1823, message to Congress came in at 937 words, the Blue Jays' 2003 message to Shannon Stewart and his representatives weighed in at twenty-five pages, heavy on diagrams and charts for simplification's sake. They knew that they shouldn't take anything for granted, especially after hearing stories about arbitrators asking the two parties during one case, "What's a save?"

Forget fending off European colonization, the Blue Jays needed another starting pitcher, and saving a couple of million dollars might just do the trick.

Toronto would have been afforded one hour to compare Stewart's upcoming salary figure to the likes of Anaheim's Darin Erstad's latest contract, as well as the recent free agent deals signed by Cliff Floyd and Edgardo Alfonzo. Still, even the most exhaustive preparation wasn't everything, as the Seattle Mariners found out a few days later in their arbitration hearing with pitcher Freddy Garcia. The word around baseball was that the Mariners' proposal blew away the argument set forth by the pitcher's representatives, but the panel chose to side with the player's request of $6.875 million, not the team's figure of $5.9 million.

As far as the Blue Jays were concerned, there were some pretty major reasons why they felt they should win. Stewart didn't have a good arm. Stewart had a history of injuries. Stewart hadn't proved himself to be a $7.5 million player. These were going to be some of the Toronto quartet's points when it faced off with Moorad's group. But just like eighty-eight of the ninety-three arbitration cases filed the season before, neither side got to set off their factual fireworks.

"I kind of wanted to do it just to see what it was like," said Ricciardi, taking a healthy sip of his Sunkist.

The Stewart scenario had been unique to the one-year-old Ricciardi regime, in that it potentially represented the GM's first foray into Major League Baseball's arbitration system. Under the league's rules, after playing three seasons in the Major Leagues, a player has to be offered salary arbitration by his team or he is entitled to file for free agency.

Three days before the Tampa-based arbitration hearing was scheduled to be heard, Ricciardi had mixed feelings concerning the process. While some general managers fear the repercussions of bombarding their player with the reasons why they aren't worth what they and their agent are asking, the no-nonsense, forty-three-year-old seemed more concerned that he would have to break into his necktie collection for the February 21 showdown. He had a lot of ties, more than a hundred of them, but not a lot of occasions to use them.

Ricciardi may not have labeled the other side's feelings as a priority, but that was partly because he shared the views of such experienced front office men as Mike Port, who described the process simply as "an exploration of facts."

Port, now the Red Sox's vice president of baseball operations, was three hours down Interstate 75 in Fort Myers. The fifty-eight-year-old was one of the most experienced, still-active front office employees in baseball, having served as general manager for the California Angels and Boston after starting in the San Diego organization in 1975. As much as Ricciardi was a neophyte to the arbitration process, Port had experienced more cases than he cared to remember.

The even-keeled, dry-witted Port, who had filled in as the Red Sox's GM after Dan Duquette's firing during the 2002 spring training, had seen the best and worst of arbitration since the process began twenty-eight years before. "Back then, however, we were debating over $2,500 to $5,000," the California native explained. Port insisted that if both sides dealt with documented cases then there would be little room for bickering. But that didn't mean he wasn't dealt a few eyebrow-raisers in his time.

There was the time Dave Skaggs, an Angels catcher, had already been released after the 1980 season, but he still had to go to arbitration to settle on his termination pay. And in one of Port's last cases with the Angels, he thought he had a slam dunk when the player's agent stood up at the end of the proceedings and declared, "We really blew that one!" Yet, even with the statement (and the absence of the player) the arbitrator's decision went against the club.

But in Port's mind, nothing could ever compare to one particular '80s arbitration dealing. "We both finished our presentation and the arbitrator stood up, turned to us and thanked us," he remembered. "Then he turned to the player and said, 'Can I please have your autograph?' How do you compete with that?" It certainly painted a picture that perhaps the Jays were fortunate to avoid the trip to Tampa this time around and turn their attention toward other contractual peccadilloes.

"Now I want to make a run at Kenny Rogers."

—J.P. Ricciardi

THE TALK REGARDING the particulars in the Stewart signing set off a round of smiles around the picnic table. It was a feat that probably wouldn't have elicited a peep twenty miles southeast in the New York Yankees' Tampa camp, the home of the $150 million payroll. But this wasn't the Yankees; it was the $53 million budget of the Blue Jays, and potentially saving $1.3 million was a big deal.

After locking up Stewart for another year, the Jays' GM was $1.5 million under his team's self-imposed budget. It was money he still had left to play with, and he wanted to use it on the undeniable weakness of his team entering the 2003 season—starting pitching.

For most teams, the thirty-eight-year-old Rogers wouldn't have garnered such anxiety, but Ricciardi had to cut corners somewhere, and three days into spring training it appeared he had done so in the starting pitching staff.

"Rogers can flat-out pitch. Forget No. 3 [starter], he could be our No. 2," Ricciardi insisted. But the GM also knew that obstacles stood in the way of Rogers agreeing to come to Toronto. The money appeared to be short for a player who had turned down $10.2 million for two years from his previous team, the Texas Rangers. The lefty, who relied on finesse rather than fastballs, also had put it into his contract when with Oakland that Montreal and Toronto were the two places he could not be traded to.

"I don't think [the Jays' offer] will be enough, but I wouldn't be doing my job if I didn't at least pick up the phone and find out," Ricciardi explained to his lunchmates. "I'm happy with our team, but Kenny Rogers would just be the icing on the cake." Twenty-seven days later, Ricciardi would have to settle for a different kind of icing as Rogers signed a one-year deal with Minnesota for $2 million.

Like the Blue Jays, the Twins were watching every penny, maintaining a $55 million payroll. They, however, had two things working for them that Toronto couldn't match. First, Minnesota was coming off a season in which it finished atop the American League's Central Division. And second, and perhaps most important for the Twins' cause, was that the $2 million Rogers was being offered was being entirely financed by the team's insurance policy on Eric Milton. Rogers would be replacing Milton in the Minnesota rotation after the team's staff ace was lost for the season with a knee injury.

While the Stewart signing was being celebrated at and around the Dunedin picnic table, Minnesota GM Terry Ryan had no idea that Ricciardi had interest in Rogers, and he didn't really care. But when Milton went down, the pitcher's suitors quickly increased by one. Ryan immediately called his ownership group and asked what his financial limitations were. The Twins' boss was told he didn't have much time, but he did have an extra $2 million.

"Here's what I got, do you have any interest?" Ryan told Rogers and his representatives. That was it. There was no more money to be had. As it turned out, it was enough.

Ryan and Ricciardi understood that, as was the case with finding a veteran pitcher like Rogers, obstacles are a way of life for franchises outside of New York, Boston, Texas, and Los Angeles. It was J.P.'s job to navigate his way around them, which he and McCleary had managed to do in the Stewart case.

The good-natured McCleary, who possesses an unassuming air about him despite having been entrenched in the baseball industry since interning for MLB commissioner Peter Ueberroth in 1986, had already logged more than his fair share of arbitration experience while working for the Yankees from 1992–95. In one season alone, he had to present four separate cases, which equaled the total number of cases heard in '03.

There was one instance with New York, however, that actually taught McCleary his most reassuring lesson—that animosity doesn't always have to linger in the baseball business.

It was the off-season between the 1993 and '94 seasons, and the Yankees had just traded with the Philadelphia Phillies to acquire lefty pitcher Terry Mulholland. The problem for McCleary was that Mulholland was headed for arbitration just six days after the deal had been finalized. The assistant GM would have to meet his team's newest player for the first time in a New York City meeting room, where McCleary would be trying to show all of Mulholland's faults.

After a pair of very businesslike presentations, both sides left the building and headed for their respective flights. Much to McCleary's dismay, he was forced to share a cab to the airport with the subject of his factual assault, Mulholland. Once at La-Guardia Airport, the two discovered while in line that they were on the same flight to the Yankees' spring training site in Fort Lauderdale. As cordial as the pitcher had been to that point, there was still some level of discomfort in McCleary's mind.

Just before arriving at the ticket counter Mulholland suggested the pair sit together on the plane. McCleary explained that as nice as that might be, he was scheduled to sit in coach, not first class like Mulholland. Without hesitation, the player took a wad of cash out of his pocket and threw it down on the counter. "Have him sit with me," Mulholland told the ticket agent, pointing to McCleary. In the end, the Yankees would win the arbitration case, but, in McCleary's eyes, Mulholland had won something even better—his respect.

Since the Mulholland case, the arbitration oddities hadn't let up for McCleary. This time around, just a few days before Stewart had agreed to terms, Moorad employed a particularly unusual tactic. Sitting across the table from the Blue Jays representatives, the agent took out the stacks of paper which made up his side's case in a pending arbitration hearing, and slid them across the table toward Ricciardi and McCleary. It left the Toronto gang a little confused. The only thing that the Toronto executives could figure was that Moorad wanted to make it clear Team Stewart was ready to mix it up at the table in Tampa. In any event, it was a preemptive negotiating strike none of the team's representatives had witnessed before.

Two days later, Stewart signed a contract. Thirty-two days later, the outfielder was breaking spring training with the highest batting average of any Major League player.

"It's nothing personal, just business."

—Michael Corleone from *The Godfather*

RICCIARDI'S CURIOSITY when it came to experiencing an arbitration case not only exemplified his confidence in his team's case against Stewart, but his comfort in dealing with all players and their agents. "When you come down to it, everybody is a person and should be treated like one," he said. "Everybody wants to know where they stand. As long as you are honest and create dialogue, there isn't a problem."

In the Stewart case, Ricciardi would have been swapping proposals with the only agent with whom he had experienced a conflict throughout the 2002 season. Moorad had also represented outfielder Raul Mondesi, the biggest albatross on the Blue Jays' payroll as the 2002 season had gotten under way.

Moorad had made it clear from the beginning of spring training in 2002 that Mondesi wanted out of Toronto. And with two years left on a contract, which called for the thirty-one-year-old to be paid a very unparsimonious $11 million in '02, there was no bigger favor Ricciardi would have liked to do for the agent and his client.

The problem was that, as Ricciardi found out, nobody thought Mondesi was worth the money the Blue Jays were paying him. J.P. reached the conclusion that would probably never be able to jettison the contract, but he also knew that getting out from under it was his top priority.

Then came a blessing straight from the heavens—a misplayed fly ball in Yankee Stadium.

The "drop" came in the midst of the New York Yankees' June 29, 2002, game against their crosstown National League rival, the Mets. All season the Yankees had been looking for the chance to replace the retired Paul O'Neill in right field, relying on the talents of Shane Spencer and John Vander Wal. But neither player had seized the opportunity, leading Yankees manager Joe Torre to play utility infielder Enrique Wilson out of position in the outfield in the weekend series against the Mets. Wilson responded by playing like there was a circus tent over the stadium, circling fly balls aimlessly until they finally dropped in.

While Wilson's misadventures were taking place, Yankees broadcaster Tim McCarver started to suddenly sing the praises of Raul Mondesi. McCleary was watching the broadcast and immediately called Ricciardi. "You aren't going to believe this," said the Toronto assistant GM. "It's like McCarver is working for us!"

Paul Godfrey had no idea about Enrique Wilson or his adventures in the outfield at the time. He was immersed in his own concerns, the Blue Jays' late-afternoon game against their Canadian rival the Montreal Expos. But Rob Godfrey, the son who had joined his father in bidding the corporate world a fond farewell in exchange for life in the Blue Jays' offices six months earlier, changed his father's focus for the next twenty-four hours with the delivery of one phone message—"Randy Levine wants to talk to you."

Randy Levine was the Yankees' equivalent of Paul Godfrey in their chain of command, serving as the president of the club. But while the men's titles may have been the same, the dynamics of their jobs were very different, with Levine's world skewed by the presence of baseball's one-word lightning rod, "George."

Levine had to answer to George Steinbrenner, and after the Wilson misplays, George was calling—calling for Levine, calling for Mondesi, calling for someone's head on a plate, and he wanted answers now.

"Paul, I want to talk to you about one of your outfielders," said Levine upon receiving the return phone call from Godfrey.

"Shannon Stewart or Jose Cruz?" responded the Blue Jays' president, still wondering why Levine was calling him, instead of New York general manager Brian Cashman putting out a feeler to his peer, J.P. Ricciardi.

"No, I want to talk about Mondesi," responded Levine.

"Mondesi! Holy shit!"

The words never came out of Godfrey's mouth but they wanted to. The closest holiday was Canada Day on July 1, but after hearing the name of Toronto's most unwanted outfielder come out of his office's phone Godfrey was ready to start drawing up a new proclamation: "The Day Someone Wanted Raul Mondesi and His Goddamn Contract."

Levine was proposing that the Yankees take Mondesi off the hands of Toronto, and in return pay for the second half of his remaining salary. No player, just money. Sweet, sweet, American money.

Godfrey's first instinct was to finish the impromptu phone call with a verbal handshake. But it's a funny thing about human greed and how it can detour what appeared to be common sense just a few moments earlier. The answer was, "I'm going to have to turn this one over to J.P."

"Either you and I are going to make this trade or the trade is not going to take place," yelled Levine, clearly upset that George's directive might get derailed. Still, Godfrey didn't waver. He was a chemical engineer by trade, not a general manager. J.P. was going to have to be involved.

The initial phone call between the presidents took place at 6 o'clock on a Saturday evening. Two more calls would be placed to Levine that night, only after, of course, getting the words for the exchange passed along from Ricciardi. One more bit of dialogue Sunday night, along with a few more dotted i's and crossed t's, and the deal was done. The Yankees would pick up some of Mondy's money, and they would send Toronto a twenty-six-year-old Double-A lefty hurler named Scott Wiggins.

Godfrey's greed had gotten Toronto a left-handed pitcher.

A seventh-round pick in the '97 draft, Wiggins had solid numbers (2–1, 2.45 ERA in twenty-four appearances) at Norwich. Nevertheless, he was hardly the key to the deal for the Jays. Gone was the $11 million contract Mondesi held for 2002, along with his $13 million commitment for '03. Toronto did have to agree to pay $6 million of the '03 figure, but as far as the Jays were concerned, it was money well spent. Ricciardi knew that once the deal was consummated, his plan for the future of the entire roster could really be set in motion. "It was probably the most important thing that happened to us," said Ricciardi.

The final step of the process, however, wasn't an easy one. Ricciardi had to head into the dank hall of green concrete that was the runway to the visitors' clubhouse in Fenway Park to deliver the news to Mondesi. The GM was now thinking less about salary structure and more about Michael Corleone's mantra. As much as

Ricciardi disliked Mondesi's contract, he liked the person and player who possessed it. "Raul always played hard and he never gave us a hard time," said the GM. "But the faster the changing of the guard was, the better off we were going to be."

Just fifteen minutes before Toronto's July 1, 2002, game against the Boston Red Sox, Ricciardi joined Toronto manager Carlos Tosca in delivering the news to Mondesi outside the Blue Jays' locker room. As relatively new as his tenure was, this wasn't a new situation for Ricciardi. He had also informed relief pitcher Dan Plesac that he had been traded to Philadelphia for relief pitcher Cliff Politte just five minutes before a game the month before, although it had been in Toronto instead of on the road. Beyond that, by the time the Mondesi deal had been consummated, trades were old hat for Ricciardi, who had already made seven deals involving eighteen players since taking over in November 2001. His don't-look-back attitude had even alarmed his wife, Diane, who told him a month into his tenure, "You're trading everybody!" His response was predictable, "I didn't take this job to sit around."

But something strange happened in the case of Mondesi, the player who had begged to be dealt from Day One of the '02 season. Upon hearing the news that he was going to be playing for the team everybody wanted to play for, he broke down and cried, wrapping his hulking, 5-foot-11, 230-pound frame around Ricciardi and manager Carlos Tosca, dispensing spine-crushing hugs.

"I think Raul wanted to be traded to a contending team and we were able to get that done, but at the same time he's an emotional guy and he has a big heart," Tosca explained. "He was very emotional about it."

As moving as the moment was for all parties involved, there were certainly no tears shed by either side once reality set in. Mondesi became the everyday right fielder for a Yankees team that was favored to win the World Series, and Ricciardi could focus that much more on building the Blue Jays up, instead of finding ways to tear them apart. So with a huge obstacle removed, in came an equally big building block by the name of Josh Phelps.

Ricciardi called up Phelps from Triple A Syracuse to replace Mondesi on the Jays' roster. The catcher/designated hitter had tortured minor league pitchers with twenty-four home runs, sixty-four RBI, forty-five extra-base hits and a .658 slugging percentage. The call-up would play a key role in the Jays' second-half success, as Phelps went on to hit .309 with fifteen homers and fifty-nine RBI in seventy-four games, entrenching himself as one of Tosca's middle-of-the-order guys in Toronto's 2003 lineup. With Phelps' arrival, the Blue Jays had officially stopped stalling, and were now heading down the road that Ricciardi was hoping would lead to consistent respectability.

While the Mondesi and Phelps situations played a large part in the Blue Jays reconstruction, the Toronto brass's days were also loaded with a fair share of under-the-radar transactions. An example of the seemingly mundane roster maneuvering came in the form of a call McCleary had to make to pitcher Brandon Lyon back on October 9, 2002.

The season had just ended for Lyon, a good-natured, twenty-three-year-old right-handed pitcher who Ricciardi liked to compare to the laid-back character 'Spicoli' in the movie *Fast Times at Ridgemont High*. Although he had been demoted to Triple A Syracuse for the second half of the 2002 season, Lyon was feeling confident about his career. After all, it hadn't even been three years since Toronto had picked him in the fourteenth round of the 2000 June Amateur Draft, and he'd reached the big leagues.

Lyon had made a resolution to take his conditioning to a new level after his toughest season as a pro, proving it on the early October day by checking in at his gym in St. George, Utah. But before one weight had been lifted, Lyon's cell phone rang.

"Brandon, it's Tim McCleary," said the voice on the other end of the line. "I've got bad news and good news. The bad news is that we've taken you off the forty-man [roster], but the good news is that you've been picked up by the Red Sox." McCleary went on and talked to Lyon for a few more minutes before allowing the now-former Blue Jay some time to digest the developments before getting in some very unfocused exercise.

Then, just twenty minutes after McCleary's phone number had popped up on Lyon's caller ID, it was his new team's turn to interrupt his weight lifting. This time it was Boston interim GM Mike Port, who was in the last month in his role of running the Red Sox before handing the reigns to Epstein.

The day before that pair of life-altering phone calls, Lyon was playing golf when his agent, Matt Sosnick, had started the series of momentous messages. "All of these GM's keep calling me," Sosnick said. "I think you might be getting traded."

Sosnick and Lyon didn't realize it, but the pitcher had already been placed on waivers by the Blue Jays.

The reason Toronto wanted to put Lyon through waivers was more because of its desire to add players to its forty-man roster and less due to its disdain for the pitcher's performance. The Blue Jays needed the roster spot, and moving the kid who liked to pull his hat's brim over his eyebrows was the means to secure the space.

When a player is put on waivers, the rest of the Major League teams have forty-eight hours to make a claim. It was during the two-day process that five teams took a stab at Lyon, four from the National League and a lone American League representative, the Red Sox. The franchise with the lowest win total from the season before would be awarded the pitcher, although the Blue Jays were the only team who knew what teams were involved.

Ninety-three wins might not have gotten the job done a week before, but that record, along with a $20,000 claiming fee, were enough to deem Boston the winners this time around.

The Lyon deal may have lacked the bungee-cord excitement of other McCleary endeavors, but it still remained the media guide–filling transactions that were subtly playing a big role in Ricciardi's vision of the Blue Jays achieving consistent contention throughout the latter half of his newly signed five-year contract.

"I'm not saying we're right or we're wrong, but this is our plan and this is our direction," the Toronto GM said. "I did it for sixteen years in other places and we had some success. And you know what, we're having success here."

*"If you're interested in continuing to do things the
same way they've been done around here, then
I'm the wrong guy for the job."*

—J.P. Ricciardi to Blue Jays CEO and
president Paul Godfrey

THE MONDESI AND STEWART predicaments weren't unlike
many of the decisions facing Ricciardi since he made the leap from
player personnel director for the Oakland A's to the fourth general manager in the Blue Jays' twenty-six-year history. While
interviewing with Godfrey, the longtime Oakland A's employee
had walked in and flatly told the Blue Jays' president and CEO
that Toronto had to come around to his way of thinking.

By the time Ricciardi came into the picture, the Blue Jays were
a mess, both on the field and in the team's financial reports. In
2001, the first full year in which the Rogers Communications
Group owned the team, Toronto reported a $52.9 million operat-
ing loss. That same year, the Jays finished 80–82 under first-year
manager Buck Martinez.

Not helping the bottom line for the Blue Jays was a weak
Canadian dollar, which Godfrey estimated accounted for $38.9
million of the team's losses in '01. Then, of course, there was perhaps the biggest problem—the fans, or increasing shortage thereof.

Attendance at SkyDome, the Blue Jays home stadium, had
dipped to 1.9 million in Martinez's first year, well below the four-
million-per-season average during Toronto's two world championship seasons in 1992 and '93. Group sales had plummeted, going
from an average of 750,000 in the early '90s to just 165,000 in '01.

So when Ricciardi told Godfrey what he needed to hear,
instead of what he might not necessarily have wanted to hear, the
Blue Jays finally swallowed hard and braced for the dirtiest of
words among baseball fans—rebuilding.

By the time Ricciardi's second spring training rolled around,
the Blue Jays' ledger had a decisively different look. The Blue Jays

were still claming a loss, but it was $17 million less than the previous year. And, just for good measure, the team was coming off a season in which it had the best post–All Star break record of any nonplayoff team, capped by winning its last seven games of the 2002 season.

Yet, even with the Ricciardi plan in place, some solutions hadn't been found after one year. Interest in the Jays was still a serious problem, with attendance in 2002 hitting the lowest mark since strike-shortened 1981. The team's fan club was also boasting just 750 followers, far less than the 10,000-member club of the early '90's.

With the position players scheduled to report to spring training in two days, there were just more than twenty people watching the Toronto workout. It was a tremendous contrast to a team such as the Boston Red Sox, who had more than a thousand fans roped in their Fort Myers training camp the same day.

"Ideally, you hope people are patient enough to see the master plan," Ricciardi said. "But in the end, my wife and family will still love me, and that's what counts."

The good news for Ricciardi was that his family finally showed up in Dunedin on March 1 and they still loved him. The bad news was that the GM knew the Toronto fans' patience would be a lot less easy to come by if the momentum from September 2002 didn't carry over to April 2003.

"So let me get this straight, our priority is to scout college kids, hang out at the mall, then, if there's nothing else to do, scout high school players."

—Rob Godfrey

WITH TINNISH set to leave the lunch and head off to another scouting assignment, the talk turned to his priorities. "Are you going to any high school games?" Ricciardi asked. When it was explained that the boyish-looking scout's schedule didn't include many, if any, high schoolers, Ricciardi responded, "Thattaboy. If you've got absolutely nothing else going on, go to a mall or to the beach. Then, if you've got nothing else going on, go to a high school game."

Godfrey, the son of the Jays' president and CEO, couldn't resist the opportunity to joke about the mandate set out to Tinnish. But while the Jays' new scouting philosophy offered some levity in between sips of Diet Coke, the importance of understanding was no laughing matter to Ricciardi.

Ricciardi knew that if the cash-strapped Blue Jays were going to be able to become legitimate players in the annual American League playoff push, a big part of the solution would be to come up big in the draft. And in the GM's eyes, the best way to hit a home run in the two-day event was to look primarily at college kids, and be very judicious when it came to the high schoolers. That's what they did when he was with the A's, and that was going to be the Blue Jays' way.

The college kids had the track record, plain and simple. Ricciardi's favorite analogy was the one pertaining to purchasing a car—if you're going to put down the money, then you're going to get something that is tried and true. You're going to buy on its track record. It was all about managing risk.

Ricciardi had already made his presence felt in the 2002 draft, taking University of North Carolina shortstop Russ Adams in the first round with the fourteenth pick. The GM had seen Adams play four times in person and felt confident in giving the MVP of the prestigious Cape Cod Summer League the $1,785,000 signing bonus such a pick demanded. As Ricciardi explained, "If I'm going to give a kid a couple of million dollars, then I'm going to have to feel comfortable enough to sign off on it." In all, the GM saw fifteen different players in person before the 2002 draft, a number which by many accounts represented more firsthand scouting than any other general manager in baseball.

There couldn't have been a better poster boy for Ricciardi's approach to the draft than Adams. The twenty-one-year-old lefty hitter was a college guy (University of North Carolina) who hadn't even been selected in the draft coming out of high school. He was an athlete, the second-highest rated college player in the '02 draft, and, above all, the kid oozed baseball instincts. The hard-nosed shortstop was, as his new boss described, "everything you look for in a player."

The compliment afforded Adams was considered high praise throughout the league considering Ricciardi's reputation for eyeing baseball talent. From early on during his days with Oakland, where he had unearthed shortstop and four-time postseason participant Mike Bordick from the University of Maine, Ricciardi displayed an ability to find the baseball in the player. His reputation for outworking the other scouts was so well-known that teams started instituting the "J.P. Rule," stating that their guys had to not only see the games, but get there early enough to witness warm-ups.

"J.P. might be the best I've ever been around in terms of evaluating talent. He's got a real knack for it," Tosca would say. "Early on in your career, you're looking for the five-tool animal. The one thing J.P. has an eye for is not only finding talent, but also finding baseball players, guys who do things that don't necessarily show up in a box score. You don't find too many scouts who can do it. If anybody epitomizes J.P.'s ability to scout, it's Russ Adams. It took a keen eye to recognize that talent."

It wasn't just Adams who drew rave reviews when the picks were made on June 2nd and 3rd. The entire Toronto 2002 draft turned out to be a critical success, with *Baseball America*, the longtime authority on all things baseball, ranking the Blue Jays' draft as the best in all of baseball. Yet, Ricciardi's first foray into running his own selection show wasn't totally mishap-free.

Through the first six rounds of Ricciardi's inaugural draft, the plan had worked to perfection. Six picks, six college players. But then came round No. 7. Ricciardi left the room, and that's when, as he explained it, "there was a big misunderstanding."

With Ricciardi gone, the old remainder of the Jays' Loyal Order of Player Pickers unintentionally reverted to the organization's old philosophy of freely drafting high schoolers, selecting high school pitchers Brian Grant and Russell Savickas with the next two picks. This was not part of the plan.

Keith Law had only been in professional baseball for six months, but he knew there was going to be trouble.

Law is a Harvard graduate who just turned twenty-nine the day before the draft began. At just 5-foot-8, maybe 150 pounds, his presence was already tough for some of the draft room's participants to fathom, perhaps because many of them didn't know where the New York native had come from, or why he was there. And if they did know just how Law arrived as one of Ricciardi's chief sounding boards, it wouldn't have helped anyway.

Law, a recently unemployed tech worker by day, and writer for the statistical analysis baseball supernova *Baseball Prospectus* the rest of the time, began his new life with an unsolicited phone call to a Major League general manager he had never dealt with before. What he didn't know was that J.P. Ricciardi, the just-on-the-job GM in question, was familiar with Law's writings, and was looking for someone like his caller to use his perspective for the good of the Toronto Blue Jays. Fifteen minutes into the impromptu phone call came an impromptu job offer. The tech worker was unexpectedly helping run the rebuilding of a Major League franchise . . . and, by all accounts, doing a pretty good job of it.

Acceptance would come with knowledge and information, which had been brewing in Law for years and was now just getting out, courtesy of the discretion of the Blue Jays' general manager. The newcomer's job was to give Ricciardi another angle when it came to looking at players. J.P. had always been able to visualize talents firsthand, but now he wanted to get the fourth dimension, one that resided in the performance numbers. That was where Keith fit in.

If you're going to buy a house, you're going to want all the information you can get on that house. Now the Blue Jays were in the midst of selecting the equivalent of more than forty homes, and Law was doing his best to inspect them all.

Law remained silent during the selection of the high schoolers because of his newness, but what he did know was that Ricciardi was not going to be happy upon coming back into the room. He was right.

When the new Toronto GM reentered the Blue Jays "War Room," a twenty-foot-long office not nearly big enough to comfortably house the day's contributors, he was not at all pleased that his edict to pick the college kids had been overlooked. The general manager was infuriated that the message of not dipping into the high school pool of players was either ignored or not understood. Shortly thereafter, an organizational meeting was held, with Ricciardi having to reannounce his "it's my way or the highway" declaration.

By the time the following March rolled around, more than forty-five scouts and other members of the previous regime either were jettisoned or left on their own. The draft debacle may not have been the sole impetus for every departure—in Ricciardi's view, the department was dramatically overstaffed—but it signified the reason for the exodus. That, however, didn't mean that all was copacetic. Late in 2003's spring training, the GM was informed just outside his spring training office that his scouts had high schoolers rated in among the team's top amateur prospects.

The news prompted Ricciardi to slump his shoulders, shake his head, and dip in to his movie-quote archive. When in doubt, J.P. turned to the classics. "What we have here is a failure to communicate," he said. "You know what movie that is from?"

Bart Given correctly answered, *Cool Hand Luke*. "Nope," Ricciardi responded. *Smokey and the Bandit.*

They were both right. But, as Ricciardi was trying to impress on his rapidly changing staff, there can only be one final answer—his. "You have to have someone out there in the lead," the GM explained back at the picnic table. "I'm pretty sure [University of Louisville men's basketball coach] Rick Pitino doesn't ask someone if they think it's a good idea to press. Right or wrong, someone has to make the tough decisions."

Ricciardi already knew that the first year was going to have the kind of logistical problems that popped up in the '02 draft. But he also realized that with time and a few personnel changes, his organization could soon be operating in unison. "Now I understand why people want to bring in their own people," Ricciardi says. "The people around you have to know what they're doing. With all the things that are going on, I don't have time to guide everyone through everything."

Helping Ricciardi's quest for continuity entering his second season was the addition of a new right-hand man, Tony LaCava.

LaCava had been the second-best player on his high school baseball team, behind a shortstop and pitcher named Dan Marino. Like many of his teammates, Tony had been caught in the whirlwind that had enveloped the future Miami Dolphins quarterback. LaCava was a good athlete and a good baseball player, manning both third and first base. And with Marino around, plenty of scouts at least got a taste of what the kids behind Big Danny could do. So did the photographers.

Life magazine had decided to follow Marino around everywhere he went during his senior year. The fields, the hallways, and the houses, it didn't matter where, the photographers would be there. The problem for those same photographers was that usually everywhere Marino was, so were his buddies. By the end of the magazine's stay, LaCava and the boys had come away with their own souvenir from Marino's documentation—an entire trash barrel of wasted film. Frame after frame of unwanted backgrounds and misguided directions reeked havoc.

LaCava later felt bad about contributing to Operation Interference, but he also knew that the behavior was a product of his high school–level maturity. It was a level that Tony dramatically improved by the time his two-year professional baseball career had ended with the Pittsburgh organization. He was getting married, and the fun of baseball didn't appear to be an option, leading him to partner up with his brother and run a Dunkin' Donuts. Unfortunately, "Time to make the donuts," didn't elicit the same goose bumps as a good old-fashioned "Play ball!"

So LaCava, like many a scout before him, slowly got into baseball, slipping into the industry side of the game. After talking up some baseball types at his younger brother's high school games, Tony got a job as an associate scout for the Angels. After 1989, he started getting paid as a part-time scout, leading up to a full-time position in '91. Five years later he had signed three future big leaguers, pitchers Brian Anderson and Mike Holtz, and first baseman Mark Sweeney.

Tony had first met Ricciardi in '91 at a showcase for players up and down the East Coast called the Coco Expo, down in Florida. The pair's personalities and passions blended perfectly, leading to their vow of someday working on the same team with the same goal. The year 2002 was that time.

But like much of the Blue Jays' transformation in Ricciardi's first season, securing the forty-one-year-old took a little more elbow grease than had been previously anticipated.

In Ricciardi's mind, LaCava's job would mirror what the former A's director of player personnel had done for Oakland GM Billy Beane—combining the roles of sounding board, talent evaluator, confidant, and all-around right-hand man.

As one of his first orders of business, the Toronto GM placed a call to Montreal general manager Larry Beinfest to ask for permission to bring LaCava to the Blue Jays as an assistant general manager. Permission was denied. That prompted Ricciardi to make another call, this time to Expos president David Samson to explain that this was a chance for LaCava to move up the executive ladder. Again, the plea fell on deaf ears.

So, as was the case for many of Ricciardi's early moves, the Jays decided to take the long-term approach toward solving the problem. LaCava handed Montreal his resignation and became a free agent. Ricciardi knew, however, that if the Jays scooped up LaCava right away, they would be opening themselves up to potential tampering charges. So, with the Blue Jays still in his sights, LaCava went to Cleveland to become the Indians' national cross-checker for one year. It could have been more than just the one season (the Indians offered a three-year deal), but Tony hadn't forgotten his unwritten pact with J.P. to someday join forces. Even when the

Red Sox came calling prior to the 2003 season, asking LaCava if he wanted to join up with the staff being assembled around Theo Epstein and make more money in the process, the answer was "thanks, but no thanks."

They hadn't carved their contract in any tree, or used a dull glass bottle to become blood brothers, but ten years before, there was an understanding. Someday the two scouts were going to build something—together.

Ricciardi had his man and another piece to what was becoming Toronto's ever-changing puzzle.

"He's a dead ringer for that guy from Home Alone.*"*

—Tim McCleary

THE TALK AT THE picnic table had turned to actor Daniel Stern and the man the Blue Jays' executives considered his twin, pitcher Gary Majewski. "Yeah, Majewski looks exactly like him," said Ricciardi.

"It's pronounced Ma-jes-ski," explained Given. "Really?" asked Rob Godfrey, quickly adjusting the pronunciation of the pitcher's name. Ricciardi continued, "He was also the guy from *Breaking Away*. 'The damn cat's name is not Felipo!'" Such lines from the 1979 movie were no problem for Ricciardi. Now his challenge was to remember another "cat," the pitcher who looked like "that guy from *Home Alone*."

For good reason, everyone knew who Majewski was after just three days. The 6-foot-2, right-handed pitcher, just eight days away from turning twenty-three years old, was one of three Rule 5 draftees that Ricciardi had brought into camp. Just like fellow pitcher Aquilino Lopez and outfielder Jason Dubois, Majewski had to be on the Blue Jays' roster for the entire 2003 season or be sent back to his previous organization.

Major League Baseball's Rule 5 draft has been a regular occurrence at every one of its winter meetings since 1950. The draft allows teams to select players from other teams who haven't been placed on their organization's forty-man roster after three to four years of professional experience. The draft, which is named for the rule number it represents in the Professional Baseball Agreement, goes in order of the previous season's records, from worst to first, with the American League and National League alternating the top pick from year to year.

The Rule 5 extravaganza has more often than not been dismissed by fans as something not worthy of putting on their off-season radar. Usually, the chance of the players sticking with their new team is slim because of their relative inexperience. But, as Toronto found out in the 2002 season, there is reason to care. Ricciardi's first foray into the Rule 5 draft resulted in the Jays grabbing Corey Thurman, a twenty-three-year-old righty reliever who pitched in forty-three big-league games for Toronto after toiling in the Kansas City Royals minor league system for six seasons.

Thurman was only the most recent example of Rule 5 success for the Blue Jays organization. Toronto had hit it big before in the draft, picking up longtime contributors Willie Upshaw (1977), George Bell (1980) and Kelly Gruber (1983). As far as the rest of the league went, the far-and-away most successful selection ever made came when the Pittsburgh Pirates chose a young outfielder named Roberto Clemente in 1954.

Ricciardi didn't have delusions about finding another Hall of Famer when he chose Majewski, Lopez, and Dubois on December 16, 2002, but he did see them as additional rays of hope within the Blue Jays' building process. It only cost the Jays $50,000 to select each player, $25,000 of which would be sent back to Toronto if they didn't make the team. In the GM's mind, it was money well spent.

All three of Toronto's picks had shown signs of promise in the previous season. The pitchers both threw well at Triple-A, with Majewski going 5–3 with a 2.65 ERA in fifty-seven games with Birmingham, and Lopez finishing at 4–4 with a 2.39 ERA in thirty-four games at Tacoma. Dubois, while only at Single-A, had finished his 2002 campaign by hitting .321 with twenty home runs and eighty-five RBI in 361 at-bats in the damp, heavy air of the Florida State League.

A few hours before the mid-February picnic table feast, Lopez was walking toward Ricciardi when the GM made a fifty-yards-away observation. "Boy, doesn't he walk like Pedro," said Ricciardi, comparing the pitcher's 6-foot-3, 165-pound frame to three-time Cy Young Award–winner Pedro Martinez. "Now if he can just pitch like him." Lopez just about fulfilled the wishes of Ricciardi in spring training, finishing with nineteen strikeouts and just two walks in his twelve innings of work.

A soft-spoken pitcher who had grown up thirty miles down the coast from the Dominican Republic capital of Santo Domingo, Seattle had soured on Lopez because he had lied about his age when he had originally signed. During Major League Baseball's crackdown on foreign players' birth dates after the September 11, 2001, tragedies, Lopez became one of almost three hundred players whose real dates of birth were found out. In the blink of an eye, his birthday went from July 30, 1980, to April 21, 1975.

Ricciardi, on the other hand, didn't care about age. All he knew was that the potential reward was well worth the risk. As a month of spring training had proven, it was a risk worth taking.

"Whew, it's hot today," Lopez had said in broken English while passing by Ricciardi before a late-March spring training game. "Wait until you get up North," responded the GM "But you know what? It's better to be *frio* in the Major Leagues than *caliente* in the minors." Lopez just smiled the smile of a player who knew his days of weathering any kind of temperature in the bushes were a thing of the past.

Unlike Majewski and Dubois, Aquilino was not going back to his former organization or to the minor leagues. He had made it to the bigs.

This was life with a Rule 5 player—hope for the best, and don't worry about the worst. This was also life in the Toronto organization. The resurrection had begun and there was no turning back.

"One day at a time, right dad?"

—J.P. Ricciardi

"ALL THESE GUYS are coming in early," said Ricciardi to his father as he got ready to leave the picnic table and head to one of the adjourning fields one day before all of the fifty-five Major League candidates were to report. "It's awesome!"

On this February day everything was copacetic. But would Ricciardi get that same feeling when September rolled around? "You need anything else?" the GM asked, patting John Ricciardi on the back before heading back off to the practice fields. The elder statesman of the luncheon had his Blue Jays jacket and another piece of cornbread; he was all set. His son, on the other hand, could still use a little pitching.

"Back off to work," exclaimed the younger Ricciardi.

Another day, another devalued Canadian dollar.

CHAPTER 4

A General Manager's First Game

"That's baseball."

—Theo Epstein

The gray suit in Section 102, Row U, Seat 2 couldn't stay still. Back and forth. Forward and back. The suit was usually immobile at baseball games, reserving sudden movements solely for entrances and exits, but this was different. This time it was residing on the back of a real, live Major League Baseball general manager.

The suit's owner, Theo Epstein, failed to mask his anxiety as he sat in the hard, plastic blue seat behind home plate at St. Petersburg, Florida's Tropicana Field. It had been four months since the combination of his youth and job title had thrust him into baseball history, months that had been saturated with a year's worth of problems and the most unwelcome feeling that every clock had implemented 180-second minutes.

Now, however, time stood still. The Boston Red Sox had accumulated twenty-six outs from the bats of the Tampa Bay Devil

Rays and were just one more away from successfully completing their day . . . Opening Day.

The calendar squares leading the twenty-nine-year-old to this early-season punctuation hadn't generated any of Epstein's father's gray hairs, but Theo knew that at this rate they would be introducing themselves to their sun-soaked brown brethren well ahead of schedule. Now the stress had morphed—almost without notice—from what might have been anticipation to what definitely was anxiety.

It was time to find out if this collection of ballplayers Epstein had helped put together to form the Red Sox could get one more out, and give Theo a perfect record as the game's youngest GM.

The only thing that now stood in the way of history was a second-year left fielder named Carl Crawford.

With Tampa Bay base runners Marlon Anderson and Brent Abernathy standing at first and second base, respectively, Crawford, a strapping, athletic, 6-foot-2, 220-pound Texan, was dealing with a 1-and-2 count after fouling off four straight Chad Fox pitches. A three-run Red Sox advantage had been turned into a 4–3 affair by Devil Ray doggedness, a change that was just enough to set the pores of Sox fans everywhere to sweating, regardless of the outcome.

While the previous innings had resulted in simple, slight seat adjustments by Epstein, the offerings to the Devil Rays' leadoff hitter had elicited a new set of subtle mannerisms. As badly as Theo had wanted to win while watching the final outs of his Brookline High baseball team, or during the waning moments of a Yale University men's hockey game, or even the last inning of a game of "Gutterball" back on Parkman Avenue, this was a different level of eagerness entirely.

Finally, Fox delivered an eighty-seven-mile-per-hour slider right at the lower-left corner of the left-handed hitter's strike zone. Epstein wasn't alone in his thoughts. The GM, the players, and the 34,390 fans in attendance for the teams' first game of the 2003 season undoubtedly figured the worst damage Crawford could inflict was a tie-inducing base hit, considering that the speedster had managed just two home runs in his brief big-league career.

That Crawford, only four years out of high school, was in a Major League Opening Day lineup had surprised most baseball insiders. Among them was Epstein, who had known about the Texas native's unmatched athletic abilities from his work in preparing the San Diego Padres for the 1999 draft. Theo remembered the debate among the Padres' room full of executives concerning whether or not they should use their first pick on the raw talent of Crawford, who had already been offered scholarships to play quarterback at the University of Nebraska and point guard for UCLA.

In the end, the Padres decided to select another high school outfielder, Vince Faison, with the twentieth pick in the draft. That left Crawford available to the Devil Rays by the time they chose in the second round's first slot, thirty picks after the Padres' decision. Now Crawford was playing in his sixty-fourth big-league game, while Faison was on the conservative track to the majors as a member of the Double-A Mobile Bay Bears.

Everyone knew Crawford had the potential to be special, but was Tampa Bay trying to uncover the outfielder's destiny too soon? For one swing of the bat, the answer was all too clear to the Red Sox.

Crawford's left-handed, uppercut swing at Fox's offering had sent the ball sailing toward the domed stadium's right field fence, 370 feet away from home plate. He had never hit a game-winning home run, not once. Not in Little League or high school. But he also hadn't received such a gift in any of his previous chances at long-ball heroism. This time Carl got a lefty hitter's dream—a pitch that was nestling itself two feet off the ground, five inches from his right knee, and right in the path of the rapidly accelerating Louisville Slugger.

Except for the National Anthem and the seventh-inning rendition of "God Bless America," Epstein hadn't moved around much at all. But now, with his hopes of a 1–0 start to the 162-game regular season heading over the head of Boston right fielder Trot Nixon, he needed to get the perfect view.

When you're a kid, every fly ball hit by a Major Leaguer seems like it could go forever. The majesty and altitude of the ball off these larger-than-life ballplayers always appear to be far too well struck to be held by conventional baseball measurements. This is why, at every ball game, a pop-up to the infield will lead to the inevitable screams of home run hopes, followed by the predictable sighs of inning-ending disappointment.

Epstein had passed the fly-ball fantasy stage long ago. He now dealt in the reality of simultaneously trying to watch the ball in flight while gauging the distance it had to go before reaching its landing spot. Unfortunately for Theo, there was no need for last-minute, geometric analysis in regard to Crawford's blast. The arc wasn't a fly-ball out, but a three-run, game-winning home run, producing a 6–4 win for the sad sack Devil Rays.

The moment took everyone by surprise. The slider was Fox's best pitch, and this had been a good one. The right-handed pitcher, whose face consistently had the appearance of the sadness experienced throughout a career that had included four surgeries, was making his inspiring return to the mound after rebuilding his rotator cuff the season before. Now, against Crawford, his stuff looked good; good enough to at least keep the ball inside the ball-park.

Tampa Bay bench coach John McLaren and Devil Rays first-base coach Billy Hatcher had both thrown Crawford hundreds of batting practice pitches and knew the likelihood of what was going to transpire. It had been their job to drill the mind-set of a leadoff hitter into their young outfielder—hit it on the ground, or in the gaps, use your speed and, whatever you do, don't try and hit the ball over the fence. Crawford's fence-clearing hits were always an afterthought, for both the player and his teammates. As McLaren later admitted, "A home run was the furthest thing from my mind."

Over at first, Hatcher's main concern was to keep warning Anderson to be ready for a shot into the outfield gap since that was the batter's forte. Anderson, on the other hand, wasn't as optimistic, remembering Crawford's penchant to ground the ball to the left side of the infield. His motivation was to get to second base before a force play could end the game.

The pride of Arlington High's Class of 1999 surprised them all.

After the ball had reached the seats above the sign advertising Progress Energy, the Boston players trudged their way to the visitors' dugout while the collectively lowest paid team in all of baseball leaped and bounded its way toward home plate to greet the hero of the day. The entire population of the Devil Rays' fandom would never admit it, but they knew that even with 161 more games of potential euphoria staring them in the face, this was as good as it was going to get.

In Boston, however, a March triumph wouldn't have meant much. A March loss—especially to a group carrying a microscopic $4 million worth of pitchers—was another matter entirely.

Epstein was suddenly enveloped by a sea of happily surprised winners, Tampa Bay fans emptying out onto Tropicana Drive, basking in the glow of their mythical Opening Day championship. Theo was oblivious to the celebration. He simply stood and stared out onto the scene for ten seconds, attempting to digest what had transpired, why it had happened and, more importantly, how it could be fixed. When you're a general manager of a Major League Baseball team, you have to keep your focus on solutions.

After realizing the only short-term answer to the dilemma was to win Game 2 of the new season, Epstein patted the most veteran member of his executive support system, Bill Lajoie, on the back and headed through the screaming throng of Devil Rays celebrants. No one seemed to notice the Boston Red Sox general manager's exit. He walked right by with the inauspiciousness of an anonymous peanut vendor, leaving the rest of the witnesses to their crazed disbelief.

If it had happened four hours later, it would have been perceived as the greatest April's Fool Day joke of all time. Unfortunately for the Red Sox, reality had come well before midnight.

Moments after the stands had finally cleared, while the players dressed in preparation for taking their bus back to The Vinoy Resort three miles away, Epstein sat in Boston manager Grady Little's office. Little was off in another room, conducting the obligatory postgame press conference, leaving the isolated GM with a stream of thoughts. Once Little finally did return, Theo joined the manager in going through the laundry list of mighta, coulda, shouldabeens.

Finally, with the visitors' locker room clear of all of Boston's twenty-five players, Theo emerged into the stadium's vast hallway. The easygoing demeanor of spring training that had allowed him to adeptly handle the slings and arrows of the spring's building process was diminished but not entirely displaced.

"It happens," he said, seemingly reminding himself that there were still six months of baseball to be played. And with that, off Epstein went, walking toward the exit of Day 1 with his eye set on Day 2.

"The funny thing about experience is that at one time or another none of us had it."

—Tampa Bay general manager Chuck Lamar

AS UNSAVORY AS the ending to the season's opener had been for Epstein, its events perfectly typified the GM's four-month tenure. "Plain" has never entered the job description for general managers of the Red Sox, as was once again exemplified by Epstein's variety pack of an introduction to the 2003 season.

Epstein slept appreciably well in the days leading up to the opening series in St. Petersburg. That hadn't necessarily been the case in the previous two weeks, when three of his proposed trades to bolster Boston's pitching staff had been rebuffed. During that span, the GM had exuded public confidence regarding his roster, but privately, he told the team's ownership group that he thought that the Red Sox didn't have quite enough pitching, and that it might be wise to do something sooner rather than later.

It had become clear since he had taken the job that Epstein wasn't going to sit still. By the time opening day rolled around he had already painted an entirely new face on a Boston team that had won ninety-three games the season before, but had not made the playoffs. "Theo was as active as anybody," said J.P. Ricciardi in hindsight. "He had a plan, and he was going to get it done."

Although he was relatively new on the job, Epstein had already established a reputation around the league as someone who systematically targeted elements he thought would enhance his organization. When the 2003 season arrived, general managers such as Tampa Bay's Chuck Lamar were well aware that Epstein was much more interested in making history with a Red Sox World Championship than with his birth certificate.

"When I first met Theo his reputation had preceded him. We had heard that there was a very astute young baseball guy in San Diego," Lamar said twenty-four hours before beginning his sixth season as the GM of the Devil Rays. "Theo is and has been tremendously respected around the world of baseball for his knowledge and his work ethic. Whether he's twenty-eight, thirty-eight, or forty-eight, I just don't think age is a factor."

Epstein's inability to secure a few more arms entering the season was influenced less by age and more by the other teams' lack of interest in what he had to offer in exchange. The rejection was hardly a surprise to the Boston GM. Ninety-nine percent. That was the number Theo had surmised fit the amount of times the first draft of a trade proposal gets shot down.

An example of Epstein's analysis regarding the deliberations that precede the consummation of deals came twenty-three days after the '03 season had begun. While sitting at McCoy Stadium in Pawtucket, Rhode Island, his cell phone rang. "Hey, Billy," he said, addressing the off-season titleholder of Red Sox GM For a Day, Oakland's Billy Beane.

The Boston GM's good friend and West Coast counterpart was shopping for some position players and wanted to give Epstein first crack at them. Just a month before, Beane had offered Theo something of much more value than a mid-March transaction. Billy had passed along the warning not to try to overhaul a roster because of spring training peaks and valleys.

Beane was adamant about this—do not make a trade in spring training. April, on the other hand, was another matter.

"Right now I'm going to have to say no. I think we're pretty happy with our offense," said Epstein after a few seconds of pleasantries. "You guys take care of the West and we'll work on everyone else." And with that Beane's five-minute inquiry was done. Both parties knew that it never hurts to ask. Unfortunately for one member of the conversation, it also always never hurts to say "no."

Even with preseason deals nixed, the Red Sox seemed to be on solid footing. Boston had easily handled the Braves in Atlanta in the final two preseason tune-ups, and staff ace Pedro Martinez, who hadn't walked a batter in the entire spring training, was slated to go on Opening Day.

As they rolled into St. Pete, the Red Sox and their new GM appeared ready to take another crack at bringing back the world championship that had left town 85 years before.

Epstein's comfort level only increased upon arriving in St. Petersburg, thanks to the posh surroundings of The Vinoy Resort. Whatever kind of ESPN sexiness that was lacking in Boston's Opening Day opponent, it was more than made up for in the eyes of the organization, thanks to the pinnacle of what would be a season-long hotel sampling.

The Vinoy was a bright pink, 360-room monstrosity that had been hovering over St. Petersburg Harbor since opening its doors on New Year's Eve 1925. Its inception had been the result of the partnership of businessman Aymer Vinoy Laughner, financier Gene Elliott, and legendary golfer Walter Hagen. Hagen had so enjoyed hitting golf balls off of Laughner's pocket watch into the yard of a Mr. Williamson that the trio decided the balls' usual destination alongside the city's scenic waterfront would be a perfect venue for the hotel of all hotels.

Williamson succumbed to the trio's inquiry, signing over the deed to the land on the back of a brown paper bag. The venture yielded one of the country's most desired relaxation destinations, with the likes of Babe Ruth frequently paying the $20 per night room charge.

But by the time 1974 rolled around, the extravagance of The Vinoy's early years had been lost for some time, and the hotel shut its doors. It wasn't until 1992 that the Stouffer hotel chain found out what Major League teams already knew—adding $93 million into your foundation will go a long way toward turning things around.

Now seventy-eight years and two months after its ground-breaking, The Vinoy hosted what Epstein hoped was a much more economical reclamation project, the Boston Red Sox.

What Boston traveling secretary Jack McCormick didn't know when he booked the amenity-laced Vinoy was another not-so-publicized aspect of the resort's history—it had been included by various groups in their list of Florida's most haunted. Visions of such inexplicable oddities as an early twentieth-century couple residing in the complex's bell tower had added to The Vinoy's legend. It was a label that was only enhanced later in the 2003 season thanks to another Mr. Williamson, a Cincinnati Reds pitcher who went by the first name of Scott.

Williamson and the rest of his Reds teammates had taken up residence in The Vinoy for a mid-June three-game series. The pitcher, a hard-core southerner who embraced the remembrances of Confederate generals Robert E. Lee and Stonewall Jackson, always believed in UFOs, but never really thought too much about the return of other historical figures in the form of ghostly figures. That was until the night of June 9.

Williamson had turned in just hours before his team's three-game series in St. Pete. His rapid eye movements never quite got untracked, however, since every so often he felt the push of hands on his back. His eyes would close and the feeling of discomfort would begin. Finally, Williamson, unnerved enough to forgo valuable rest, swung his head up and focused in the corner of the room. There he saw a man, dressed in the garb befitting the previous property's original Mr. Williamson, standing in a ghostlike state.

Word got out about Williamson's sighting, with the power of the electronic media making the experience a quirky little side-note for ESPN and other news-starved organizations. By the time the Devil Rays' next opponent, the Pittsburgh Pirates, came into The Vinoy, the story had leaked to enough of the Pirates that their infield coach, Alvaro Espinosa, was talking about it during the team's batting practice.

"Did you hear about . . . ?" asked Espinosa, going on to explain Williamson's well-publicized tale.

The mention of the ghost turned Pittsburgh strength and conditioning coach Frank Velasquez white as a Halloween costume's sheet. "You're kidding me, right?" he deadpanned.

Velasquez hadn't heard about Williamson's experience, but he did know a little bit about the subject. The night before he had also seen a man, of the very same description as that told by Williamson, but had hesitated to tell anyone.

The news quickly spread among the Pirates, prompting Velasquez, Espinosa, and Pittsburgh catcher Jason Kendall to ask teammate Scott Sauerbeck if they could stay at his Bradenton home for the rest of the series. Suddenly, trips to the usually docile city of St. Petersburg had taken on a whole new face for members of the Major Leagues.

Epstein, on the other hand, had no ghostly encounters, or fear-inducing late-night awakenings while staying at The Vinoy. Yet, Theo did know he was going to experience another aspect of the resort's uniqueness for the next four days—it just happened to have the same model of bed that could be found back in his apartment in Boston.

It had been just more than one year since he had purchased the piece of furniture Epstein viewed as the bed to beat all beds. He adored that bed. The tale that went with it was another story entirely.

Upon being hired as interim general manager Mike Port's assistant, Epstein was forced to move all of the belongings he had accumulated throughout his five years in San Diego across the country. So, while he went ahead to settle into his Fenway Park office, the moving truck filled with everything from his 1998 National League Championship ring to his car made its way from coast to coast.

Epstein would make it back, raiding his parents' refrigerator in Brookline without suffering a scratch, but the same couldn't be said for the carrier of a lifetime of possessions, the moving truck. The mammoth eighteen-wheeler hit a patch of ice somewhere just outside Rochester, New York, denting, scratching or somehow defacing virtually all of Theo's belongings.

How could this have happened? Did that last six-pack of beer from Epstein's abandoned refrigerator play a role in the mishap? Boston's new assistant GM couldn't help but wonder. He had warned the driver not to polish it off on duty, but the question still had to be asked: Was it really black ice, or maybe Black Label?

The frozen road alibi had proven to be acceptable, but that didn't make the damage done any easier to digest. Not all was completely lost, however, as the harm done to Epstein's Volvo was repaired with $4,000 of work. His bed also made it.

After a few weeks of scrambling to replace or repair his possessions, Epstein was finally getting settled into his new place. With his trusty, form-fitted bed moved in, he was ready to put his relocation disaster in the past and get a good night sleep. He lay down, closed his eyes and . . . dropped to the ground. Evidently, the bed hadn't weathered the accident quite as well as anticipated.

The brief fall left Epstein staring at the ceiling, wondering if this was a sign of things to come. Judging by his presence in The Vinoy on the opening day of the '03 campaign, the bad luck appeared to have ended with the broken furniture.

"Theo, it's Jim."

—Red Sox trainer Jim Rowe

IT WAS THE DAY of his first game as a general manager and Epstein was comfortable—in both his surroundings and his title as the boss of the Boston Red Sox.

The dawn of a new era in Boston baseball history had started with Epstein waking up an hour early on the morning of March 31 after putting an end to his previous day at about 2 A.M.

Usually Epstein's status as a night owl would allow for a morning wake-up call no earlier than 8:30, but with the excitement waiting on the final day of March, five hours of sleep would be plenty. Sleep is never high on the list of priorities for a Major League Baseball general manager, not during the season.

The alarm clock read 7:45 A.M. and Opening Day's ceremonial first pitch wouldn't be thrown by the head coach of the Super Bowl champion Tampa Bay Buccaneers, Jon Gruden, for another nine hours. Epstein rose from bed and turned on CNN to watch the latest developments in the war in Iraq when his phone rang. It was Boston trainer Jim Rowe.

Just fifteen minutes had passed since Epstein had opened his eyes to the Major League Baseball regular season and he had already had to dismiss the game itself. Rowe had gotten a call earlier in the morning and now it was his job to pass on the news: Cloninger, the sixty-two-year-old pitching coach who epitomized everything that was right with the game he had lived among all of his life, was sick. Really sick.

Unfortunately, cancer doesn't discriminate, as the Red Sox found out in Cloninger's case. Smack dab in the middle of spring training, there had been a two-inch tumor, which was later determined to be cancerous, found in the Boston coach's bladder. It was a scenario that hardly seemed likely considering the man involved.

Cloninger's place in baseball had been branded in the record books thanks to one game back in 1966 in which he hit two grand slams, along with posting a twenty-four-win season in '65. The performances had showcased a Thorpean level of athletic ability, which appeared to fit more beautifully on the baseball diamond than any other playing field.

It was, however, one of Cloninger's defeats that had defined the North Carolina native.

Tony was the kind of guy that blends into a baseball clubhouse as easily as a tin of Skoal or well-placed curse word. He was a likable tough guy who spoke with the drawl of someone whose words meant a lot, but whose actions you knew were going to mean more.

Cloninger hadn't pitched much at all during the Atlanta Braves' '66 spring training. He had been holding out for an extra $10,000 on his contract, which only seemed proper considering his mind-boggling 279 innings of work the season before. By the time the season began, he had only stretched his right arm out to six innings, well below what was thought to be needed if Tony was to match his total of sixteen complete games the year before.

It just so happened that Cloninger's first start in '66 was a showcase event for the Braves, the day the team was unveiling its new home, Atlanta–Fulton County Stadium. The 51,500-seat park had cost the city $18 million and, if the Braves had their way, it was going to open with a win, courtesy of the franchise's ace pitcher.

Cloninger pitched well that day, a cool April 12th. Well enough to carry Atlanta into extra innings with a 2–2 tie against a Pittsburgh lineup that boasted the likes of Hall of Famers Willie Stargell, Bill Mazeroski, and the world's greatest Rule 5 draftee, Roberto Clemente. But that wasn't good enough.

Cloninger had been regularly visited on the mound by Braves' manager Bobby Bragan since the seventh inning, with the pitcher predictably responding to the age-old question of "How do you feel?" with the answer that every hurler worth his salt is trained to shoot back with. "Fine, Skip," he kept saying.

Finally, in the thirteenth inning, after throwing more than 200 pitches, Cloninger's day was finished when a fastball didn't quite get in enough on Stargell's fists, resulting in a home run over the brand-new stadium's brand-new right-field wall.

Five days later, Cloninger was back on the mound to pitch against the Mets and their starter, Dick Selma. Tony not only lost the game, 4–1, but also perhaps his career's momentum. With every pitch against New York, it felt as though knives were being stuck in his shoulder, a feeling that stayed with him far too often before he finally had to call it quits at the age of thirty-two in 1972.

Cloninger's toughness had been his downfall. And now it was coming to get him again.

The afternoon before Opening Day, Cloninger, much wider than his playing days but just as clubhouse cool as thirty-seven years before, appeared no different than at any other time during spring training; sleeping soundly on a recliner chair in the middle of the visitors' locker room before Boston's optional Tropicana Field workout. The next morning presented a different picture.

By the time Epstein met up with Cloninger in Red Sox manager Grady Little's room, the pitching coach's suite looked like a murder scene. There was blood everywhere. Bladder cancer may be the fourth-most prevalent malignant tumor in the United States, but, as the Red Sox and Cloninger found out, it was no less demoralizing than any other forms of the disease.

The Red Sox decided that it would be best to send Cloninger back to Boston, along with Boston CEO Larry Lucchino, aboard Sox owner John Henry's private plane on April 1. Tony would stay in The Vinoy for the entirety of Opening Day, ultimately fading in and out of consciousness with every Pedro Martinez pitch. He wanted to witness his spring training handiwork, but even the pomp and circumstance of the opener couldn't derail the reality of the disease's cold embrace.

The pitching coach who had entered the world of professional baseball in 1961 needed some time away.

When Epstein left Little's suite the clock was still in the A.M., but Theo yearned for the distraction of baseball nonetheless. The park, however, would have to wait. There was more to be done at the hotel. Next on the agenda: A man named Fernando.

Early in spring training the thirty-one-year-old Pedro Martinez had stated that if Boston didn't pick up his $17.5 million
option on his contract for the 2004 season by the start of the season, he was going to bolt for another team when his contract was
through. On paper, Boston didn't have to make a decision on the
contract until November 5, but in the eyes of the player it was
going to be now or never, and it was up to Martinez's agent, Fernando Cuza, to find out the Red Sox's answer.

As gifted a talent evaluator as Epstein had become, he also possessed a fair share of experience involving the legalese of baseball.
The Padres had given him the freedom to attend the University of
San Diego School of Law, where he did well enough to pass the
bar for the state of California. He was perhaps the only one of the
No. 2 pencil-carrying crowd taking the test that day whose career
goal revolved around the benches belonging to dugouts, not court-
rooms.

Epstein's dad, a man who has lived his life within the circles of
academia, calls Theo "the smartest person I know." And while
some may chalk that up to the typical kind of gushing a father
often affords one of his children, it's been hard to argue with the
senior Epstein's analysis of the kid who got an SAT score well into
the 1400s. It was those smarts that were now being counted on by
the Red Sox organization to keep its star pitcher, along with fiscal
sanity.

Cuza's voyage to John Henry's room had taken dramatically
different detours than his contractual counterpart. The passion for
his and his client's goal, however, was identical to Epstein's.

There was perhaps no better sports agent to represent Martinez in his quest to extend his commitment to Boston than Cuza,
for reasons that stretched well beyond his Spanish-speaking roots.
The forty-six-year-old had experienced a healthy chunk of the pitfalls Pedro had had to endure since transitioning from the poverty
of the Dominican Republic to his current state. Cuza had also
dealt with the tragedy of life's mishaps, and now was trying to
shield his client from unforeseen monumental setbacks.

In the first two years of Cuza's existence, his family had experienced the good life thanks to a family-owned sugarcane ranch in Cuba. Then, in January 1959, Fidel Castro took control of the country and, subsequently, the Cuza family's fortunes. The lifestyle change ultimately led Fernando, his brother, Rafael, and his mother, Isabel, to Miami, where the family took up residence with Isabel's sister, Yvonne, and her husband, Eduardo.

Just as Martinez would experience years later when leaving the Dominican Republic, Cuza discovered the difficulties that went along with the inability to speak the language of those around him. Upon entering kindergarten at St. Rose of Lima, in Miami Shores, his learning curve was increasingly hampered by his inability to speak English. It wasn't until second grade that Fernando, with extra help from his teachers, was able to adequately communicate, although his continued trouble reading his new language left him playing catch-up throughout his formative years.

Cuza also learned how exactly to determine which athletes were worth fighting for well before meeting Pedro in 1987. Back at North Miami High, Fernando had formed a friendship with a girl named Terri Dundee, who decided one day to introduce Cuza to her parents, Angelo and Helen. Without any kind of warning, Fern struck up a fast friendship with Terri's dad, who just happened to be the trainer for the athlete all others would measure their hearts against, boxer Muhammad Ali. It was during his visits to the Fifth Street Gym to watch Angelo (who would serve as Fern's best man at his wedding) elicit the best from his fighters that Cuza discovered the inner aptitude of the great ones. That's what he saw in Martinez.

As Cuza spoke with Epstein he also remembered another childhood friend, Greg Stead, and the lesson he had taught Fernando regarding the unpredictable nature of life. Stead was a star ninth-grade football player who had earned the admiration of Cuza, an aspiring athlete two grades behind him. However, Cuza's hero worship turned to deep concern when Stead was left paralyzed from the neck down after his helmet slid off while making a tackle.

More than eight months later, Stead had ventured out of the

shadow of death at a Houston rehabilitation center, but moved into a life far different from the one he had planned for himself. Greg Stead's story was dramatically different from Pedro Martinez's, but it was because of his lifelong friend's sudden misfortune that the need for security had been ingrained in Cuza's psyche.

Greg had gone on to enjoy life, albeit in a wheelchair. It was now Fernando's job to lock Martinez into his own sense of security via a new, multiyear contract.

For four hours Theo and Fern talked. The dialogue wasn't about picking up the option—that was going to be the fallback scenario for the pitcher whose worth when healthy was unmatched, but who wasn't quite healthy enough to make the monetary commitment a no-brainer. Both sides wanted Martinez to stay in Boston well into the back-end of his career, but on slightly different terms. The difference was small in Major League superstar terms, but just big enough to be a deal-breaker.

On this day the only agreement made was to try and agree another day.

"We've got the right man for the job."

—Red Sox vice chairman David Ginsberg to Theo Epstein
moments before Boston's March 31 game

BY THE TIME EPSTEIN hopped in a car with Lucchino and Henry and made it over to Tropicana Field to be greeted by well-wishers such as Ginsburg (a Winthrop, Massachusetts, native who had come from the Florida Marlins to join John Henry), the idea of playing a baseball game was nothing but an afterthought.

But finally, at 2:35 P.M., Epstein was able to step onto the simulated grass in the home of the Devil Rays, and witness honest-to-goodness baseballs being slung about.

Another piece of advice Beane had given to Theo was that the two days in which he would most be nervous as a first-year GM were his first day of spring training and his first Opening Day. It was just two hours before the opening pitch and he insisted there was no anxiety to be found. Perhaps his calmness resulted from the day's already unnerving schedule of events.

The baseball game was the release . . . at least until the media arrived.

As had been the case since arriving in Fort Myers, a trip near a baseball field also meant a swarm of information gatherers following not far behind. Not only did the Red Sox have five newspapers consistently following them on the road, but, since it was Opening Day, virtually all the other print and electronic media outlets within the reaches of Route 128 or the Mass Pike had paid the $240-per-person plane ticket to send their people to Florida.

In the public eyes, Epstein was the man to look for in, at, or around a Red Sox game. He was young, smart, and personable. Dan Duquette, the Boston GM from 1994 until he was let go during spring training in 2002, had been considered standoffish, to both the fans and the people holding the tape recorders and microphones. The Duke's answers had most often merged less with the questions being asked, and more with whatever message he wanted to relay.

By comparison, Epstein's appeal to the public had no bounds. This is a lesson the GM had learned ad nauseam in his first months in Florida.

One spring training day, after Epstein had watched his Red Sox beat the Reds, a twenty-year-old student from Emory University, Brian Wolfe, waited out the throngs of well-wishers and autograph seekers who bombarded the most popular man in City of Palm's Park following the game's final pitch.

Finally, Wolfe approached with camera in hand. Epstein gladly had his picture taken with the college student, who informed his "Brookline High rival" that he had recently graduated from nearby Newton North High School. After the exchange Epstein moved on, but Wolfe wanted to relay his experience to anyone who would listen.

"He just wrote a letter to the Orioles, got an internship and worked his way up," said Wolfe to some nearby onlookers who didn't know Epstein's story the way the kid from Newton did. "It's a great lesson for all kids like me." Wolfe then walked off, smiling with the expression of someone who thought he had just witnessed his own future.

He might not have won a game as general manager for the Red Sox yet, but Epstein had made his imprint on at least one member of Boston's fandom.

The GM's magnetism wasn't just limited to the Red Sox youth, either. The next morning after meeting Wolfe, Epstein walked on to Boston's spring training home field typically carrying a notebook full of organizational information.

"Who is that?" asked the sixty-year-old Jerry Sheindlin from the Red Sox dugout, picking out the person receiving a wave of attention.

"That's Theo Epstein," a reporter responded. "He's the general manager."

"You're kidding," Sheindlin said. "But he's so young!"

Five minutes later and Sheindlin, a celebrity in his own right for having hosted the television show *The People's Court*, was snapping photos of Epstein with his even more famous wife, Judy (known to midday television viewers as "Judge Judy").

Four months before the spring training rendezvous, Epstein had turned down a chance to appear on *The Tonight Show*, and now he was being tracked down by television's most recognizable courtroom couple. The verdict was in: Theo was sick of the attention, but nobody was sick of Theo. "Wait until we're 35–45," he said walking up the stairs to his office moments after meeting the Sheindlins. "We'll see how popular I am then."

The attention had started with a November 25 press conference and hadn't let up by the time he oversaw his team's first pregame batting practice of the season atop the top step of the visitors' dugout two hours before his team's March 31 opener.

"How they do colors our whole day."

—Leslie Epstein regarding his son's team,
the Boston Red Sox

BY THE TIME Tampa Bay starting pitcher Joe Kennedy threw a first-pitch strike to Red Sox leadoff hitter Johnny Damon, Theo had taken his place among the Opening Day crowd. To the left of him was Lajoie, while another baseball operations assistant Jed Hoyer sat on his right. The Boston baseball executives were charting, writing, and talking about everything that had to do with what transpired on the field. The glitz of Opening Day had given way to the business of baseball.

Leslie Epstein's focus wasn't so straightforward.

Theo's father didn't have the luxury of solely concentrating on his son's debut. The game began at 5:17 P.M., and as the head of Boston University's Creative Writing Program, he had a graduate student class to instruct thirteen minutes after Kennedy threw his first pitch.

Fortunately for Leslie, a soft-spoken gentleman who appears to analyze every spoken word before respectfully (and often passionately) responding, he had earned a Rhodes Scholarship, taught at B.U. since 1978, written nine books, and had a fair amount of leeway when it came to his classroom. Therefore, the evening session in the antiquated building on the south end of the Boston University campus was going to be complete with a portable radio and Red Sox hat.

Professor Epstein listened as the Red Sox jumped out to a 3–0 lead after just one inning. With Martinez on the mound, it appeared as though there was going to be time for some teaching after all.

Every lull in the two-and-a-half-hour class allowed Epstein to turn up the volume and listen to Red Sox announcers Joe Castiglione and Jerry Trupiano relay what had been a stream of good news. By the time class had adjourned, the Red Sox ace pitcher was just completing his seventh and final inning of work. Martinez had left Boston with a 4–1 lead and Theo's father with a confident two-mile drive back to his Brookline condo.

The Epsteins' modest, yet smartly decorated, place of residence had been the sight of many sports-induced celebrations and disappointments. The most memorable of which, the night Bill Buckner allowed Mookie Wilson's ground ball to find its way through his legs during Game 6 of the 1986 World Series, was viewed only by Theo and his twin brother, Paul, at the residential three-condo, side-street structure.

Leslie and his wife, Ilene, had committed to attending a party on the same night as Boston's potential world championship–clinching showdown with the New York Mets. The couple stayed throughout the game, dodging the stares of the other partygoers who were growing impatient with the Epsteins constantly trying to get a glimpse of the television.

Theo and Paul, both by now diehard twelve-year-old Red Sox fans, had stayed behind to hold their own sort of celebration. The pair had decided that they would climb to the top of the family's couch and simultaneously jump off when the final out was made.

As it turned out, the Epstein boys were left perched atop that couch for more than a half hour. And when Wilson's grounder found its way through the legs of Buckner, allowing Ray Knight to come in with the game-winning run and ruining New England sports fans forever, the two boys did exit the couch in unison, except that it came in the form of a tumble of disbelief.

Now it was Leslie's turn.

Just about seventeen and a half years after the Buckner error, Epstein got home just in time to see the final inning of his son's opening day. There would be no celebrating, just concern. While the television showed images of Crawford circling the bases and Tampa Bay fans going berserk, all Leslie could envision was Theo's reaction.

Leslie knew that Theo's short reign had been partially identified in the media by the decision to go without a designated closer in the bullpen. The Boston GM had instead chosen to use the more economical approach by having the likes of Mike Timlin, Ramiro Mendoza, Alan Embree, and Fox to combine to handle the job of the previous season's closer, Ugueth Urbina. That's why watching Embree and Fox turn a three-run, ninth-inning lead into the first loss of the season was like digesting a three-day-old Fenway frank. It was a bit tough to swallow.

"The bullpen can't be doing this. They've got to do it for Theo," thought Leslie, the father not the fan. The Epsteins were much more upset for their son than worried that the Red Sox were a game back in the American League East standings.

Leslie fought the temptation to call his son. He had learned that it was better for Theo to use his parents as a sounding board, instead of the other way around. Unfortunately for the Epsteins, there was no blueprint as to how to relate to your twenty-nine-year-old son who happens to be a Major League Baseball general manager.

In fact, the Opening Day debacle was just the latest aspect of Leslie and Ilene's having to deal with Theo's newfound celebrity. Leslie had experienced life as a relative to someone in the public's eye as the son of Philip, who had teamed with his identical twin, Julius, to cowrite the screenplay for *Casablanca*. But this was different.

Fortunately for the couple, Theo the son, not the general manager, called his parents two weeks after Boston's first game to get everyone back on the same page.

"It was a changed relationship, so he called us . . . and it was not an easy call to make," Leslie said. "It's more like our son is our son now. We sort of lost him for a while."

Even after a month of watching his son's team take shape, Leslie admitted that there was "a real air of unreality to it all." It wasn't until after a few tough weeks that the Epsteins learned that the trick was putting games like Opening Day in the background, and making their family's relationship the real must-see event.

"It wasn't like I didn't like the guy. We just couldn't afford to have him back."

—Theo Epstein regarding Ugueth Urbina

LESLIE EPSTEIN had endured the Devil Rays' comeback while sitting in front of a television screen in Brookline, Massachusetts. His son had to watch the drama unfold in the ultimate high-definition setting—from fifty feet away.

By the time the home half of the ninth inning started, things didn't look that bad to Epstein. Pedro had pitched great for seven innings, and Mendoza needed just nine pitches to dispatch the Devil Rays in the eighth. Going into the ninth, the Red Sox had the match-ups they wanted, with the left-handed Embree slated to face lefty hitters Travis Lee and Al Martin.

At that point, nobody was missing Urbina.

Epstein had been tired of the "bullpen by committee" questions before the end of the first day of spring training. But, as he said, "Just because you're sick of them, doesn't mean you don't have to answer them."

Just in dealing with the media before Opening Day alone, the Boston general manager was asked by three different media outlets about his philosophy regarding using a few different relievers to close out games. It was seemingly every reporter's repertoire to first ask about Epstein's age, and then come in with the bullpen question. "Where was the creativity?" he often thought.

Outsiders pointed to the influences of Bill James, the author of *The New Bill James Historical Baseball Abstract,* as the chief influence for Boston's new-age bullpen. The fifty-three-year-old had been hired by Boston as a senior advisor. The James hiring was a product of an off-the-cuff remark made by Henry to Epstein in the midst of a seemingly innocuous conversation.

"Why hasn't this guy worked for a team?" Henry had asked Epstein, the then-assistant general manager. There was silence. Theo did not have the answer. The question lingered with the owner until he decided to whip off a lengthy job proposal to James via e-mail.

Henry had made his money by having an uncanny knack for investments, but he also could lay claim to the fact that he was banned from playing blackjack in Las Vegas because of his ability to count cards. Like James, Henry knew that baseball was in large part about figuring out the odds.

It was James who stated in the book's section, "Valuing Relievers," that one-inning closers aren't the best way to use a bullpen. In that section, he stated that it's "far better to use your relief ace when the score is tied, even if that is the seventh inning, than the ninth inning with a lead of two or more runs." It seemed like a good enough idea. The problem was first keeping the game close, and then realizing exactly who that relief ace is.

Epstein's actions toward forming his bullpen were somewhat steered toward James's ideology. "Ten years from now that's going to be how bullpens are going to work," the GM said. "But that doesn't mean it's going to be successful every given year."

The more pressing concern when it came to the Red Sox's 2003 bullpen was financial. Urbina, who had saved forty games in '02, had been up for arbitration, and he was asking for $8 million after making $6.7 million. As Epstein explained, that wasn't a realistic figure. "There is no way I would ever pay Ugueth Urbina $8 million, not in a million years."

Boston, however, had to decide whether or not to offer Urbina arbitration, or to non-tender him and let him go as a free agent well before the reliever's market value had been set. Epstein and Co. decided to let Urbina test the market, where he signed with Texas for right around what the Red Sox had been previously offering ($4.5 million).

This was the reason Embree was starting the ninth inning on Opening Day. If Urbina had been in there in the ninth, the likes of Kevin Millar, Bill Mueller, and David Ortiz would be celebrating their season-opening optimism in just about any other uniform except one belonging to the Red Sox.

There would be plenty of days to sing the praises of the $5 million trio and forget The Committee. Opening Day just wasn't meant to be one of them.

Embree, a flamethrower whose fire had been cooled by more than five miles per hour due to shoulder tendonitis, allowed a lead-off single to Lee. The lefty then grooved a high fastball to pinch-hitter Terry Shumpert, who deposited it in the left field seats. After the home plate celebration, the Devil Rays got a single from Ben Grieve, who now represented the game's tying run.

Epstein instinctively finally broke off from his fixation on the field and looked toward the Red Sox dugout. He was thinking the same thing as Little—it was time to get Embree out and Fox in.

The day before, Little had been talking to some reporters in the visitors' dugout when one of them asked if he had decided on who he would bring in for a tight game in the ninth inning. Little said he had an idea, but wanted the opinion of the writers.

"Embree and Fox," said Sean McAdam of the *Providence Journal-Bulletin*. "Sounds good to me," was Little's response. And when Fox struck out the first batter he faced, Toby Hall, it looked good to everyone else as well.

Then came the ground ball that, as Epstein later described as the one, "everyone thought had ended it."

With pinch-runner Damian Rolls at first, Abernathy hit what appeared to be a tailor-made ground ball to Boston shortstop Nomar Garciaparra. Garciaparra gathered in the ball, took a few steps to tag second base for the force play, but then double-clutched just long enough to allow Abernathy to beat the throw to first.

This wasn't any shortstop. This was Nomar Garciaparra, Boston's annual link to baseball's All-Star Weekend. The screams from the Boston bars could be heard clear down the East Coast: "Aaah, Nomaaahh!"

At the play's inception, Epstein had leaned forward in anticipation of the game-ending double play. It wasn't much of a movement, but it was more animation than the GM had shown at any other time in the game.

Once the safe call was made at first, Theo leaned back and

regained his focus on the task at hand. Everyone else around him had all turned to the general manager and smiled, knowing that the process had been prolonged.

"Welcome to the big leagues," said Lajoie, leaning over to his new boss. Ageless words of wisdom, right on cue.

When the Red Sox ownership group gave Epstein the go-ahead to build his own staff, Lajoie ended up being building block No. 1. The man who built the 1984 World Champion Detroit Tigers team had no relationship with Epstein. He did know Ricciardi, whom the new Boston GM had asked to help formulate a list of names to interview for his support system.

Ricciardi had given Epstein about twenty names to choose from, the former Detroit general manager being one of them. Lajoie had been introduced to Epstein by the Toronto general manager at the Winter Meetings while hovering over a plate of pastries, but never thought twice about the meeting until he got a phone call from "J.P.'s friend" a few weeks later.

After talking with Lajoie on the phone, the Boston GM was sold. "He was the best guy out there, by far," Epstein said. "He has a strong desire to kick ass." Young or old, white hair be damned; if you were on board with the new Red Sox, the urge for some organizational ass-kicking was a priority.

Back in 1984, in his first year as a general manager, Lajoie had begun the season watching his team win thirty-five of their first forty games, and now Theo and Bill planned to win. They did not plan on Carl Crawford hitting a walk-off home run on Opening Day.

Upon leaving the site of the first day's disappointment, Epstein, Hoyer, and Boston bench coach Jerry Narron convened back at the hotel for a late dinner and a couple of beers. The conversation was led by Narron, whose North Carolina drawl had already summed up his eight previous Opening Days as a Major Leaguer. The underlying theme? It's just one of 162.

Epstein eventually adjourned to his room, turned on ESPN and immediately saw *Baseball Tonight*'s replay of Toronto catcher Ken Huckaby landing on New York Yankees star shortstop Derek

Jeter's right shoulder, dislocating it in the process. The early word was that Jeter might be out of action for a couple of months.

Unlike Yankees general manager Brian Cashman, Epstein's star shortstop was healthy and would be playing in the very next game. Maybe things weren't so bad after all.

Twenty-four hours later, Epstein and Lajoie were back in Section 102. This time it was the sixteenth inning, and the Boston bullpen was being represented by guys most didn't even mention as being part of the bullpen's committee: Brandon Lyon and Steve Woodard.

Back in Boston it was well after midnight, but Leslie and Ilene Epstein were still awake, watching for their son's first win as a GM At one point, Leslie turned away from the TV and couldn't find his wife. She would finally be discovered, hiding under a quilt on the couch, hiding from anticipation of the Red Sox's fate.

With the score 8–8 and the count on Kevin Millar 1-and-2, Epstein reversed the exchange from the night before and turned to Lajoie.

"Millar is going to hit one out right here," the Boston GM predicted. Three hundred and seventy-one feet later, Millar had his home run, and Epstein had his first win after a five-hour-fifteen-minute thriller.

For four months he had called the shots, now he had called the shot.

Game 2 and Win 1 were in the books. A run on contention had officially begun.

CHAPTER 5

New Beginnings Getting Old

*"They probably have signs of Osama bin Laden,
Saddam Hussein, and Ken Huckaby up in
New York right now."*

—J.P. Ricciardi

There was no simple explanation to Rob Godfrey's friendship
with Ken Huckaby, other than they were both into their early
thirties, and shared a passion for the art of the practical joke.

Godfrey had lived the life of a businessman, first in the realm
of secondary education and then in amongst the management of
various corporations. His easygoing demeanor, however, lent itself
to the relaxed atmosphere anywhere but the button-down world
of nine to five. That was thanks in part to the constant presence of
his dog, Bailey. Outside the enormous wooden double doors of
the Blue Jays' executive offices on the third floor of SkyDome, a
bird resided as the franchise's symbol. Inside, however, the mascot
had no feathers and frequently took naps at the feet of the team's
receptionists.

When Rob did have to attend to the formalities of his job, the chocolate Labrador Retriever would usually be ready to greet any newcomers while lounging in and around the team's front desk. In the world of Major League Baseball, almost nobody put more hours in the office than Bailey.

Huckaby, conversely, checked into his occupation with the seriousness of a slave to Wall Street. He knew an overabundance of frivolity might mean the crossing of that thin line between the majors and the minors. After all, it was in the latter he had spent all but eighty-nine of his 950 games since entering professional baseball in 1991.

Huck had accumulated all but one of his big-league appearances with the Blue Jays the season before. Toronto farm director Dick Scott recommended the catcher to J.P. Ricciardi, leading Toronto to sign Huckaby away from Arizona. But when he didn't make the team out of Toronto's '02 spring training, he had had enough. As far as Ken was concerned, it was quitting time. That's when J.P. stepped in.

"Listen, you can stick around and when we need someone at some point you'll be the guy, or you can quit and it will be someone else out there," Ricciardi had told Huck. "It's up to you."

Huck decided not to let someone else get his chance. And when the '03 spring training rolled around Ken was back again, this time taking up residence with his casually businesslike new front-office friend. The Grapefruit League's comedy warehouse was now open for business.

The jokes began innocently enough, with Godfrey making every trip to a restaurant Huck's birthday, eliciting an endless stream of songs and free desserts. Ken's countermeasure included dumping ice cold buckets of water on Rob each time he ventured into the shower. It was subtle, yet effective in an early-morning, heart-stopping way.

The pace picked up exponentially as the month of March wore on, with Rob finally bringing the feud into the public eye. Godfrey got a hold of a picture of the catcher, signed Huckaby's name to it and tacked it on the clubhouse's bulletin board, accompanied by a letter.

"Dear Teammates," the posting read. *"As the 2003 season approaches, I know you will be asked by friends and family for photos of some of the more popular players. With that in mind, I have made this task convenient for you by providing you with a color photocopy of myself."*

The gauntlet had been thrown down. Huckaby answered with a vengeance, albeit after he had changed his sleeping arrangements to somewhere other than Godfrey's condo. Rob came home, Rob turned the key, Rob opened the door, and Rob found a hundred live crickets jumping in, on, and around his entire living space. A day later, an exterminator had moved in, and Rob and Bailey had moved out.

By the time Toronto headed north, with Huckaby coming along as the team's third catcher, the friendship had endured (although perhaps only because Godfrey hadn't managed to paint flames on Huck's new black Lincoln Navigator, as planned). Opening Day was serious business, and for good reason.

In '91, Huckaby was the twenty-second-round pick of the Los Angeles Dodgers, an organization he would remain with until hitting one point shy of .200 in his third year at Triple-A Albuquerque. It wasn't until the final game of the '01 season that he earned the right to enter the *Baseball Encyclopedia,* striking out in his only at-bat as a member of the Diamondbacks.

But now Huck and his strong right arm had made it. He hit .289 in the spring, appreciably better than either of the team's other two big-league catchers, Greg Myers and Tom Wilson, and he had earned the right to be introduced to a Major League crowd on a Major League Opening Day for the first time in his life. Forget the $313,000 salary Ken was now drawing: seeing "Huckaby" in black pen on Carlos Tosca's first lineup card of the year was the real payoff.

Most thought it was impossible for it to rain on the Blue Jays' Opening Day parade. They did, after all, have the retractable roof protecting the festivities from the snow-filled clouds above.

Unfortunately for Huckaby, his perfect storm couldn't be turned back by even the thousands of pounds of concrete and steel that made up the team's mobile rooftop.

All it took to transform Huck's dream day into the equivalent of a ten-hour, un-air-conditioned, Single-A bus ride through the heart of Mississippi was one seemingly innocent play in the midst of the practical joke–playing backstop's first Opening Day.

The incident: Third inning, New York Yankees leading the Blue Jays 1–0. Toronto was employing three infielders on the right side of the infield because of batter Jason Giambi's propensity to pull the ball that way; Derek Jeter stood at first. Giambi grounded harmlessly back to Jays' pitcher Roy Halladay, who was forced to settle for a throw to first, because Jeter had broken for second on an attempted steal. But by the time Toronto first baseman Carlos Delgado completed the putout of Giambi, Jeter was taking advantage of the dearth of infielders on the left side of the diamond, and started heading for a vacant third base.

Jeter, a runner unmatched in his intelligence going base to base, had successfully enacted the maneuver against Toronto the season before, and appeared to be on his way to doing it again. Except this time, Huckaby had correctly raced from his usual territory around home plate and was heading all-out to third in order to accept a throw from Delgado.

As Huck gathered in the throw, Jeter was sliding headfirst into the bag. The catcher's instincts took over, lunging down to position himself into a spot where he could block the path of the base runner. Instead, Huckaby landed with enough force to dislocate the Yankees' captain's right shoulder and simultaneously paint himself as the target of New Yorkers' venomous expletives for the next six weeks.

In the aftermath, Huck was shaken, waiting out Jeter's medical assistance by nervously chomping a towel in the Blue Jays' dugout. Godfrey, on the other hand, was already working on perhaps his first plan involving Huckaby that didn't include a semblance of a practical caper.

Rob quickly got in touch with a Toronto woman whom he knew possessed Jeter's cell phone number. Once he secured the shortstop's digits, Godfrey waited until the completion of the 8–4 Blue Jays' loss, raced down to the clubhouse before the media arrived and ushered Huckaby into the adjacent video room. Jeter wouldn't answer, he was already at the hospital, but at least a sympathetic message could be left, tempering any kind of abrasive questioning planned by the oncoming masses.

"Derek, this is Ken Huckaby," Huck said into Godfrey's cell phone. *"I'm sorry things happened like they did. I never meant to hurt you, buddy."*

Meanwhile, Ricciardi was also going into mother hen mode, declassifying the mishap as the dirty play many of the Yankees were trying to label it as. Huckaby had to be somewhat compassionate, thereby weakening his argument that he was a victim of circumstance. J.P. only had one choice—full-on protection of his player.

Before the game, Ricciardi had apologized to Yankees' manager Joe Torre about an ad portraying a Blue Jay shitting on a New York hat, accompanied by the slogan "Boo Matsui!" Torre, his team, and especially Japanese rookie Hideki Matsui didn't deserve that. But there was no way J.P. was going for a two-fer in the apology department. Anybody else but Jeter, any other team but the Yankees, and everybody still remembers Huckaby as the guy who couldn't hit .200 in Albuquerque.

In a franchise that was being run by a man who had built a career off of finding, signing, and developing the little guys, the star system might have well carried an "out of order" sign. J.P. told Huckaby he liked his hustle, gave his sympathies to Jeter and the Yankees, and returned to worrying about his own tribulations. After one season, Ricciardi reasonably wondered, wasn't it supposed to be easier the second time around?

"They've got the best pies."

—J.P. Ricciardi

THE UNEASINESS that accompanied Huckaby's putout at third had originally got off the starting blocks three days earlier in Dunedin, a town that resided geographically in another country, and psychologically in a different world, from the real games in Toronto. At least helping ease the pain were those pies.

It didn't matter what kind—peanut butter, chocolate cream, coconut cream, strawberry rhubarb, pecan—the pies were the escape, and Iris's Restaurant was the purveyor of each trip from reality.

People turn on to Douglas Avenue from Main Street in Dunedin, Florida, for two reasons: A game at Grant Field and to chow down at the little food joint that had resided across the street from the Toronto Blue Jays' spring home for the past eighteen years. The baseball complex had changed, getting a $5 million face-lift over the winter, but Iris's remained the "come on in and stay a while" lunchtime crutch relied upon by Ricciardi and the rest of the organization's crew for their meat and potatoes. But by March 25, spring training was almost over, and so would be the trips to Iris's.

Where had the innocence of spring training gone? Probably out the door with the reality that in seventy-two hours the New York Yankees would be the team rolling out the welcome mat for the games that really counted.

Ricciardi was just returning from his last across-the-street lunch of the spring when Tim McCleary called out. "Boss," said the assistant GM from his immaculate, neatly organized office. "Here it is."

J.P. swung around and hovered over the piece of paper McCleary slid across his brown, wooden desk. "Oh!" said Ricciardi with a concoction of anticipation and trepidation.

The sheet was the official twenty-five-man roster McCleary

had prepared to fax into the offices of Major League Baseball. This was it. Months of work had come down to this one single-spaced collection of names. Ricciardi already knew what resided within the list, but still felt obligated to reflect with one more perusal of his Opening Day charges.

Finally, J.P. looked up with a smile. "Anybody got some holy water?" he asked, simultaneously conducting a halfhearted blessing with his right hand. "Looks good. Ship it out."

The affirmation that an ending to spring training was in sight buoyed Ricciardi. But even the finality of Toronto's submitted roster, coupled with the comfort of a slice of coconut crème, couldn't hold back what was a growing wave of tribulations.

Thirty minutes before sending in his team to the league office in New York, the conversation at the lunch table was perhaps an omen that despite a respectable, and relatively seamless, 13–10 spring training, trouble was brewing. At the end of the table, Rob Godfrey had talked about his frustration with a local radio station. He had sent the disc jockeys an Eric Hinske bobblehead doll, the same kind SkyDome fans would be receiving upon attending the season opener. The move had backfired, as all that was heard over the radio waves was the mocking of Hinske's likeness and everything else that was associated with the ceramic doll.

"So you know what I'm going to do," said Godfrey, with a hint of the devil in his eye. "I'm going to send them 100 more." Problem No. 1 solved, thanks to the quick wit and mischievous nature of Ken Huckaby's housemate.

Then came word of two Toronto minor leaguers who had been hauled into the Dunedin police station after getting into a fight with a collection of locals. The report was that the players weren't to blame, putting this problem way down the list of the days' troubles. "Did they at least win?" joked Ricciardi, knowing the situation would most likely be resolved without his involvement.

Even back in the solitude of his picturesque, yet somewhat barely decorated, office, Ricciardi couldn't escape. "Good news," Rob Godfrey said while taking a step into J.P.'s doorway. "We think we've got Fergie Jenkins." Thirty years ago, the news would have made any pitching-starved general manager break into a celebratory dance. But the man who handed the Blue Jays their first-ever shutout twenty-six years earlier while hurling as a member of the Boston Red Sox had lost his fastball. Sixty years of life will do that.

Jenkins was now getting the call from the proverbial Blue Jays' bullpen this time around for one not-so-simple reason—international diplomacy.

Since the September 11 terrorist attacks, the word had come down from the MLB boys in New York that all teams were requested to stand at attention for the playing of "God Bless America" during the seventh-inning stretch.

The tradition of standing following the visitors' half of the seventh inning has been embedded within baseball since a member of the sport's first professional team, the Cincinnati Red Stockings, mandated the in-game reprieve in 1869. Its revival came in 1910 when the twenty-seventh president of the United States, Howard Taft, duped the crowd at a Washington Senators game into believing that he was getting up to leave in the seventh inning, when all he was doing was stretching his fleshy legs. It would take another ten years after the president's fellow fanatics rose out of respect, but the term "seventh-inning stretch" was finally woven into baseball lingo.

The in-game exercise has always been nothing than a nice little reprieve before heading into the game's final moments. It had been totally controversy free . . . until Toronto's 2003 Opening Day.

The trouble revolved around Canada's noninvolvement in the war in Iraq, which was at the heart of baseball's desire to continue the playing of "God Bless America." Just days before the American national anthem was booed soundly by a hockey crowd in Montreal, and now the Blue Jays were staring at the possibility of another similar scene during what was supposed to be the most festive of their 162 games.

J.P.'s initial reaction was to not play the song out of respect to the Canadian fans. Team president Paul Godfrey, on the other hand, was worried about having the highlights from the Blue Jays' opener revolve around the fact that Toronto was the only Opening Day venue not to follow the company directive. It was decided the tune would be played, with someone of Canadian fame (enter Fergie Jenkins) tempering the crowd's potential reaction with an introduction. It seemed like a no-win situation, but at least the Blue Jays were going to make the final margin as palatable as possible.

By the time March 31 rolled around and the Blue Jays in-game entertainment crew cued up a tape of Celine Dion, Jenkins was nowhere to be found. He had been unavailable. But at 9:14 P.M. the Honorable Lincoln Alexander uttered the words, "we stand on guard for Canada as we present 'God Bless America.'" Nobody booed, so Godfrey was pleased. At the same time, Toronto was losing to the Yankees 8–0. Ricciardi was not pleased. It was already an all-to-familiar feeling.

"Success is how high you bounce after you hit bottom."

—General George Patton

THE DISCOMFORT of the spring's final days, along with the Opening Day mishaps, could be temporarily excused thanks to the remembrance of an accomplishment much more important than any pitch count or practical joke. It was a moment that would help Ricciardi weather even the bleakest of moments among the 162 struggles with sanity. It was, in the world of the Blue Jays, every bit as good as the day Raul Mondesi left town.

Back on March 17, nearly a year and a half after he had been introduced as the Blue Jays' general manager, Ricciardi nailed down the first two substantial pieces of his regime's foundation in the form of a pair of five-year contracts. Eric Hinske and Vernon Wells were in fold, and so were J.P's hopes for the future

The culmination of the project was a $14.5 million contract for

Wells and Hinske's $14.7 million deal. How the parties arrived to the point of signing on the dotted line was a process that began in October, involved a sweaty, last-minute agreement and ended with a bit of conference-call chicanery.

The first step was Ricciardi's walk down the hallway in the Blue Jays' offices and into Paul Godfrey's inner sanctum just days after the 2002 season had ended. They were not an easy twenty-or-so steps to make, but were utterly necessary, nonetheless.

The message was that in order for the Jays to stop the stripping and go full steam ahead with the building, Toronto had to start signing some of the players J.P. deemed the team's future annual All-Stars. It would be a gamble for both sides. The team would be committing to unequivocally unproven players. Hinske and Wells, on the other hand, might be sacrificing the prospects of big-time cash via arbitration, and eventually free agency for a slice of security.

In J.P.'s eyes, one thing was certain: The status quo was not the Blue Jays' ally.

Godfrey agreed to support Ricciardi's premise, which was subsequently broached to Ted Rogers and the boys down the street. It was decided that J.P. would team with Tim McCleary and Keith Law to draw up a five-page proposal stating everything that was right with the idea. How much would Rogers be saving by not going to arbitration? Has this worked in the past with other young, premium talents (Oakland's Eric Chavez, Miguel Tejada)? What were comparable players (Minnesota's Torii Hunter) making going on year-to-year deals?

Rogers's cooperation was only half the battle. Ricciardi still had to convince Hinske and Wells that signing up for the next five seasons, at terms palatable to the Blue Jays, was the right thing to do.

The negotiating starting gun was officially sounded when Ricciardi met with each player individually on February 25. Numbers were not uttered, but philosophy, approach, and intention were. From now on in, Hinske and Wells were not going to be bothered by the boys in the front office; their representatives, however, were another matter entirely.

First was the call to Hinske's guy, Dan Lozano.

Part of the preemptive process included the determination of who would be paid more, the 2002 Rookie of the Year, or the out-fielder whose potential knew no bounds. McCleary favored Wells as the leader in the contractual clubhouse, going by the premise that his mixture of home run and RBI capacity would mean more in the world the assistant GM knew best—the arbitration table. Ricciardi, on the other hand, kept coming back to his statistical staple, on-base percentage.

For years, Eric had taken pitch after pitch, and because of it he was now on the verge of taking something much more palat-able—a five-year, multimillion dollar contract.

Hinske's father, Mark, knew baseball. His dad, George, had gone to spring training with the New York Giants in 1948 and later started Menasha's Little League. Mark had continued the family's passion by participating at Division III University of Wisconsin-Oshkosh before playing for the local summer league team, the Menasha Macs, into his forties. So when Eric's dad started the process of molding his son into a duplication of his own baseball being at the age of three, hardly an eyebrow was raised around the fields of the 15,000-person Wisconsin town.

Lessons were learned on those baseball diamonds, first in Little League, then onto Babe Ruth, Legion, and high school. One of those bits of hardball knowledge was the art of deciphering a strike zone. Mark would tell his son, "Take the first pitch, bunt the second and then you can swing at the third." This made Eric Menasha's preeminent leadoff hitter. It also made Eric mad. He wanted to swing freely and hit balls out of the park, not consis-tently make his reputation off the guilty pleasure of jogging down to first base after siphoning four non-strike calls from the umpire.

Eric finally broke free of his father's coaching upon enrolling at the University of Arkansas, albeit just for one, memorable moment. It was in his first at-bat with the Razorbacks that he enacted his own brand of teenage rebellion, swinging at his inaugural collegiate offering. The result was the antithesis of a one-base free pass. This time the ball sailed more than 410 feet, up and over a fifty-foot screen. It sure felt good, undoubtedly better than all those hard-to-distinguish walks.

But Eric never forgot his roots, or the teachings that had gone along with them. He continued to take pitch after pitch, a trait that drew the interest of an Oakland A's representative while watching Hinske play for the team's Triple A affiliate in Sacramento. A's general manager Billy Beane had sent his right-hand man, Ricciardi, to check out some of the organization's almost-but-not-quite talent in the midst of the 2001 season and it was the Bees' third baseman whom had been embedded in J.P.'s list of future favorites.

So once Ricciardi took up residence in the catbird seat on the shores of Lake Ontario, J.P. called Beane about Menasha's favorite son, and Billy was hardly surprised. Ricciardi's best buddy already had a building block third baseman named Eric in young Mr. Chavez, and he also knew Hinske was a logical choice to help secure a missing piece of Oakland's puzzle, an end-of-the-game reliever.

Subsequently on December 7, 2001, sadly seven days after the passing of the Hinske family's first baseball star, George, Eric was traded along with pitcher Justin Miller to Toronto for relief pitcher Billy Koch in a deal that took barely more than five minutes to consummate.

The plate discipline ingrained into Eric by his father had distinguished him as Ricciardi's first transaction as a Major League general manager. Now, the hard-to-find talent was also the impetus behind justifying giving Hinske more money than the all-encompassing ability of a player one locker over, Vernon Wells.

By the time March 3 rolled around, Ricciardi wasn't getting anywhere with Hinske. The plan had been to agree to terms with the third baseman and then turn the ledger toward Wells and his agent, Brian Peters. But what J.P. didn't know was that the delay was already on a road of inevitability thanks to Eric's father.

Lozano had called Mark to let the family know of the Blue Jays' initial offer of $12 million over five years. According to the agent, it was an embarrassment of a travesty of a disaster. Just renew for a one-year deal and then work on the subsequent four years next spring, advised Lozano. But twenty-four years of playing baseball for free with the Macs had taught Mr. Hinske that these kind of dollars don't get introduced to baseball players from Menasha too often.

"I don't care if you negotiate for a couple more weeks, but Eric is signing this contract," Mark insisted. So Lozano talked the figure up to $14.75 million and Hinske and the Blue Jays had their agreement. The problem was that Wells and Peters now knew what the outfielder's counterpart was about to pull in, allowing Vernon to aim just a bit higher.

Unlike the Hinske family, Wells had been familiar with the inner workings of professional sports since the days his father, Vernon Jr., played in the Canadian Football League. Even after the senior Wells' gridiron glory, which had included a record-setting, ten-catch performance at the University of Tennessee, the interaction with the highly-paid matinee idols hadn't ceased.

Mr. Wells had begun to master the finer points of sketch drawing and painting, allowing for a most-unexpected career in portraying pro athletes on canvas and, later, trading cards. His first subject, his son, was portrayed at the age of three while wearing Spiderman underwear. Twenty years later Minnesota's Torii Hunter would be the next subject to don the symbol of the web-slinging superhero, except this time it was in tribute to the Twins' star's ability to climb outfield, not kitchen, walls.

By the time he was ten years old, Vernon III was impressing his youth league baseball teammates with visitors such as then–Oakland A's Cy Young Award–winning pitcher Dave Stewart thanks to his father's artwork. "No way," his friends would say in disbelief upon the promise of Stewart's arrival before one early summer game. "Look," responded Wells, pointing to one of the first to jump aboard the increasingly loaded-down Vernon Wells bandwagon. The Wellses had cracked the inner sanctum of professional athletes, many of whom never had the kind of zeroes being thrown Vernon's way by J.P. and the gang.

Knowing Hinske had let his teammate in on his numbers, the

Jays didn't have time to beat around the piggy bank with Wells. The offer was fast and firm: $14 million over five years. The response from Peters was, "Not enough."

Time was ticking. McCleary understood why Peters was pigeonholing his client above Hinske; that was his job. Back in 1995 the Toronto trio of Carlos Delgado, Alex Gonzalez, and Shawn Green were in the same kind of race for stature, each stating a case that they brought more to the table than the other two. Delgado brought the power, Gonzalez the glove and Green an all-around promise of potential. McCleary's response? "Why don't you all get together and decide how you want to slot it and that's how we'll do it." To nobody's surprise, each agent had their client topping the list. Predictably, the end result was a dead-heat, $500,000 apiece.

Now, every time Peters tried to eclipse Hinske's $14.75, the Jays came back to the same two centerpieces: the Menasha High leadoff hitter's .365 on-base percentage and that Rookie of the Year plaque that resided in on the family's mantel. Toronto would go to $14.5 million and give Vernon a $850,000 signing bonus ($350 K more than Hinske), but that was it.

Suddenly, there was thirty minutes for Wells to decide, then fifteen, then ten, nine, eight, seven, six . . . "OK," Peters relented. "We'll do the deal."

Both players had agreed to serve as the franchise's preeminent building blocks. Little did Ricciardi realize, but that would be the easy part.

With Hinske and Wells in line to sign on the dotted line, Ricciardi still couldn't break out the pens until he got permission for the financial terms from the Rogers people. The ownership group was a publicly traded company, so any kind of financial layout would have to be approved by a board of governors. J.P. would have to dip his toes into a baseball man's most unfriendly of venues—the boardroom.

In the end, it all came down to a twenty-minute video conference call between Ricciardi's Dunedin office and the Rogers higher-ups. Paul Godfrey had done quite a bit of selling on his end in Toronto, but now the onus was on J.P. to close the deal. Thanks to some flash cards and two impromptu mimes, that is exactly what the general manager did.

While J.P. sat at his desk, stating his case to the team's money men, McCleary and Law sat on the other side of the video phone. For twenty minutes, while Ricciardi put on the hard sell, his two assistants furiously wrote notes on cards in an effort to fill their boss's mouth with the words that would secure two future stars. First, McCleary, then Law, then McCleary, then Law. It was the equivalent of a pitcher and catcher working in perfect harmony, with no signs being shaken off and every offering placed perfectly in the glove.

Two days later, while J.P. was watching his team take batting practice in preparation for a spring training game with the Yankees, the GM's cell phone rang. It was the team's senior vice president of finance, Richard Wong, with the news—the money had been approved. Nerves had been frayed with pure pennant-race precision. But it was all worth it.

Unfortunately for the Blue Jays, it was the kind of good news that was few and far between as the season's first few weeks unfolded.

"Our GM couldn't field like that."

—Red Sox catcher Jason Varitek

THE BALL WAS SENT out like a rocket toward Fenway Park's left field wall. It was only batting practice but the awaiting fielder took no chances, adeptly moving his feet, crouching in a perfect infielder's stance and gobbling up the white sphere without a hint of a bobble.

As is the case with anybody gathering in a batting-practice offering, the person shagging the errant ball immediately threw the ball toward the nearest player, in this case Red Sox catcher Jason

Varitek. Upon receiving the toss the catcher offered an extra long stare at his outfield partner. The player's brief thought process centered around who this person wearing a black leather jacket, jeans, and certainly no baseball uniform was who had joined him in the shadow of the Green Monster.

Finally, after a few uncertain seconds, Ricciardi was recognized. The identification almost immediately elicited Varitek's comparing the Toronto general manager, the former minor leaguer, to Red Sox GM Theo Epstein. "I did used to play," Ricciardi responded while stepping into the bowels of the wall through the small hidden door next to the "At Bat" portion of the scoreboard. Branch Rickey, baseball's Babe Ruth of general managers, also played, just long enough to allow thirteen Washington Senators to steal off of him in one game while catching for the New York Highlanders.

J.P. knew a pro baseball pedigree wasn't a prerequisite in the job, but Varitek's acknowledgment was still a much-welcomed bit of affirmation. It also exemplified the GM's first return of the season to his youthful stomping grounds—the best of times before the day's first pitch, and equaled agony in the hours thereafter.

By the time Ricciardi stepped into Fenway's archaic, manual scoreboard on the late April Saturday morning, his Easter weekend homecoming had already been tainted. The night before, Toronto relief pitcher Jeff Tam's control had gone astray to the tune of four seventh-inning walks. In the process, the thirty-three-year-old righty, whom Ricciardi had brought in as a free agent after witnessing his work in Tam's three seasons with Oakland, allowed Boston to turn a one-run deficit into a 7–3 Red Sox win.

"I've never seen him like that," Ricciardi said of Tam while walking through the Fenway stands the day after the bullpen implosion. "But like I told Carlos [Tosca], you can't have both offense and defense on a $53 million payroll. You have to cut corners somewhere." When Toronto finally left Boston and headed to St. Petersburg for the final three games of a season-long eleven-game road trip, the Blue Jays had made errors in eight straight games and were last in the league in fielding.

The frustration that flew through the visiting manager's office after the first game of the Jays' and Sox's four-game series had made for a long thirty-minute drive to his house in Worcester. "I don't care if it's riding home on the school bus after a high school game or in the big leagues, that ride home after a loss is never easy," Ricciardi admitted the next morning.

He knew the early going was going to be tough, starting the season by exclusively playing the Yankees, Twins, and Red Sox. Everybody did. "You've got it brutal early on, huh J.P.," former Blue Jays manager Jim Fregosi had mentioned to Ricciardi before another spring training meatloaf dinner. "But, boy, does Boston have it easy," Fregosi added, referring to the Red Sox's April series against Tampa Bay and Baltimore. By the time the day before Easter rolled around Toronto was 6–11, having lost eight of its last nine. Boston, on the other hand, had won five straight on the way to an 11–5 mark.

The once-comforting momentum from the year before was now well beyond the memory of those who needed it the most, the Blue Jays.

"This place is special to me."

—J.P. Ricciardi

THE EARLY MORNING WALK through the only Memory Lane located on Boston's Lansdowne Street was a welcome diversion for Ricciardi. Diane was happy to have the family back in Worcester for the holiday weekend, using the Saturday to take the kids to a friend's birthday party. J.P. was just happy to sign his name on the inside of the left-field wall. When you're losing, every little piece of salvaged sanity counts.

With a Toronto camera crew in tow, Ricciardi scaled parts of Fenway he had not seen since first soaking in the park's greenness. One of the stops was to the new seats atop the Green Monster. It was there where he predictably was greeted by a vendor who, like many who would converge on the Sox–Blue Jays game, knew Ricciardi more as the guy who used to coach Holy Name basketball for eleven years and dabbled in scouting some baseball games. The conversation was another welcome distraction for Ricciardi, who seemed to prefer breaking down the problems with the Massachusetts Interscholastic Athletic Association than present his "we know we're not going to win the World Series" speech to another follower of Major League Baseball.

For many of the Worcesterites who knew of Ricciardi, it was more difficult to believe that he wasn't coaching high school basketball anymore than it was to fathom that he had become the Blue Jays' general manager. Just a few months before the start of his second season with Toronto Ricciardi had gotten a call from his local paper, the *Worcester Telegram and Gazette.* The fact that the paper of a 100,000 circulation was touching base with one its highest-profile subjects wasn't out of the ordinary, the line of questioning was another story.

"J.P., how's the team going to be this year?" asked the reporter.

"Pretty good, we just signed Cory Lidle and Mike Bordick and it looks like we've got a pretty good line on Catalanotto," Ricciardi responded.

"Um, you are still coaching Holy Name, aren't you?" said a now very confused inquisitor.

"No. I'm the general manager of the Toronto Blue Jays," Ricciardi laughed.

The bad news for the reporter was that the *Telegram and Gazette's* high school boy's basketball phone list hadn't been changed. The good news was that neither had Ricciardi. As the misguided reporter, the Fenway Park vendor, and the other well-wishers had discovered, the Toronto GM might have known he had made the big time but he sure didn't act like it.

Ricciardi's genuine nature was easy to spot on days like the one he took his Fenway Park tour. The stories of having to leave early from his first game only to hear the roar from a Ray Fosse home run, or how he refused to take his sons to Fenway until they were old enough to appreciate it, rolled off his tongue and illuminated his eyes. Talking about his baseball team also excited Ricciardi, it was just that the tales would be a lot easier to tell if Toronto had started the season like it had finished the year before.

"You can learn little from victory. You can learn everything from defeat."

—Christy Mathewson

THE UPS AND DOWNS of an entire season had also infested themselves in the Red Sox's first month, albeit from a much different perspective than their Toronto counterparts. Even with the successes of the Easter weekend series, there was an uneasiness that surrounded the team's Fenway Park offices. The bullpen hadn't deviated from its opening day impression and starting pitcher Derek Lowe, the nineteen-win anchor of the year before, failed to look like the horse Boston was planning to strap its five-man rotation to.

The concerns grew exponentially on April 24 when Lowe turned an afternoon's series-ender in Texas into the poster for the Sox's early-season inconsistencies. The 6-foot-5 pitcher, whose repertoire was built more on the sink of his fastball than its sheer velocity, was prone to put his emotional state on display for all in attendance to see. Now, against the Rangers, the image showed a series of disgusted hat-tugs and disappointed dirt kicks.

Seven runs on six hits in just two innings of flat fastballs and sinkers with no sense of gravity.

Back in Boston, the warmth and sunshine of the spring had been secondary in the minds of the locals thanks to the anticipation of watching the Red Sox's afternoon baseball game. By the fifth inning, however, the viewers had been forced to turn their attention toward that night's Boston Celtics playoff game at the FleetCenter against the Indiana Pacers.

When it came to priorities in the eyes of Boston sports fans the Celtics, even in the crazed enthusiasm of the postseason, couldn't keep up with the regular season Red Sox. Theo Epstein was no different than the followers of his team, although his apathy toward the town's professional basketball team had taken root long before Larry Bird left town. The C's just never did it for him, not like the thrill of a Sunday afternoon Patriots game, anyway.

Still, regardless of the interest level, Epstein was ready to jump aboard the Celtics playoff express for this one game. The plan to follow the Sox's game in Texas with a Celtics ticket–chaser was not because of a sudden 180 degree turn in his pro sports loyalties, but more due to a welcome chance for some valuable family time with his dad. Boys night out hadn't been often enough for the Epstein family since the second son's November press conference, and watching a game at the FleetCenter (in down-by-the-court seats, nonetheless) seemed like the perfect springtime tonic.

That was until Lowe's hat-tugging, dirt-kicking afternoon.

By the time a final score had been affixed to the Red Sox–Rangers game, Theo didn't feel much like pretending his attention was on a basketball game. He was also wary that one camera shot of him doing something other than righting all that was wrong with the Sox might not be the best picture to paint. So he called his dad, who agreed to save the get-together for another time.

Later that night, still trying to convince his mind that sleep was more important than worrying about the day's game, Theo turned on the television and saw some familiar faces. There, on the stage of the Jimmy Kimmel Show, were Red Sox players Todd Walker, Johnny Damon, Kevin Millar, and David Ortiz.

Walker's agent had connections with the show and asked his client if he would be interested in rounding up some of his teammates for the late-night production's introduction. So, as the team bus motored from the Los Angeles International Airport toward the next series' living quarters, the Sox second baseman asked who would be interested in appearing on national television.

Getting blown out, like they had hours before in Texas, was going to happen at least a few times. Entering the inner-sanctum of network TV was a rarity.

The night of television had allowed for another reminder for Epstein. The season may be long, but the memory doesn't have to be.

"Caught off first, he leaped to run to second, but then struggled back to first."

—from the poem *Ball Game*

THE CHALLENGE OF PUTTING the April 24 loss was hard enough for the Red Sox front office, but the news it was saddled with the next morning made a healthy, levelheaded mind-set almost impossible.

Manny Delcarmen, one of the most promising pitchers in the Sox organization, would not be able to pitch for a while . . . a long while.

The burning sensation Delcarmen had been feeling in the elbow of his oh-so-promising right arm had been diagnosed. The twenty-one-year-old from Boston's West Roxbury district (the first native of the city to be drafted by the Sox in forty years) would have to be introduced to the three ugliest words in a pitcher's vocabulary—Tommy John surgery.

Tommy John's moniker had entered the world of medical science in 1974 when Dr. Frank Jobe performed a then-experimental procedure on the left-handed North Carolina native. John had blown out the ligament in his pitching elbow, opening the door for Jobe to replace the injured body part with a tendon from the patient's wrist.

The impending surgery would link Delcarmen and John, albeit solely because of the pair's broken down ligaments. When Jobe put John under the knife, the patient was told a resumption of his pitching career would be one in 100. Yet, even if the operation wasn't a success, John still was heading to retirement with 124 Major League wins in 355 games.

Delcarmen, conversely, had barely made it three weeks into his third years in the minors. What he had going for him was the history that John gave birth to, winning 164 more games after serving as Jobe's Frankenstein. Now, the success rate for pitchers' returns was closing on ninety-five percent, a number that made Delcarmen's flight from Fort Myers, Florida, to Birmingham, Alabama, two hours of little worries.

Meeting Delcarmen and his parents at the HealthSouth Medical Center was Boston's director of player development, Ben Cherington. The initial blow to the organization regarding the news of its promising young pitcher had been digested and now it was time to deal with the yearlong road back. Part of that job fell on Cherington, who was going to make sure Phase 1 went off without a hitch.

Like many of the Red Sox's new wave of decision makers, Cherington had experienced a somewhat swift rise toward the front office. Just five years before, the twenty-eight-year-old had begun his professional baseball career as an advance scout for the Cleveland Indians. That initiated the progression with his new team, the Red Sox—scout, baseball operations assistant, and then in '02, assistant director of player development.

As was the case with some of the Boston front office's brotherhood, the dark-haired, former collegiate pitcher whose every movement appears to be linked with a sense of purpose grew up a fan of the team he now received his paychecks from. Cherington's hometown of Meridan, New Hampshire, was a good four hours from Boston, hovering near Vermont and Dartmouth College, but it was still entrenched in Red Sox Nation.

Another similarity Cherington shared with at least one of his coworkers was a bloodline link with greatness. Not only did Theo's family possess an Academy Award, but Ben had been calling a Pulitzer Prize–winner grandfather for the past quarter century.

The person Cherington designated as his maternal grandfather, Richard Eberhart, was a man who was deemed the Poet Laureate for the John F. Kennedy administration. In other words, he was the nation's No. 1 starter when it came to poetry.

Eberhart's most momentous achievement came in 1966, when he earned his Pulitzer Prize for the selected poetry he spun from 1930–1965. But in the world of baseball and his grandson, the words that truly exemplify Eberhart's true worth stemmed from watching Ben play a baseball game at Plainfield Elementary School.

On that mid-1980s afternoon, a ten-year-old Ben Cherington was poetry in motion . . . literally. It a moment that, while seemingly innocuous at the time, was even afforded a title—*Ball Game.*

> *Caught off first, he leaped to run to second, but*
> *Then struggled back to first.*
> *He left first because of a natural desire*
> *To leap, to get on with the game.*
> *When you jerk to run to second*
> *You do not necessarily think of a home run.*
> *You want to go on. You want to get to the next stage,*
> *The entire soul is bent on second base.*
> *The fact is that the mind flashes*
> *Faster in action than the muscles can move.*
> *Dramatic! Off first, taut, heading for second,*
> *In a split second, total realization,*
> *Heading for first. Head first! Legs follow fast.*
> *You struggle back to first with victor effort*
> *As, even, after a life of effort and chill,*
> *One flashes back to the safety of childhood,*
> *To that strange place where one had first begun.*

The poem was born for Cherington, but now carried its meaning to another young baseballer, Manny Delcarmen. His was a career that had gained momentum, only to be reeled on in by a plane ride to Birmingham.

Delcarmen not only entered the 8,500-square-foot rehabilitation center with the affirmation of Cherington, but also the knowledge afforded him by peers such as fellow Red Sox minor leaguer Jerome Gamble, who had also undergone the elbow surgery. So when Dr. James Andrews, the preeminent baseball surgeon who was asked by the organization to perform the surgery, told Manny to touch his pinky finger to his thumb, it was no surprise. This was the first step in the tendon scavenger hunt.

The first option for the tendon donation is the subject's wrists. If a respectable replacement isn't found there, the search continues to the back of the ankle and then the hamstring. In Delcarmen's case the wrist would suffice, a fact made perfectly clear by the word "correct" labeled on the body part in magic marker.

The warm-up act's information was all very interesting to Cherington, who had engaged in a conversation regarding the operation in the middle of a suite of four of the practice's sixteen operating rooms. Then came the curveball. "Do you want to watch?" asked one of Andrews's coworkers.

In the times of previous Red Sox regimes, if it was learned that a member of the front office witnessed one of the team's top prospect's surgeries, the public outcry might classify the attendance as paranoia. These days, however, it was what it was—another afternoon of information-gathering.

New and different never scared off Boston's new breed, and this time neither did a little blood.

In fact, the viewing was appreciably less gory than Cherington had anticipated. It went something like this: Andrews and his crew of eight or so took out the eight-inch, dental-floss-looking tendon, and placed it in a saline solution. After a three-to-four-inch incision is made along Delcarmen's right elbow, the ulnar nerve is slightly moved away from the frayed tendon so that the new one can be placed over it.

Three holes are drilled in the bone, which will serve as the anchor for the new tendon. Andrews fastens the replacement via a figure-eight weave and that is that. Just more than an hour of surgery was a piece of cake, both for the patient and the peanut gallery. There was some discomfort for Delcarmen and Cherington, but it was a pain that revolved less around the operation's numbing effect and more among the next year of monotonous rehabilitation.

At least the sting of Delcarmen's hiatus had a potentially happy ending. Many of those who come back from Tommy John's medical claim to fame are eventually stronger pitchers within three years of the first incision. It is an increased velocity due less to advanced science and more because of the opportunity for athletes to use the time to recondition their entire bodies. Go in for thirty minutes of work on the elbow, stay for four more hours to fine-tune everything else.

It was nice to see the young pitcher manage to smile thanks to the prospects of a silver lining. Seeing the light at the end of the dugout tunnel in the majors, however, wasn't as easily mustered by Epstein and the boys back up in Boston. Not with 119 games still left to dissect.

"Please come to Boston for the Springtime."

—David Allen Coe

BY THE TIME THE Yankees came to town for the first time on May 19, Theo at least looked the part of a man who had settled into his lot in life. His tan had gotten a head start on the rest of the Northeast thanks to a scouting trip to the University of Houston, where his only other general managerial company was Ricciardi. They both went to see a pitcher named Brad Sullivan. As it turned out, the game between the Cougars and Southern Mississippi didn't exactly reach the crescendo most anticipated as the object of both GM's attention lasted just three innings, giving up eight runs on seven hits. Scouting was an inexact science, and so was time management.

Theo might not have gotten a good read on Sullivan, but he did at least return to Fenway with a new goatee and a first-place team. The Yankees made it through April having lost six of their twenty-seven games, but they were now in a dead-heat with their American League East neighbors. The Sox had played well enough to match New York's 27–16 record, even with the continued woes of Lowe.

No matter the margin in the standings, Red Sox fans were going to buy every ticket Fenway Park had to offer upon the arrival of the Yankees. With each purchase the patrons knew they were getting a baseball rarity—playoff atmosphere before the first day of summer—and the inalienable right to yell "Yankees Suck" regardless of score or state of the respective teams.

This time, however, the Boston fans' credo carried at least a little weight. The Yankees did suck, or at least, in the words of their general manager Brian Cashman, "stink." New York had lost six of its previous seven games, having been introduced to the Red Sox immediately after getting swept in Yankee Stadium by the Texas Rangers. It was a joyous scenario for Red Sox Nation.

Adding to the optimism in and around the Fens was the Red Sox's bullpen's slow-but-steady journey to decency. Sure, it had started with the idea of ignoring a job title born from the days of Three-Finger Brown, Chief Bender, and Firpo Marberry, all of whom started relief pitching's closing craze in the early stages of the twentieth century. But, after toiling through the agonizing inconsistency of Mike Timlin, Chad Fox, Rarmiro Mendoza, and Alan Embree, Boston decided the committee was to be downsized.

Just like the rest of baseball, Boston finally had one closer. But unlike the most of baseball, their closer was a waiver-claim afterthought who was listed more prominently in the Pawtucket Red Sox's media guide than that of the parent club.

"Don't look back. Something might be gaining on you."

—Satchel Paige

BRANDON LYON was used to living on the edge, a welcome personality trait for all relief pitching game-enders.

Lyon's affection for bordering himself one step away from disaster perhaps stemmed from the day he decided to snowboard off the roof of his family's three-bedroom, white brick, Utah home. The daredevil lifestyle was also surely harvested when the family succumbed to the youngest son's pleas to build a skateboard ramp in the backyard.

And like the pitfalls that lay before him while filling a reliever role he had never once delved into before coming to the Red Sox, Lyon knew how to bounce back from falling off the wrong side of that fine line.

The first rendezvous with resiliency came just fourteen years into Lyon's life. It was a time when he liked playing baseball, a sport he had mastered both on the mound and at the plate as a shortstop. But he loved skateboarding and rollerblading. It was on his field of dreams, a half-pipe ramp, that the desire to stretch his expertise in shows with four wheels went a bit too far. A day later he had two broken bones held together by a plate and six screws.

The breaks weren't in his bread-and-butter right arm, but it still put baseball on hold for six months. But, in the beginning of a recurring theme, Brandon bounced back.

Lyon pitched well enough to be drafted after his senior season of high school by the New York Mets. Brandon instead chose to head to Dixie Junior College, a nearby school with a solid baseball program and all the amenities needed to build his stock in the eyes of the Major Leagues. It seemed like the right thing to do, until Christmas break, anyway.

Just days after Christmas of his first collegiate year, Lyon's decision to go snowboarding with some friends would provide the next great impediment. On the first run of the day, Brandon did nothing more than just slow down to allow his buddies to catch up. He was, after all, pretty good at the snow-induced discipline, having taken up the sport five years before. But just like the unpredictability of a midsummer bullpen session, Lyon knew that he could never be totally certain what kind of obstacles the mountain's snow-covered landscape presented. That's why he wasn't totally befuddled when an edge was caught and his tumble ensued.

When Lyon got to his feet he knew his right shoulder wasn't all together, a fact confirmed after taking X-rays later at the lodge. And when New Year's Eve rolled around, the scene only had gotten worse thanks to the image of Brandon lying on an operation table. He had torn the ligament that held the bone down in his shoulder, a condition the doctors decided warranted using a sort of tape to hold the parts in place while they regenerated. It looked as though living on the edge outside baseball had swiftly put Lyon over the edge in the realm of a baseball future.

It was one thing to be saddled with an eight-inch, rollerblade-induced scar on his left arm, but now the deformity was on the only body part that mattered in the eyes of the baseball world—Lyon's pitching shoulder. To make matters worse, the skin discoloration wasn't the only souvenir from the accident. Also making an appearance was the protruding bone, giving Brandon a permanent lump where the end of his collarbone and top of his appendage came together.

It wasn't until the following summer that Lyon threw a baseball again, taking a lot longer to shake off his subconscious woes than anything milling about in his pitching shoulder. But he did throw again, and again, and again. He threw until the mental cobwebs were gone, along with the soreness in all the muscles and joints. Finally, he was back to form as a member of the Dixie Junior College pitching staff, a position he used to segue into the Major Leagues just one and a half years after taking his final snowboard run.

In the world of Lyon, he had accomplished the equivalent of landing on his head while attempting a Stale Fish Grab off a mountain's mogul, only to get back up and back on board without hesitation. This was Boston's new closer—the weebles-wobble-but-he-won't-fall-down waiver claim.

The metamorphosis from snowboarder with a good arm to a close-the-door Major League relief pitcher appeared to be nailed down in the second game of the Sox's first Yankees series. By the

Blue Jays GM J.P. Ricciardi. *Toronto Blue Jays*

Red Sox front office members (left to right), Josh Byrnes, Theo Epstein, Jed Hoyer, and Galen Carr. *Julie Cordeiro/Boston Red Sox*

J.P. Ricciardi with his father, John. *Toronto Blue Jays*

The Beaumont Basher, first baseman Kevin Millar of the Red Sox. *Brian Babineau/Boston Red Sox*

The Menasha Masher, Blue Jays third baseman Eric Hinske. *Toronto Blue Jays*

The World's Greatest
Snowboarding Waiver
Claim, Brandon Lyon.
*Julie Cordeiro/Boston
Red Sox*

Cy Young Award
Winner, Harry Leroy
Halladay III. *Toronto
Blue Jays*

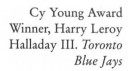

The Red Sox's second third baseman of the season, Bill Mueller. *Julie Cordeiro/Boston Red Sox*

Triple Crown winner and Blue Jays prospect Vito Chiaravalloti, shown with the Auburn Doubledays. *Toronto Blue Jays*

The ankle-breaking lefty, Casey Fossum. *Steve Babineau/Boston Red Sox*

Red Sox prospect Abe Alvarez of the Lowell Spinners. *Lowell Spinners*

time Lyon stepped on the Fenway mound, staring the responsibility of protecting Boston's three-run lead squarely in the face, all doubts concerning his big league worth had vanished.

Then came the exclamation point: Robin Ventura—strikeout on four pitches; Alfonso Soriano—strikeout on four pitches; Derek Jeter—strikeout on four pitches. Lyon suddenly had six saves and a tag affixed by The Nation that began with an "s" and ended with "avior."

Once Jeter was punched out, the questions elevated from the press box almost in unison. How could a twenty-three-year-old pitcher, with stuff good enough to strike out the meat of the New York Yankees' order with the game on the line, be available in the sometimes-hit, usually-miss world of waivers? Was he really a lot more experienced than the team was indicating? Did he have some sort of sordid past? There must be a story behind the pitcher who was thought to be lowered from the baseball heavens into the troubled bullpen of the Boston Red Sox. And there was, although unless good, old-fashioned physical fitness is considered the equivalent of international intrigue, there was going to be some disappointment.

The simple explanation for Lyon's revival—he got Hurt.

Lyon was familiar with Ken Hurt through his time at Dixie Junior College, where the aptly named trainer performed his practice. After suffering the indignity of surfing the waiver wire, the pitcher decided it was time to take his conditioning seriousness and hire someone to oversee his new seriousness. It sounded like a good idea, until Brandon spent nearly every day of two weeks hunkered over a toilet bowl, enveloped in a sea of pain and exhaustion.

Mr. Hurt wasn't going to let his pupil off lightly.

The sessions only lasted about one and one half hours each day, but what a ninety minutes they were. Lyon's frame might have been ideal for doing skateboard tricks, but when it came to working off a pitching mound his legs were more suited to riding four wheels supplying the impetus behind a ninety-three-mile-an-hour fastball. And boy, did Brandon hate when Hurt showed just exactly how inadequate all those muscles were.

According to Sir Isaac Newton's Law of Inertia, "All objects tend to travel in straight lines, unless acted upon by an unbalanced outside force." This is why baseball pitchers are so dependent on using their legs to drive the rest of their body toward the plate until finally the arm completes the deal. In Lyon's case, his unbalanced outside force needed a little work.

Lyon resisted the temptation to throw up, repeatedly. That was progress. A month later he developed again, this time actually looking forward to see the intensity of Mr. Hurt. And when the exercises started getting easier, and the fastball began to take off just a little faster, the evolution was complete.

It was the evolution of a player, a bullpen and, most importantly to everyone at 4 Yawkey Way, a team.

CHAPTER 6

Fourteen Days to Sanity

*"The grand essentials of happiness are: something
to do, something to love, and something
to hope for."*

—Allan K. Chalmers

The top-floor apartment normally couldn't have been distinguished in the street-block-size building just a matter of yards away from Fenway Park. But this night was different, thanks to a lone open window letting in the sixty-five-degree evening air.

Theo Epstein walked by, ridiculing himself for not remembering to close the window upon leaving his two-bedroom space nearly fifteen hours before. When you're a Major League Baseball general manager, even the most perfect of days can be thrown off by the triviality of a window crank. It was a fact Epstein reminded himself of constantly, whether because of a pitcher's sore elbow, or a nuisance such as having to prove his age to some doorman just 170 paces from his own ballpark.

But on this evening, where June 11th met the 12th, Epstein's good times couldn't be derailed. In a deluge of sleepless nights, this was not going to be one of them. The Boston Red Sox were in first place.

It would have been ample reward for the day to include Boston's 13–1 win over St. Louis. Yet, that was just the appetizer for a full-course meal of satisfaction.

The starting pitcher for the Red Sox, Pedro Martinez, added to the evening's festivities, even though he had thrown just forty-nine pitches in three innings. The mere fact that Boston's starting rotation's superstar had entered the clubhouse at 4:32 P.M. ready to pitch for the first time in twenty-seven days was good reason to rejoice.

For the fourth time in the past five seasons Pedro visited the disabled list, this time because of a sore right side. The official term was an inflammation of the latissimus dorsi, but to Red Sox fans it had been just another pain in the ass.

Now the throbbing was gone . . . from Pedro's side and The Nation's psyche.

The night only got better for Epstein and his Red Sox. By the time the final pitch was thrown, new second baseman Todd Walker, new designated hitter David Ortiz, new first baseman Kevin Millar and new third baseman Bill Mueller were all hitting over .300. They were statistics that, for the time being, elicited a smidgeon of sense of accomplishment.

The off-season had clearly been kind to Theo, both in the realm of player acquisition and property acquisition. Epstein was living in the same apartment building as the year before but had upgraded to a space that included a private gym. The workout center was the second biggest perk, with an inexplicable inability for his radio to pick up the sometimes venomous talk stations being the biggest benefit. And even if Epstein's clock radio's reception had been keener, listening these June days wouldn't have been such a painful experience thanks to the Red Sox's new formidable foursome.

The pennant race began, and the Red Sox had suddenly grabbed the pole position.

By the time Epstein reached his postgame destination, a neighborhood restaurant, his brother, Paul, and his wife had joined six other acquaintances, whose occupations ranged from social workers to college professors. The get-together offered the group a chance to bask in the excitement that was a Red Sox win, while also allowing Paul to decompress a bit. His teaching job may have been on summer hiatus, but there was always time to take thirty needy youngsters to a ball game. Theo's brother was truly one of the good ones.

While conversation filtered throughout the group, Paul turned to his twin with a big news-type of expression. "Did you hear about the Yankees?" he asked.

Theo got word regarding the team now known throughout the Fenway offices as the second-place Yankees. New York, which went into the evening a half game ahead of the Sox, not only lost, but had gotten a no-hit by six different Houston pitchers. It was the first time a Yankees team had been held without a single hit in 6,980 games. The night was just getting better and better.

Such a rare occurrence was actually leading some fans, such as the ones sitting with Paul and Theo Epstein, to believe that a change of power in the AL East was in the offing. It was, if nothing else, a nice thought. It took a good two weeks, but now the Fens District of Boston was finally rediscovering its anything-but-the-end-of-the-world tranquility.

The transition began fourteen days before, and involved the wildest of times for all involved in the American League East's race for first place.

"It was a quality pitch, but he called it a ball."

—Brandon Lyon

BY THE TIME Brandon Lyon took the mound for the ninth inning of Boston's May 28th visit to Red Sox's fans' annual gateway to misery, Yankee Stadium, he was still the world's best snow-boarding waiver claim.

With his hat's brim consistently pulled even with his eyes, and a tuft of blondish brown hair jutting out from his chin, the laid-back Lyon was living the life of a big-league closer. He had saved five of Boston's thirteen May wins, while posting a more-than-respectable 3.09 ERA.

This was why, when Boston scored four, game-tying runs off of the man Lyon aspired to be, Yankee closer Mariano Rivera, Brandon was Sox manager Grady Little's guy.

But Lyon got into some trouble in the ninth, allowing a leadoff double to New York's Hideki Matsui. The hit was made tougher to digest when Boston's left fielder Manny Ramirez threw wildly toward the Boston dugout for no apparent reason, handing Matsui third base. Unfortunately for the Sox, Ramirez wasn't getting paid more than $17 million per season for his ability to hit the cutoff man.

The no-out scenario prompted Little to put his young relief pitcher in a most uncomfortable predicament, intentionally walk-ing the Yankees' two most powerful hitters, Alfonso Soriano and Jason Giambi, to load the bases. The strategy was hatched so that an out could be made via a force play at any base. That is the reward. The risk is walking the batter to force in the game-winning run. Simply put, it was a baseball manager's version of Russian Roulette.

Days after the decision, *Baseball Prospectus* writer Nate Silver took a sampling of fifteen seasons in which managers were pre-sented with similar scenarios to the one Little faced against the Yankees (tie game, home team at-bat, ninth inning or later, runner on third, fewer than two outs). It was determined that teams that took the Sox's route, walking two batters, had a 38.4 percent chance of sending the game into extra innings. The best bet appeared to be walking just one hitter, putting the chances at extending the game at 43.4 percent.

(As much as most want baseball to be run by romanticism and instinct, it is stats that really rule the roost. This is why in every major league dugout you can find these enormous fact-filled note-books resting alongside pouches of chewing tobacco.)

But what wasn't deciphered into the equation this time, by either Little or Silver, was the success ratio when a snowboarding waiver claim throws a 2-and-2 pitch right down the middle of the plate with a country music–singing umpire behind the plate.

Joe West was fifty-one years old, had been umpiring in the Major Leagues for twenty-five years, and was immune to virtually every kind of pressure or controversy (a quarter of a century of deciding between out and safe will do that).

The former Elon College quarterback hadn't settled solely for the life of a baseball decision maker. He was also venturing into the world of patenting sporting goods and recording the type of songs he grew up listening to in North Carolina. West had per-formed with industry heavies such as Merle Haggard, Bobby Mackey, Bonnie Owens, Mickey Gilley, and Box Car Willie, while also reaching country music's pinnacle—the Grand Ole Opry stage.

But now West was on baseball's biggest regular season plat-form—before 44,617 fans at Yankee Stadium—and as far as the Red Sox were concerned, Country Joe was about to hit one of the sourest notes of the season.

Lyon's 2-and-2 fastball appeared to slice through the middle of the strike zone, past a frozen Jorge Posada and into catcher Jason Varitek's still mitt. "Ball," West said. Varitek's glove stayed there, hoping its position would somehow change the umpire's mind. The pitcher also stood motionless, not believing the offering hadn't at least partially gotten the Sox out of its bases-loaded pre-dicament.

While the Boston dugout voiced its displeasure, Lyon was just pleased that Varitek hadn't made a big fuss. There was, after all, still another ball or strike to be called. Unfortunately for the Red Sox's battery, the reliever's decisive pitch wasn't nearly as close, eliciting a "Ball Four," from Cowboy Joe. Posada took his base, Matsui came home, and the game was over.

Lyon still didn't say a word as he trudged off the mound (it just wasn't his way). Varitek, as fiery a competitor as there was on the Boston roster, threw the ball down at the feet of West while voicing the pent-up anger from the lost strike call.

Moments after the Red Sox dropped to 31–21, just a half game in front of the Yankees, Lyon got Hurt, again. Ken Hurt, the trainer who had transformed the former Dixie Junior College standout into the Boston Red Sox's present relief pitching standout, had made the trip to New York with his wife and wanted to catch up with his pupil. Unfortunately for the visitor, conversations with closers after a game are a 50–50 proposition, and on this day Lyon was on the wrong side of the equation. The visit was brief as Boston headed to Toronto and away from the memory of Cowboy Joe's call.

Back in Boston, the boys in the front office decided to watch the game in Epstein's two-television set office. Frustration was at an all-time high. This was not only a bad call, it was also something much worse—a bad call that helped lose a game to the New York Yankees.

But then suddenly the misery was put on hold thanks to a call from the 602 area code. The son of Joe Garagiola had good news for the Red Sox.

"This trade was about winning the World Series
. . . To put ourselves in that position, we needed
more pitching."

—Theo Epstein

JOE GARAGIOLA JR., the general manager of the Arizona Diamondbacks, saw the Yankees' win and all that went with it. Within the Red Sox's loss he saw a solution to his team's dilemma in the form of a twenty-seven-year-old, free-swinging third baseman named Shea Hillenbrand. The Diamondbacks flat-out could not hit, were on the verge of falling to 24–29 and viewed the kid from down the road in Mesa as a possible solution.

"How did you like that slide?" Epstein asked his Arizona counterpart, referring to an immaculate (albeit unsuccessful) hook-slide Hillenbrand had made in Boston's comeback. The third baseman who called himself baseball's version of an "entrepreneur" back in spring training was opening himself up for business.

The fact that Hillenbrand notched two hits (including a home run) against the Yankees to raise his batting average to .303 after the season's first fifty-two games wasn't the impetus behind the phone call. Neither was the fact that the Red Sox third baseman had as many RBIs by April 15 (seventeen) as the mish-mash of Diamondbacks' three-baggers totaled at the time of the May 27 late-night communication. And while knowing Hillenbrand was Arizona born and bred (even winning the title of the state's best high school soccer player as a senior) was nice, it didn't make Garagiola Jr. dial one single digit.

Hillenbrand was cheap (making just more than $400,000), he was a good hitter, would make an aging Diamondbacks team younger, and, most importantly, had gotten the stamp of approval from Arizona owner Jerry Colangelo. A deal would be done—the 1993 Arizona high school soccer player of the year for perhaps the most unusually effective pitcher in the Major Leagues, Byung-Hyun Kim.

Hillenbrand was drafted as a shortstop, then moved to catcher before landing in the big leagues at third base. But in comparing the back-story of the beefed-up, line-drive hitter to his counterpart in baseball's first big deal of '03, Kim, the journeys weren't even close. Very few had a yarn like the one this pitcher possessed, and he was just twenty-four years old.

Kim's trail to Boston started innocently enough, a college pitcher getting attention from big-league scouts for his uncanny ability to throw a baseball. But hidden inside the obvious resided the uniqueness.

First, Kim wasn't at University of You-Name-the-State, he was in South Korea, a no-man's land for scouts. He was also absent of the pitcher's mold, standing at 5-foot-5, while whipping his offerings virtually underhand. It wasn't that the submarine style was so out of the ordinary, it was that his radar gun readings were about ten miles an hour faster than that of any of his sidearm-tossing brothers. Submariners' inability to throw hard was always accepted as a physiological compromise . . . that is until Kim showed up.

Appearance wasn't Kim's only separation from other Major League dreamers. Then again, potentially pitching for your life will often pluck someone from a crowd.

It was 1998 and a nineteen-year-old Kim was pitching for his country in the Asian Games. On the horizon wasn't the chance to become South Korea's second Major Leaguer (Chan Ho Park arrived in 1994), that future was reserved for a commitment to the military—unless, of course, his team won the gold medal. So said the nation's president.

Kim won the tournament's semifinal game, his team won the whole ball of wax, and with it the pleasantly powerful pitcher won a chance to enter the world's premier baseball-playing league in the United States. Firing ranges were dismissed, fastballs weren't.

Kim signed a four-year, $2.4 million contract with Arizona, took a thirteen-hour plane ride from his home to Phoenix and soon thereafter threw twenty-six pitches in Bank One Ballpark's home team's bullpen. As much as he didn't know what to make of his new surroundings, the people who now made up his backdrop didn't quite know what to make of Kim.

Blue Jays's hitting coach Mike Barnett still remembers coaching first base in Tucson, where Kim began his rapid ascent to the majors, and standing in awe not only of the pitcher's pitches, but the hitters' reactions. The ball would start out heading for the low, outside corner of the plate and end up buzzing underneath the batter's chin. Kim was good at making the seemingly impossible anything but.

"What was that?" opponents and teammates alike would ask Barnett.

"That's his 'Shooto,'" responded the coach. Barnett had no idea what the pitch's name meant, but it appeared fitting since something like that couldn't dare carry around a traditional tag. This was also a pitcher whose peculiarity begged for a nickname, which he would ultimately receive courtesy of his new American teammates. In the world of the Diamondbacks' clubhouse Kim was "The Lion."

For those who enjoyed simplifying things, the name didn't exactly fit the stocky-legged, vertically challenged pitcher. Kim was far from ferocious. But in the world of the baseball fraternity, creativity counted for a lot, and this was a good one.

As the Diamondbacks soon discovered, Kim slept like crazy. To say that he had his eyes closed more than they were open wouldn't be an exaggeration by any means. It wasn't a problem (after drilling it into his head that naps during games were off limits, that is), but his propensity for slumber was comically eyebrow-raising, nonetheless.

So along came the nickname, stemming from The Tokens' 1961 song "The Lion Sleeps Tonight." It was what Kim did when he was awake, however, that was the real music-maker.

After taking over for Matt Mantei during his rookie season of 2000, Kim saved fifty-five games as the Diamondbacks' closer. The partnership of the relieving role and the pitcher only made sense—he threw hard, he struck people out, and he wasn't averse to sampling a bit of pressure now and again. Unfortunately for Kim, there were two of those "agains" that his young career had been defined by.

First came Game 4 of the 2001 World Series—game-tying two-run homer by New York's Tino Martinez with two outs in the ninth, and then a tenth-inning game-winning solo job by Derek Jeter. The next day came Game 5—another game-knotting, two-run homer with two outs in the ninth, this time off the bat of Scott Brosius. Suddenly, that military commitment wasn't looking all that horrendous.

But background and age are beautiful things when looking for resiliency, and Kim had them both in his corner. He pitched well out of the bullpen again in 2002 and looking forward to segueing into Arizona's starting rotation in '03. (The goal was to become the best Korean Major Leaguer ever, a task that couldn't be accomplished as a reliever.) By the time spring training rolled around, Jerry Stephenson certainly didn't see any problems with the baby-faced, frisbee-thrower. Relieve, start, Kim still looked as unexplainable as ever.

Stephenson was a Boston scout whose responsibility was following the National League West Division. He first saw Kim in '01 and never forgot the 145-pound kid who regularly reached ninety-three on the gun. Then in the spring, he got another glimpse of the kid and there was a subtle difference, although it had nothing to do with psyche or shellshock. Kim just wasn't throwing as hard as he used to.

The change wasn't a huge concern. It was only a couple of miles an hour, and Stephenson thought he had an explanation: overuse. Kim had not only pitched in 150 games over the previous two seasons, but he couldn't go a day without throwing to something—a batboy, a wall, his interpreter, anything or anybody. This was the same guy who left the legend of throwing more than two hundred pitches in one game on one day's rest back in South Korea.

Someone else who wasn't concerned about Kim was Boston's new general manager.

Epstein saw the value of Kim right away, a pitcher who could start, relieve, and come right back on short notice to do it again. And he was good, to boot. That's why, in the winter trading months, offers kept coming from Boston toward Garagiola Jr. Prospects, money, whatever. The Red Sox wanted Kim, but the Diamondbacks weren't biting.

But while in Texas watching his future No. 1 draft pick, David Murphy, Epstein finally got the word he was waiting for from Garagiola Jr.—a Kim for Hillenbrand deal was a possibility.

The initial groundwork had been added to by an old acquaintance of Garagiola Jr., and Epstein's newest ally, Bill Lajoie. Before Garagiola Jr. became the general manager of the Diamondbacks he had made a living in the realm of the other side—the life of a player agent. One of his clients just happened to be a Detroit catcher named Mike Heath, who just happened to be working under the watch of then-Tigers' GM Lajoie. Contracts were negotiated and a friendship was struck. Now one friend was asking the other about his team's interest in Kim.

In the world of baseball, deals like this were rarely made before June. There was always the hope that things might straighten themselves out. But Boston needed pitching, both to start and close games, and with the Yankees and Blue Jays one winning streak away from grabbing the division by the balls, it appeared to be a necessity.

Lajoie stepped into the fray once again, this time to give Epstein some advice: Sometimes it's better to make the trade too early rather than too late.

So Stephenson got the call.

The Sox scout followed Arizona for ten days, all of which were Kim-free thanks to his stint on the disabled list. The injury was a fluke. He had hurt his ankle thanks to Colorado outfielder Preston Wilson's broken bat. But just as Stephenson thought he might finally see Kim for the first time in the '03 regular season, word came down on a Friday that the pitcher had suffered another setback. The word was that Kim had suffered a groin injury running the bases in a rehab stint at Tucson and wasn't going to be available for viewing for some time.

Stephenson got another call. The Red Sox knew something he didn't—Kim was going to pitch in San Francisco on Tuesday.

Sure enough, May 27 rolled around, Kim was going toe-to-toe with San Francisco starter Jason Schmidt, and Stephenson and fellow Sox scout Jerry DiPoto were sitting directly behind home plate ready to watch the whole thing unfold. The heat was on, and "The Lion" didn't even know it.

Whether or not Kim could feel the Boston duo's eyes burrowing in on him, the performance was worth the scouts' trip. The Arizona starter pushed all the right buttons, giving up just one run over seven innings. But it was more than the final numbers that left Stephenson satisfied with his subject. The real impression maker came when Kim took the most unfettered path in the majors—going right after the walking intentional walk, Barry Bonds. The knock on the hurler was that lefties ate him up, but on this night it was his "Shooto" that was devouring the left-handed-hitting Bonds.

DiPoto got on the phone and called back to the Boston offices to tell the Red Sox front office the unfolding merits. The group gathered in Epstein's office already knew the message before the first ring. They were also watching it, 3,000 miles away on the GM's office television. On both coasts, the right pitches, and impressions, were being made.

The scouts, in San Francisco and the Fenway Park office space, had seen enough. The report was in: looked great, fastball only 87–88 but with good movement, great change-up, probably better suited to be a reliever, which might raise his velocity.

The next night Garagiola Jr. and Epstein were closing the deal among the gloom left over from the bases loaded walk–induced loss to the Yankees. Kim was going to be a starter, at least until Boston decided who would be its next pitching pick-up. That was an easy decision. How to let Hillenbrand know all of those trade rumors had become a reality was a bit trickier.

This wasn't the first time Hillenbrand had been mentioned in potential deals. In fact, way back when getting Kim seemed like an impossibility, the Red Sox thought they had another deal done with Diamondbacks—Mr. Arizona Soccer 1993 straight up for D-Backs' first baseman Erubiel Durazo.

The potential Hillenbrand transactions kept coming, and so did the third base replacements if and when a deal was struck. Boston had its backup plan in a gritty gamer by the name of Bill Mueller, a player whose propensity for injuries kept his value at a manageable level.

Epstein had eyed Mueller when in San Diego, as did Josh Byrnes while serving as an assistant to Rockies general manager Dan O'Dowd in Colorado. Byrnes, from his work with the Rockies, had a good idea what it would take to sign the third baseman, giving the Sox a head start on the impending negotiating process. (Every little bit helps in the courtship of baseball-playing millionaires.)

So at 10 P.M. on December 20, the day before Epstein's impromptu trip to Nicaragua, an agreement was struck. Mueller was going to be the Red Sox's third baseman, it was just that Hillenbrand didn't know it yet. In fact, Boston was so certain that a trade regarding Hillenbrand was inevitable it decided to sit on the Mueller deal so that not to endure an uncomfortable positional overlap.

But sometimes even the most logical of signings can breed uncertainty, which was the overriding aura circulating the Boston baseball operations offices in the waning hours of the 20th. So Epstein and Byrnes decided to elicit some 1 A.M. good feelings and popped in one of a limited collection of Bill Mueller highlight tapes. The problem was that it was anything but. Ugly swings. Broken bats. Looked hurt. "Screw this!" said Epstein. So the words "hits only" into the digital machine spewing out the images. There were hits, all right, but none of them made a single outfielder take a step back.

Maybe Hillenbrand wasn't so tradable after all. And to make matters worse in the coming days, even when the Red Sox tried to trade their third baseman they couldn't, leaving for a convoluted hot corner. So more than three weeks later, Epstein made the decision to announce the Mueller signing and use Hillenbrand's traditionally hot start to fix the roster's uncertainties. It wasn't ideal, but formulating a roster while there's snow still on the ground is rarely seamless.

But sure enough, Hillenbrand started strong, there was a hole in the pitching staff, and the Red Sox filled it with the sidewinding South Korean . . . then came the hard part.

In the midst of the trade talk, during the heart of spring training, Hillenbrand had gotten antsy and asked Epstein to let him know of any trade that was to be made. Theo agreed. The problem was that by the time the Kim deal was consummated, the Red Sox were already hunkered down in their Toronto hotel in preparation for their month-ending series with the Blue Jays.

Hillenbrand was in Canada, so that's where Epstein and his new passport were going.

No one would have held against Epstein if the hour flight to Toronto on May 29 had never been made. Hillenbrand hadn't exactly shrouded himself in sympathy in the weeks leading up to the trade, going so far as to spout off a "Yeah, trade me now, faggot," half-kidding edict to Epstein on Boston radio station WAAF. But a promise was a promise, and this being Theo's first big, in-season trade, it was going to be executed properly.

The meeting was set up in Little's suite. Somewhat to Epstein's surprise it went without a hitch, with Hillenbrand lending a seemingly sympathetic ear. The only problem of the day appeared to be that Theo couldn't arrange for a flight back to Boston that night, leaving him stuck in a hotel room sifting through the paperwork that comes with the completion of a Major League Baseball transaction.

The next morning Epstein was on his way, feeling free and clear of the potential animosity that he thought might have been waiting in Toronto. But in line to get a bagel while waiting for his flight he caught eyes with a familiar face. It was Hillenbrand. Another round of cordiality was being mustered up. This time, however, the third baseman had a sense of aloofness to his greeting. Animosity had festered overnight and had now taken up shop in the waiting area for the Delta flight to Boston. Making matters worse, the two men shared the same small plane back to Logan Airport.

Epstein had been officially initiated into a general manager's nightmare—the unpredictability of a trade and everything that went with it.

While Epstein was jetting back to Boston with his former third baseman, he had much more to worry about than just the entrance into the Kim Era. The GM may have left Toronto behind via a one-hour flight, but his team wasn't so fortunate. The Blue Jays were winning, and winning a lot. The result was a notion thought unthinkable just weeks prior—Toronto had inexplicably gained membership in the American League East pennant race.

"Realizing the importance of the case, my men are rounding up twice the usual number of suspects."

—Claude Rains playing the role of
Captain Louis Renault in Casablanca

THE FRIDAY MORNING Theo was fighting back bad airport vibes from Hillenbrand, J.P. Ricciardi could be found roaming SkyDome's outfield. It was just 10 A.M., but the Blue Jays were working out some last-minute, late-round draftees, and virtually Toronto's entire scouting think tank was on hand.

The players, dressed in their collegiate practice uniforms, were littered around the artificial turf-covered diamond, with the hopeful hitters taking their chances against an equally anxious group of pitchers. Various scouts would instruct both parties about what they were looking for—fastball, curveball, ground ball the opposite way, line-drive down the line . . . the works.

The morning workout was going as smoothly as could be expected, with the occasional pitcher shaking off the predetermined pitch selection throwing things slightly off. There was also the concern voiced by Tim McCleary, whose contractual instincts flared up when he realized there was no emergency medical staff on hand ("They signed waivers, but a good lawyer could rip through those pretty quick," he matter-of-factly admitted). When it came to covering all the legal bases, McCleary was the best.

Finally J.P. got off the phone, picked up a stray baseball and yelled to McCleary, "Hey Tim, I'm doing my part!" The retrieval was in reference to the assistant's assertion that in this cutting-coupons atmosphere of big-league baseball, the team was losing a good chunk of money in lost balls. They figured that at $10 Canadian a ball, former outfielder Raul Mondesi had cost the team about $80 per game in just the souvenirs he flipped into the crowd. Every bit helped.

After stuffing the ball into his pocket, Ricciardi strolled into the crowd to mingle with McCleary, Keith Law, Tony LaCava, and the sea of scouts hovering around the batting cage. While hitters hit, pitchers pitched, and parents watched, J.P.'s attention had been sucked in by the impending draft's top of the heap selections.

The call Ricciardi received in the outfield helped clarify the organization's focus on its draft's early rounds. The adviser for a player J.P. was thinking about taking in the third round had been on the other end of the line, and he wasn't happy about what the GM had just informed him—the Blue Jays were going to pass on his guy.

The kid had talent, maybe first-round talent, but had been kicked off of two separate collegiate teams for smoking marijuana. Making the same mistake twice was just too coincidental for Ricciardi, who slept on the positives and negatives of the selection and decided to go in another direction. It was a decision that flummoxed the adviser.

To J.P., these advisers were a necessary evil when approaching the draft. It was one of the game's great mysteries—how collegiate baseball could allow these certified agents to deal with amateurs just because they were affixed with the tag of "adviser." If any other collegiate underclassmen had met with an agent for breakfast, as was the case with the passed-on player and his adviser that morning, the NCAA would rain its wrath on all involved. But this wasn't the case inside the strange, holier-than-thou world of professional baseball.

This time, there was nothing an adviser, agent, or any other kind of mentor could do. The Blue Jays had made up their mind. One down, thousands to go.

J.P. already knew whom he wanted to pick with his first pick. It was just a matter of knowing if any other of the twelve general managers slotted before him were placing the same name atop their draft room's depth chart. Ricciardi didn't think so, but he knew from his years in Oakland that one couldn't be too careful.

Enter The Claude Rains Project.

It was a safe assumption that Claude Rains had never been affixed to the world of Major League Baseball in seventy-eight years of life. He had stood at just 5-foot-5 and was almost blind in one eye because of a gas attack suffered in World War I, not exactly the stuff of hardball legends.

What Rains did do was play a character near and dear to Ricciardi's movie memory—The Invisible Man.

For J.P., Rains's character was the be all and end all when it came to exemplifying secrecy. How much more clandestine can you get than being invisible? And that was exactly what Ricciardi and his troupe were going to be in the days leading up to the draft when it came to a shortstop named Aaron Hill—invisible. Wherever the LSU infielder went, the Blue Jays were going to head in the other direction. As far as Toronto's crew was concerned, Hill was its top guy; it was just that they wanted every other team to believe anything but.

Invisibility was the Blue Jays' ally. The word came down: Up until the June 2 draft, The Claude Rains Project would be in effect.

The plan was hatched in the midst of every team's late-May right of passage—a scouting trip. For Ricciardi, scouting trips were like a whirl on a roller coaster—do it once, have some fun; and remember why you don't like repeating the process over and over again. They did sure bring back some memories, though. Hundreds of thousands of miles of pavement, hardly groomed baseball fields, and endless trips through drive-through windows will do that.

There were days in which Ricciardi witnessed five games in one sixteen-hour span, and weeks that strung together a series of ten-hour trips. J.P. still remembered seeing shortstop Rod Correia pitch three days in a row, all at 7 A.M., or joining former Oakland A's scouting director Grady Fuson in driving over medians and past "Do Not Enter" signs just to see the first pitch of a high school game in Michigan. The thrill, thankfully, was gone.

It was all the life of a scout, a life Ricciardi had put behind him until the middle of May had rolled around.

First stop: Houston, Texas.

J.P., McCleary, and Toronto scouting director Chris Buckley joined the Epstein-led Boston contingent in viewing the University of Houston's finest, Brad Sullivan. While they were at it, there were three kids from the Cougars' opponent, Southern Mississippi, who were going to get the evaluation once-over.

Ricciardi saw what Epstein witnessed, a pitcher in Sullivan who was topping out at eighty-five miles an hour while allowing a constant stream of base runners. J.P., however, saw something else. When you've made your living on evaluating talent, there's always more than the radar gun. That's why the kid who had just thrown the worst game of his collegiate career was in the process of being labeled as Toronto's realistic Plan B first-round option.

Second stop: Starkville, Mississippi.

When the heavyset convenience store worker encountered Ricciardi on the other side of the counter buying a bottle of water, she probably thought nothing more than to give back the right amount of change. The problem for the Mississippi resident was that she couldn't decipher exactly what form of currency J.P. had placed in front of her.

"What is that?" the clerk said, pointing to the five dollars of Canadian money Ricciardi had tested her with.

"That's Confederate money," J.P. said with just enough seriousness to be believable.

"What?" she said.

Finally, Ricciardi relented, "It's Canadian money."

"That's real money?" the confused clerk continued. That was it for J.P. There was still scouting to be done and energy couldn't be wasted explaining the merits of the one and two dollar coins Canadians called the "Loonie" and "Toonie." Another pitcher, this time a Mississippi State student by the name of Paul Maholm, was waiting to be looked at.

Maholm was a Georgia-bred left-hander who pitched like the big leaguer he idolized, Tom Glavine. The stuff wasn't eye-popping, but the method to the pitcher's madness was. By the time Ricciardi and his coworkers joined the other 4,802 in attendance in exiting Dudy Noble Field, they had seen the object of their attention strike out ten in just six innings against the maroon and white of Alabama. An impression was made.

Now, the Jays were placing Maholm as their No. 1 wish-list candidate. Reality, however, suggested they had better get another name up on the top of that list, because the Glavine-worshipping lefty was going well before Toronto's turn up on the draft room's speakerphone.

Third stop: Fayetteville, Arkansas.

To get to Razorback Country, Ricciardi, McCleary, and Buckley first had to drive their blue Chrysler LeBaron three hours to the Memphis airport. That also meant navigating Interstate 55.

The road was as dark as dark could be, leaving whatever was out on the horizon unknown to the three travelers. What were out there were tornadoes, lots of them. Ricciardi heard the warnings coming over the radio, but they really didn't mean much since the Toronto trio had no idea where the twisters and their LeBaron might meet. So reinforcement was brought in via a cell phone call. Keith Law to the rescue.

By now, it was 11:30 P.M. in Law's Massachusetts' residence, but it didn't matter. The organization's hierarchy was potentially in danger and it was up to the team's stat man to guide his co-workers to safety. So Law went to work, first dialing up weather Web sites to pinpoint nature's wrath. But the problem was that the weather service only designated its natural-disaster-immersed sites by counties, and since Ricciardi was having a hard time seeing the road's mile-markers, never mind a town boundary, the computer wasn't serving as much of a help.

Law improvised, grabbing an encyclopedia to find a map of wherever a road intersected Mississippi and Memphis. By now books and Web pages were flying through the Law household, leaving Keith's wife with the expression asking what exactly was this world of baseball her husband had gotten into. Rule 5 drafts and deadly gusts of wind—that's what it is all about.

Finally, a midnight solution was passed in a final phone call to

Ricciardi—keep going straight and you will be all right. Nobody said rebuilding a franchise was going to be easy.

Ricciardi, Buckley, and McCleary got to their Baum Stadium green plastic seats in time for Louisiana State University's 1:04 P.M. game against Arkansas, a feat appreciated by each one of the tornado survivors. But, as the Jays' trio soon discovered, their reward for not being caught up in nature's fury was much more than just admittance to a Southeastern Conference baseball game. The pot of gold was a shortstop with the name of "Hill" on the back of his white, gold, and purple uniform.

Ricciardi should have known that Saturday afternoon was going to be worth the trip when he passed through the stadium's gate. There waiting for him, and the other 4,000-or-so fans of the Hogs, were the likenesses of Toronto, and former Arkansas, third baseman Eric Hinske in the form of bobblehead dolls. Evidently, Blue Jay Fever had spread 1,127 miles south.

The storm chasers' good fortune only increased in the third inning, when on a 1-and-1 count the player responsible for J.P.'s attendance turned a 92-mile-an-hour fastball into a solo home run over the left-field fence. The 5-foot-11 shortstop was now standing ten feet tall as far as the pack of scouts was concerned.

The homer was nice to see; they always are. But it wasn't until two innings later that Hill's place atop the Blue Jays' non-wish list draft board was cemented. With the count worked to 3-and-1, the shortstop drew a fourth ball to increase his already league-leading on-base percentage.

In his five at-bats, Hill had walked once, gotten two hits, and made the opposing pitchers throw him eighteen pitches while not once swinging at the first offering. In Ricciardi's mind, this kid was just waiting to be drafted by the Blue Jays, and J.P. wasn't going to let him down. It was time to get invisible.

For the seventeen days leading up to the draft, all attention was going to be thrown at Sullivan. The message given to the rest of baseball was going to be that the Blue Jays wanted the Houston pitcher, first and foremost, and had developed a case of cold feet when it came to Hill.

Ricciardi and Claude Rains hadn't been linked together since the 1936 production of *Anthony Adverse*, which costarred a man by the first name of William who shared J.P.'s bloodlines. Now the two families were back at it again.

The scouts had returned to Toronto complete with stories of confused convenience store workers, deadly spinning gusts of wind, bobblehead dolls and, most important, a plan hatched by the invisible man.

On the afternoon of the May 29 game back at SkyDome, Ricciardi's plate was full. Outside his office and down the hall were books and books, and pages upon pages of scouting reports signifying that the draft was near. On the phone were a carload of relatives who were closing in on Toronto to watch the Blue Jays' weekend series with the Red Sox. And in the back of his mind was the prospect of what might happen if the Blue Jays could actually win a couple of these games against Boston.

Toronto had already swept its series in New York against the Yankees, so what stood in the way of success against the Red Sox? Ricciardi was mildly unoptimistic. He didn't like the pitching match-ups, and Boston had seemingly straightened its act out. But the thought was still there: What if the Jays could win these three games and be in the most upscale of neighborhoods in the American League East?

Ricciardi was about to find out.

"There is no security on this earth, there is only opportunity."

—General Douglas MacArthur

TO UNDERSTAND THE PROCESS Ricciardi goes through over the course of one of his 162, nine-innings sessions, witnessing the Toronto Blue Jays' final out in the month of May would be a good start.

"Turn him over. Turn him over," were the words J.P. planted in the ear of relief pitcher Cliff Politte as the closer prepared to face Boston's Jason Varitek. The GM may have been a football field away, entrenched in the Blue Jays' in-game bunker known as the general manager's box, but he knew Politte, he knew Varitek, and he knew what was supposed to happen—a ground ball to second base.

As had been the case for most of May, when J.P. asked, J.P. received. This time the gift came in the form of a scorecard that read: Varitek, 4–3. Toronto 10, Boston 7.

"Yes!" Ricciardi yelled, pounding his fist on the same spot on the counter in front of him that had weathered numerous blows of frustration throughout the same game. In a few hours the game might have lived up to the axiom that it was simply just one of 162. But as long as there were players on the field and people in "The Box," then this was one of one.

Ricciardi was not alone in his celebration. Four stools to his left was Toronto's head of security Ron Sandelli, whose fist pound and coinciding, "Yes!" would have measured up to that of his boss' exultation if not for the laptop computer resting precariously in front of his imposing sixty-year-old frame.

Sandelli, a former member of the Toronto Police Department, clearly loved the competitive spirit that permeated the box. Born and bred in the home of the Blue Jays, he had been entrenched in the city's police department for more than thirty years before convincing Paul Godfrey that he was the right man for a position that never even existed.

Also jumping up from the front row of the box was assistant general manager Tim McCleary and farm director Dick Scott, whose verbal approval might not have registered like Ricciardi and Sandelli's, but whose smiles matched anyone in SkyDome.

As handshakes were exchanged among the four men like glasses being toasted at a graduation dinner, Ricciardi breathed the breath of someone who had gone the full twelve rounds, and then some. Whoever says that baseball is a boring game never watched the Toronto GM take in nine innings.

When a play is made in a Toronto Blue Jays' game, any play in any game, there is going to be analysis and reaction (not necessarily in that order) coming from the second row of the luxury box directly to the left of SkyDome's press box.

Tom Clark, a scout Ricciardi got into the Oakland organization, will never forget his introduction into J.P.'s in-game metamorphosis.

A transplant from Wisconsin, Clark secured a job as the junior varsity coach for the Holy Name High School basketball program. His mile-a-minute, high-energy approach to life immediately merged with the everyday energy of the school's varsity coach, Ricciardi. Discussions were plentiful; arguments were not, except when it came to Clark's infatuation with the philosophy of former University of North Carolina coach Dean Smith. J.P. wasn't a Dean disciple. Rick Pitino was his guy.

Clark fancied himself an intense coach, junior varsity level or not. It was his job to get the kids ready for J.P., and that included the apathy-free atmosphere that waited for them at the varsity level. What Tom didn't realize was that he was coming up short, maybe not in teaching the program's preferred man-to-man defense, but definitely in regard to the exultation that roamed the sidelines.

Before one midseason showdown Ricciardi asked Clark to decompress from his JV game quickly enough to assist the varsity staff. Tom had no choice but to forget the result of his game once the Holy Name's first team tipped off; J.P. made sure of that. There was stomping and fist pounding and cursing and just about everything else Clark hadn't previously seen from Ricciardi. And then came halftime.

The yelling continued, albeit at a much more intense and higher level than what was echoed in front of a friends and family filled gymnasium. "This is ridiculous!"

And with that Clark thought Ricciardi had put the exclamation mark on his midgame tirade. That was until J.P. paused, turned away from his players, and proceeded to put his fist through the propped-up chalkboard.

That was then, this was now, and there wasn't much of a difference.

Gone were the forty minutes of trying to control the action of five separate on-court entities. In their place were nine innings of much-less-controlled pitching, hitting, and running. But while the sports may have changed, the in-game wave of intensity hadn't gone anywhere.

As regular as the celebratory scene had been throughout the month of May, its emphasis was undoubtedly a bit more punctuated with the month's final victory. First, it was a win. Second, it came against American League East rival Boston. Third, it moved Toronto to within two games of the first-place New York Yankees just thirty days after trailing the league's richest team by eleven and a half games.

Then there was the record.

"We've got the record!" yelled Ricciardi in mid-handshake with McCleary. In the tidal wave of good fortune, J.P. had forgotten that the victory was the Blue Jays' twenty-first in the month of May. It was more wins than any Toronto team had accumulated in any month in any of the franchise's previous seasons.

Even though Ricciardi didn't need a second wind, the news of the record gave him just that. It also prompted the GM to do the kind of thing almost every baseball fan would certainly love to do, yet almost any other general manager might hesitate in executing.

Ricciardi broke free of the four-man celebration, glided down three steps, hung out the window with his arms spread wide and echoed the voice of every Red Sox fan.

"You're ruining our summah!" J.P. addressed the seats below.

To whatever Toronto fans were left in the stands, the exclamation wouldn't have made much sense. But to the group of Ricciardi's relatives who had made the nine-hour trip from Worcester, it was the beginning of a Red Sox fan's summertime ritual. In an odd twist of fate, the general manager of the Toronto Blue Jays had officially opened the door for Boston fans everywhere to use the phrase that traditionally became The Nation's mantra once the temperature rose above sixty degrees.

Later that night, Ricciardi met up with just a smattering of his never-ending list of relatives. Standing just feet from windows that overlooked SkyDome's field in the midst of the complex's hotel bar, J.P. laid it on his relatives again. "They're ruining our summah!"

Everyone laughed. They were having a great time, despite the fact that Ricciardi had mandated that they all had to pry off their Red Sox apparel and replace it with Blue Jays hats and T-shirts. But then, out of the crowd, came one serious-looking member of the party. He walked right up to J.P. and with an unmistakable matter-of-fact tone pointed to his host and responded, "No, you're ruining our summer!"

He was right. J.P. and his Blue Jays were ruining the early moments of his relatives' summer, and the Toronto general manager was loving every minute of it.

"Convinced myself, I seek not to convince."

—Edgar Allan Poe

As much as the Blue Jays wanted to remember (and the Red Sox wanted to forget) what turned into Toronto's weekend sweep, the organizational mind-set was going to have to be switched. The second day of June had sneaked up and with it came Major League Baseball's June amateur draft.

The origins of each teams' draft picks were set up well ahead of time, with Toronto still in its cozy twenty-foot-long room, and the Red Sox hunkered down in a, in Epstein's words, "nice fat suite," at the Copley Marriott Hotel in downtown Boston. Perhaps the only common bonds between the settings were the tension in the air and a speakerphone planted in the middle of the participants.

There was, of course, also the wall of names, hundreds of them, who made up the excitement of the present and hope for the future. The teams had an idea about which names were going to go to which teams thanks to weeks of scouting, gossiping, and analyzing. It wasn't an exact science, but it was a science nonetheless.

This year the draft figured to be slightly different than in the past thanks to the overriding trend of teams' preferring college players. A month before, a book chronicling Oakland's 2002 draft, *Moneyball*, had brought to light the philosophy to which Ricciardi had been a card-carrying subscriber from his days with the A's— high school kids presented more risk and cost more money in the long run. In this respect, both Toronto and Boston were ahead of the curve; it was just a matter of which teams were going to jump on board. Starting at 1:05 P.M., the mystery of the teams' approaches started to be unveiled.

After the draft's first few rounds it was clear that a trend had been set. In Boston, high schoolers were marked with red, and college guys were represented with blue. Epstein looked up and saw a sea of blue under each organization's roll-call of draft picks. With the exception of a few teams (Los Angeles, Atlanta) the priority had been set and it didn't include the unproven world of high schoolers.

Besides philosophy, another must when it came to approaching the day was the necessity of teams to be realistic about their lot in life. For instance, the Blue Jays would love to pull up the card reading, "Maholm, Paul" on it, but everyone in the cramped room knew full well that the Tom Glavine clone was going to be long gone by the time Toronto picked at No. 12. Their instincts were correct. He went to Pittsburgh at No. 8.

It was a realization that made little things, such as The Claude Rains Project, so important. If Hill hadn't been there, Sullivan was going to be the choice and, in the minds of Ricciardi and the rest of his staff, the dropoff between Maholm and Hill was like a jump off the couch compared to the Grand Canyon-esque chasm that resided after the shortstop.

After Blue Jays' scout Jon Lalonde leaned over and uttered the words, "Aaron Hill, shortstop, Louisana State University" into the squawk box for all of baseball to hear, the Red Sox had less than three minutes to decide the fate of their first pick, the seventeenth overall in the draft. The selection of Hill hadn't fazed the Sox because their top guy was still on the board, "David Murphy, outfielder, Baylor University." There had been some worries in Boston's nice fat suite that Murphy wouldn't make it past Cleveland at No. 11, but when the Indians went with Tulane outfielder Michael Aubrey, nerves were instantly soothed.

Murphy was a left-handed batting outfielder who stood at 6-foot-3 and weighed 195 pounds. His size didn't sway a methodical approach, which began with the bat being gently cradled by the loosest of grips, and ended with a fit of aggression toward whatever ball might come near the strike zone. As a junior in '03, he led the Big 12 Conference in batting (.420) and total bases (176), while maintaining the always-desirable high on-base percentage (.492). After getting the call from Boston scouting director David Chadd while eating dinner at the rib joint Damon's, Murphy had now accomplished something much more permanent than any statistic, a place among the nation's other thirty first-round picks.

For Boston, Murphy was a no-brainer. Its next pick wasn't so easy.

The Red Sox were picking at No. 32 thanks to the New York Mets' signing of free agent Cliff Floyd, an outfielder for whom Boston had traded right before the previous season's trade deadline. Awarding draft picks to teams having to say au revoir to departing free agents was a baseball front office's biggest ally, as Epstein and his cohorts were finding out. It was a trade-off: Forgetting the seduction of immediate dividends for a chance to build your farm system. It was a sacrifice Boston, a team with one of the thinnest group of minor league prospects in all of baseball, was glad to embrace.

Boston had two players in mind for pick No. 32: Georgia Tech outfielder Matt Murton and a pitcher from Long Beach State named Abe Alvarez. Its dilemma was designating which kid had a better chance at potentially slipping to the Sox's next selection at No. 49. The consensus was that, as much as they liked Alvarez, the

Red Sox had pretty much confirmed the identity of at least a few teams lying in wait for Murton. Alvarez was going to have to wait.

The mere notion that any team was basing a good chunk of its draft strategy around Alvarez was a sign of the times. In years past, there hadn't been much call for a one-eyed, tilted-cap, war-painted lefty who couldn't break double eights on a radar gun.

Yet, in the draft room of the Red Sox, image wasn't everything. In fact, it wasn't anything.

Alvarez, however, took the notion of performance over potential to the utmost of extremes. It was a philosophy the pitcher was dearly counting on a month before the draft when the Major League Baseball scouting service came calling. Even with the numbers befitting a first-round pick, the words uttered to the doctor testing everything about his slender 6-foot-2, 185-pound frame would raise a red flag for any organization.

"I just want to tell you ahead of time," said Alvarez. "I'm not going to be able to see out of my left eye."

He wasn't lying.

"Wow, you're blind!" the disbelieving doctor said.

It was difficult enough for scouts to overlook the ho-hum velocity, the face donned with war paint on non-pitching days, or the tinted hair that burst out from under his always-crooked Long Beach State baseball cap. Now they were being asked to recommend a soft-throwing Cyclops. Jim Woodward, for one, was ready to take that leap of faith.

Woodward had been one of Lucchino's San Diego Padres transplants, being assigned the Southern California area for the Red Sox. His history with Alvarez went back to watching the lefty throw a shutout for A.B. Miller High School in Fontana, California. It was an interest that continued thanks to a recommendation given by Woodward's cousin, a member of the St. Mary's College team who had played against the pitcher and believed he was the toughest hurler on St. Mary's schedule.

As the draft approached, Woodward didn't need to be sold anymore. He had played in the Mets' organization with the rotund, soft-throwing Sid Fernandez who couldn't even match

Alvarez's eighty-eight-mile-an-hour heat, yet went on to befuddle Major Leaguers for a good 15 years. Both pitchers had the unique talent of hiding the ball until the last possible moment before putting it exactly where the moment called for. Woodward knew the goods, and Abe was it.

The scouting report read: "Put the radar gun away and watch how he gets guys out." But how could the organization dismiss both the radar gun readings and the absence of sight in Alvarez's left eye? So, the day after the scouting service's once-over, Woodward became one of six scouts to inquire about the previously undisclosed disability.

As always, Alvarez supplied the explanation and it was quickly back to basking in the comfort of the lefty's stats.

Alvarez was born with an infection in his left eye, causing a growth that hindered his vision. Eyedrops that were prescribed to cure the infection couldn't dent the growth, forcing the son of Spanish-speaking parents to turn to a stronger form of medicine. The side effects of the new drops, however, permanently stunted his eyesight. Now everything viewed from the left side is just a blur.

Having to sway opinion wasn't anything new for Alvarez. Scouts wanted to know why his hair was so huge. Abe's explanation: Nobody had ever applied scissors to his head except for his hairdressing mom, Mercedes. Scouts wanted to know why his hat was always crooked. Abe's explanation: It just didn't fit right with the brim facing straight ahead, and it had felt that way since the days of T-ball.

It also didn't hurt that the pitcher was one of the most down-to-earth, genial players to be slotted within the draft's elite. Alvarez might have looked a little off, but his personality and performance were dead on.

Just for good measure, Woodward delved into his memory to justify his faith in Alvarez. There, among all the head-shaking hitters, was the recollection of a simple pop-up in Long Beach State's game against Cal State–Fullerton. It was a moment that wouldn't have dented the scout's mental checklist if not for the fact that

Alvarez's catcher had no idea where the ball was. Because of the backstop's disorientation, Abe was forced to race from his position on the mound and make the catch right in front of the backstop.

In Woodward's opinion, it was an unbelievable effort. Weeks later, it was an unbelievable effort made by a pitcher with one good eye. That was good enough for the Red Sox.

Boston took Alvarez, one spot in front of Toronto.

This race for the unconventional southpaw had been won by the Red Sox. The pursuit of the title of king of the hill in the American League East, however, was proceeding with unexpected proximity.

Nine days after the draft, Epstein finally walked the few steps home from his brotherly get-together. The apartment window was finally shut, and with it the end of one of the good days. Waiting for him in a few hours, however, was the next stage of the race. And much to the Blue Jays' delight, it was becoming a contest that was just way too close to call.

CHAPTER 7

The Good, the Bad,
and the Kielty

*"Success usually comes to those who are too busy
to be looking for it."*

—Henry David Thoreau

"Watch this change-up," said J.P. Ricciardi, not flinching an elbow or eyebrow.

Seventy-nine miles-per-hour. Strike three. Game over. How did he know?

The pitcher, a former Major League starter turned Double A closer named Juan Pena, hadn't tipped his hand. In fact, it appeared Ricciardi had called the pitch before the subject's head gave the obligatory nod of acceptance. But there were signs: the count, the position of Pena's glove, the pitcher's repertoire. Putting them all together was J.P.'s bag, a notion he was reinforcing in the run-down home of his Double A team.

It didn't matter whether the analysis came in Toronto or at

antiquated Yale Field in New Haven, watching a player's inner-baseball being was what made Ricciardi's professional clock tick. He loved getting inside the game. While everybody else was on the outside looking in, his thoughts were running neck and neck with the collection of fast-twitch muscles that executed the basics before him.

This time, Pena was painting the picture of a general managing prophet. Maybe it was luck, maybe good fortune or perhaps pure experience-laden skill. Whatever the source of Ricciardi's pitch prediction, it should have come as no surprise, even in the under-the-radar atmosphere of the minor leagues.

Entering the night of Pena's change-up-induced save, June 17, the Blue Jays were one and a half games behind the first-place Yankees and one game in back of Boston. In the realm of big-league baseball turnaround, this was a good one. Just weeks before, Toronto had been left (along with Baltimore and Tampa Bay) for the American League East vultures to pick on the rest of the way, but now the Jays were in an actual pennant race in the middle of a month that began with 'J.' The 2003 blueprint was being altered.

The comfort of success made Ricciardi feel a whole lot better about making his pilgrimage to Connecticut, that and the fact his attention didn't have to be split since the Blue Jays were getting rained out in Montreal. Answering the cell phone had also become much easier to digest, whether it be the bandwagon-jumping national media, other general managers who were seeing Toronto's trading strategy shift toward the "buyers" side of the ledger, or even the team doctors.

It was the latter of the three that gave Ricciardi some of the day's best news while standing on the same field once inhabited by such baseball-playing dignitaries as George Bush Sr., Babe Ruth, and Juan Acevedo, a stab-in-the-dark relief pitcher Toronto picked up that day. J.P. got the word that Eric Hinske, the reigning Rookie of the Year, might be back in the lineup within a week.

The second-year third baseman had been out throughout the Blue Jays' run of all first-half runs with a broken bone in his hand. It was an injury sustained in spring training, but not let on to until

May 23. By then his average settled in at .232 and the Blue Jays finally climbed above .500 for the first time all season. Lessons were learned, both by the aspiring Ironman Hinske, and a Toronto team that discovered it might be a bit better than even its players believed.

The injuries kept coming (shortly after Hinske's departure from the lineup, Shannon Stewart went down with a hamstring problem), but so did the wins. By the time Ricciardi found himself in New Haven, not only had the Blue Jays taken up residence in the AL East hierarchy, but had also uncovered a few assets they didn't even think they had. The nose-in-the-dirt trio of Mike Bordick, Howie Clark, and Dave Berg were holding the fort at third base, while rookie Reed Johnson expertly eased the pain of Stewart's absence.

In fact, not only was the stocky, right-handed hitting Johnson putting up Stewart-esque numbers, but his emergence also parted the clouds when it came to Ricciardi's trading strategy. Hurt or not, Stewart was a .300 hitter who could possibly bring the Toronto's most-needed elixir—another quality starting pitcher. It was all coming together.

New Haven came and went, and on the subsequent Saturday, June 21, Ricciardi was walking the streets of Montreal with the kind of smile only a baseball man could understand. He was officially the general manager of the American League East's second-place team.

"Happiness is nothing more than good health and a bad memory."

—Albert Schweitzer

SOME OF THE BLAME could be put on Brian Butterfield. Blame him for the success, the turnaround, the Blue Jays' ascension into the division's rarified air. Blame it all on Toronto's third base coach. For if it wasn't for the wide-eyed, intensely comical Maine native, the coaching staff that stayed the course long enough to see the wrongs get righted might not have yet formed the perfect storm that was the second-place Jays.

Or perhaps blame the Yankees. It was, after all, New York that executed a baseball rarity—firing its Triple A manager, Butterfield, after just one and a half months into the 2002 season—allowing for Ricciardi to form the kind of staff he envisioned. Sure, blame it on the team that was resting just one and a half games ahead of Toronto as the final days of June approached.

It was also the Yankees who originally brought the Toronto contingent together—a collection of fresh-faced, wide-eyed coaches in Ricciardi, Carlos Tosca, Mike Barnett, and Butterfield. Now they were all part of "The Plan." Ricciardi gave the directives, Tosca, the manager, executed "The Plan" from the dugout while Barnett guided the hitters, Butterfield tutored the infielders, pitching coach Gil Patterson fined-tuned the pitchers, and first base coach John Gibbons kept an eye on the outfielders and catchers.

They needed a plan, but more importantly, they needed someone to carry it out. These men were Ricciardi's messengers.

The group was anything but orthodox, if for nothing else because of a dramatic lack of experience actually playing between the lines of professional baseball. Tosca was one of six Major League managers never to have played professionally, and only Gibbons and Patterson made it past the minors (albeit for a combined twenty-eight games). But the Blue Jays weren't looking through the *Baseball Encyclopedia* when hiring these coaches. Teaching—that was the thing, and judging by their first year on the job, boy, could they teach.

It was a trait that was exemplified best by the presence of Butterfield, otherwise known as the first piece of Ricciardi's coaching puzzle.

It doesn't take long to get to know the man they call "Butter," he makes certain of that. And if you want to accelerate the process just mention the New England Patriots, the source of his sporting lifeblood outside baseball. In April he was simulating the three-point stances of potential Pats draft picks for the benefit of Hinske, a Green Bay fanatic. July brought the pregame sprints back and forth from dugout to clubhouse to check and see if New England took anyone in the National Football League's unexcitable equivalent of the Rule 5 selections, the Supplemental Draft. And then in August, Butterfield used the VCR in Fenway Park's visiting manager's office to tape what he was missing during his team's game against the Red Sox—the Patriots' exhibition game at Philadelphia.

Butter was a certifiable, football-loving, baseball-oozing ball of fire . . . and a hell of a nice guy.

Butterfield's passion for sports was first nurtured by his father, Jack, the Yankees' vice president of player development who died tragically in a car crash in '79—the same year Brian signed a professional contract to play in the New York organization. It was an enthusiasm that was so tough to picture diminished. But that was exactly what had happened upon leaving his managerial post with the Yankees.

Without baseball, Butterfield was like Superman on a bed of Kryptonite. For more than a week, he sat at his Standish, Maine, home trying to figure out where it all went wrong and where it might go right again. To make matters worse, his wife, Jan, had left him without a car. She was the Ladies Professional Golf Association's official skin, hair, and fashion consultant and was forced to attend one of the nineteen tournaments that were in need of her services. He was home alone, unfortunately without a car but with plenty of thoughts.

Butter improvised, remembering seeing a beat-up, red Nissan Sentra down the road with a "For Sale" sign painted on the front window. His inquiry to the owner elicited the asking price of $700 for the automobile. "Listen, I have $600 in my pocket right now," Butter said. It was a done deal.

The car served a purpose, not only to travel outside of his immediate neighborhood but to also take a trip from reality. It needed work, and so did Butter. That's why banging the dents out of the weathered chassis went a long way toward making him forget what had happened just days earlier.

Not too long from his Yankees exit, with the depression of the move still lingering, Butter started banging away at the Sentra. Then, one day after the car purchase, the phone rang. It was his old friend J.P. Ricciardi. The question was posed: Did Brian Butterfield want to be the Toronto Blue Jays' new third base coach? The emotions of an emotional guy took over, allowing for tears of joy to replace the hammering of the Nissan.

The timing was no coincidence. Ricciardi knew it wasn't going to work out with the manager he inherited, Buck Martinez, and that at some point during the season a change would most likely be made. He also realized that if he went too long without hiring Butterfield another member of the early '80s Yankee connection, Buck Showalter, was going to swoop in on Butter as soon as a managing position inevitably came Showalter's way. The time was right.

On June 3, 2001, Butterfield was with Toronto, along with the Blue Jays' new manager, Tosca, who had gotten the call from Ricciardi the day before while in his SkyDome hotel room. The Toronto transformation had been kick-started, thanks in part to the Nissan Sentra–pounding, New England Patriot–loving third base coach.

What experience Tosca lacked in playing in the majors, he more than made up for by managing in the minors. Something has to be said for calling the shots in 1,759 not-ready-for-prime-time games. The Cuba native was short (5-foot-8), stern, polite, patient, loved the three-run homers, and hated to steal and bunt. He was an Earl Weaver disciple and J.P. Ricciardi's first managerial hire.

Ever since the day Tosca walked from one side to SkyDome to meet with Ricciardi behind the general manager's glass-walled office, the plan had been put in place. Judging by the returns nearly three months into the '03 season, it was a design that appeared to be working fairly well. They were in second place! Second place! And directly behind a team that was shelling out $100 million more than the Blue Jays' ledger dictated, nonetheless. Not bad.

The offensive portion of the plan wasn't tough to decipher—see as many pitches as possible, bunt and steal only as a last resort, and let the runs start piling up. And they were. Only the Red Sox, a team that was executing the same sort of philosophy, was scoring at a more frenetic pace. In the month of June, the two teams dominated the league's offensive stat sheet. Home runs—both led the AL with forty-two. RBI—1. Boston 185, 2. Toronto 156. Runs—1. Boston 190, Toronto 159. Total bases—1. Boston 542, 2. Toronto 474.

The plan had its critics. How can you dismiss the basic fundamental art of stealing a base, or bunting a guy over? What in the name of all that's pure in baseball is going on? In Toronto's case, two June sacrifice bunts, two June stolen bases and a shitload of runs . . . that is what was going on. Ricciardi, Tosca, Barnett, and the rest weren't making any apologies. When you're an unexpected guest in the middle of a pennant race, explanations are best served in the morning box scores.

Pitching philosophies weren't so easily executed. You need a No. 1 starter, which Roy Halladay fit the description of quite nicely. A No. 2, the role originally pegged for free agent acquisition Cory Lidle, but now sliding in the grasp of former bullpen closer Kelvim Escobar. And then, hope for the divine intervention of two more effective arms. Normally, the quota would be for an additional three more starters after the first two, but in the World of Weaver (a place now inhabited by the Blue Jays) the former Baltimore Orioles' skipper's credos were becoming the norm.

The Blue Jays were going by the book—not that of baseball, but that of Earl. There it was, right on the coffee table in Ricciardi's office (next to Rudy Guiliani's *Leadership*), the 1984 publication, *Weaver on Strategy*. And in it were the ten laws for which Toronto were slowly starting to obey by:

> *1. No one's going to give a damn in July if you lost a game in March (Toronto 0–1, tied for second in March; an entirely more optimistic second place in June).*
> *2. If you don't make any promises to your players, you won't*

have to break them ("We know we aren't going to win the World Series this year."—J.P. Ricciardi).

3. The easiest way around the bases is with one swing of the bat (forty-two home runs in June).

4. Your most precious possessions on offense are your twenty-seven outs (first sacrifice bunt: May 26).

5. If you play for one run, that's all you'll get (ditto).

6. Don't play for one run unless you know that run will win a ball game (ditto, again).

7. It's easier to find four good starters than five (Halladay, Escobar, Lidle, Mark Hendrickson).

8. The best place for a rookie is long relief (the Blue Jays' best reliever—rookie set-up man Aquilino Lopez).

9. The key step for an infielder is the first one—left or right—but before the ball is hit (Butter wasn't on SkyDome's field with the infielders five hours before game-time for nothing).

10. The job of arguing with the umpire belongs to the manager, because it won't hurt the team if he gets thrown out of the game (fortunately, what is said in the general manager's box during games can't be held against the dugout).

It was just that Law No. 7 hadn't really been accepted on a league-wide basis since the early '70s. The common belief was that the extra work might wear out the arms of these pitchers who hadn't been trained for the rigors of pitching every fourth day instead of every fifth. But fitting in wasn't a Ricciardi priority, as was evidenced by the Blue Jays' announcement in early June that they were going to give the four-man rotation a whirl.

The thinking was logical: Toronto's starting pitching depth was as thin as its payroll, so why try and find something (a fifth starter) that isn't necessarily available? Besides, the more Halladay, a pitcher that hit June with the momentum of the league's best pitcher, the better it would be for every member of the Blue Jays' organization.

But by the time Ricciardi strolled down Montreal's Pierre De-Coubertin Avenue, the GM of the baseball's hottest team, Toronto had been forced to break Law No. 7. Unexpected ailments and nervous participants left the Blue Jays chasing the Yankees with the five-starter hand they were dealt.

Little did J.P. realize, but in just a matter of two weeks the Blue Jays would be begging for tribulations such as dissecting the merits of a No. 5 starter. As fast as the comfort of success flew into Toronto, it was going to exit just as suddenly.

"We're still open for business."

—Paul Godfrey

WHEN THE MORNING OF June 28 arrived, Ricciardi's existence in the '03 baseball season had, if nothing else, gotten him in better shape. (It's amazing how therapeutic the Blue Jays' weight room can be.) And the loop-de-loop battle with winning and losing was just a portion of the drive behind the miles of mind management.

Before the winning started, the measuring stick for the Blue Jays' woes emanated from the headquarters of a most unbaseball-like grouping—the World Health Organization. A disease called SARS (Severe Acute Respiratory Syndrome) picked Toronto as its North American ground zero. The disease was a potentially deadly (and very contagious) viral respiratory illness, which originated in Asia two months before the season opener.

Not only was starting pitching damaging the Blue Jays in the season's early months, but so was worldwide perception. Toronto was the last place Major League fans wanted to visit, a thought also shared by some Major League players. Ricciardi started getting the calls—Kansas City general manager Allard Baird wanted to know what his team could expect. Old friend, and Texas manager, Buck Showalter also rang J.P. for some peace of mind.

Teams were briefed before trips to SkyDome: Stay away from crowds, wash your hands, and don't be too concerned. By the end of May, thirty people in Toronto had died from SARS and WHO had issued a travel warning to anyone approaching the city of more than two and a half million people. To folks like Ricciardi's friends and family in Worcester, J.P. was working in the middle of a leper colony—hospitals full of the nearly dead and sea of surgical masks wherever you turned. This was the image.

Unfortunately for the Blue Jays, even reality wasn't enough to sell tickets. More than $3 million in lost ticket revenue was the organization's reality.

Toronto CEO Ted Rogers, Godfrey, and the rest of the cash-counting crew did everything to paint the picture it was viewing, one that didn't include streets full of covered mouths and petrified citizens. At Rogers' suggestion, there was a game in which tickets cost just $1, then another with a $2 admission. They were both big sellers and proved effective. Yet when a newspaper's lead sports photo the day after the first sellout included (by all accounts) the only member of the crowd who was wearing a surgical mask, the Blue Jays' battle for normalcy was dealt another blow.

The Blue Jays were baffled. If anybody should have been scared, it was the Godfrey family, whose relative actually con-tracted SARS (although while traveling from Asia to his home in Los Angeles, not anywhere near Toronto). But the Jays' president knew the disease had been contained to the hospitals, not near SkyDome, and the acts of walking, talking, breathing, and what-ever else healthy, ticket-buying human beings do weren't going to be compromised.

Tim McCleary, for another, couldn't figure it out. He would arrive at the park as early as 8 A.M. and national television shows such as *Good Morning America* would already be broadcasting from outside the visitors' dugout. What did they expect to see? A gaggle of SARS victims spewed across the infield? Sure, the box of hand-wipes in the general manager's box might have been used more than usual, and some players (such as Lidle) had sent their families home. But that was it, a fact teams soon learned upon not seeing a city decimated by disease.

By the end of June, those same clubs' worries had less to do with the pink piece of medical information handed out at the airport, and more to do with the white, statistic-filled sheet warning baseball-playing visitors of the suddenly potent Blue Jays.

Ricciardi's first primary external dilemma of the season would fade just in time for nuisance No. 2—as Ricciardi explained, "Just a bad day."

The words had been echoed over and over again by the Toronto Blue Jays general manager throughout a damp and dismal Thursday. Describing the hours of July 10 might have been initially elicited by the increasingly common nine innings of agony, but that was truly only the tip of Ricciardi's Titanic-esque iceberg.

It wasn't as if Ricciardi's anxiety quota hadn't been filled with six days left until the All-Star Game. Two losses in two days to the team (the Red Sox) that rested between Toronto and any kind of late-summer hope took care of that. But this was a different kind of bad day. This was the kind of day that made Ricciardi yearn for the 300-mile, cell phone-free scouting trips and nothing next to his name resembling a "G" or an "M."

The unmerciful onslaught of uneasiness had fittingly begun at the stroke of midnight. The Blue Jays' magical hope-carrying carriage was quickly morphing into a pumpkin thanks to a SkyDome collapse of at least demoralizing proportions just hours before. Through seven innings: Blue Jays 7, Boston 3. After nine innings: Boston 8, Blue Jays 7.

The game ended well before 11 P.M., but Ricciardi remained entrenched in the office of Toronto manager Carlos Tosca into the next day. General managers often try to analyze every game immediately following it, but when that game involves a blown four-run lead and puts you eight games out of first place the get-together can get a bit more involved than usual.

At the heart of the postgame discussion was Tosca's use of a pitcher named Tanyon Sturtze.

Sturtze was a thirty-two-year-old right-handed pitcher who, if nothing else, looked the part of a Major League Baseball player—6-foot-5, 221 pounds. The problem was that for much of his career he hadn't pitched like one. Before coming to Toronto, he had lost thirty-three of his fifty-five decisions, totaled a hard-to-figure 5.07 ERA and was arriving fresh off a hard-to-find eighteen-loss campaign with the Tampa Bay Devil Rays.

Still, here was Sturtze, making $1 million on a one-year contract while pitching for a team that had given him the third spot in its opening-day pitching rotation. Not coincidentally, that same team just happened to be run by Sturtze's radar gun–toting guardian angel, J.P. Ricciardi.

Sturtze, a strapping right-hander, first dipped into Ricciardi's memory as a shortstop for Quinsigamond Community College, a school that resided just down the road from both men's alma mater, St. Peter's–Marian High School. Remembering Sturtze wasn't difficult for the then-Oakland scout. He had all the elements of a "file-him-away" kind of player: Weird first name, similar upbringing and, above all, a rocket right arm.

So when J.P. finally saw Sturtze throw off a mound for his summer league team (one of the few clubs he had actually toed the pitching rubber for) Ricciardi's instincts started to tingle. The scout had no idea the player was perfectly content working for his friend's father's Budweiser distributorship, and he definitely couldn't have known that Sturtze's repertoire consisted of one pitch—a fastball. All of that, however, didn't matter.

Baseballs, not beer kegs, were the only thing that arm should have even come close to tossing around. Thus, the sprint across Worcester's Shrewsbury Street was made.

La Scala Restaurant would be the source of Ricciardi's report on this pitcher with only one pitch. Oakland needed to put a card with Sturtze's name on file, and the pay phone hanging on the Italian eatery's wall was going to expedite the process. There wasn't much time, since the June amateur draft was just days away, so instead of a handwritten report came the verbal description: Tall, good arm, good athlete. But the final sentence was what sealed the deal in the minds of the A's: I want him. That was good enough for Oakland.

The night of the draft, Sturtze got out of his cousin's car and was immediately greeted by his mother at the family's front door. "You got drafted by the Oakland A's in the twenty-third round," the excited mother said to the disbelieving son. The fastball-throwing shortstop was going to get a check for $5,000 to head to Arizona and make even more money by trying to become a pitcher.

Sturtze's first breaking ball as a professional ended up nestled next to the backstop. So did more than a few of the subsequent efforts. But he must have done something right by the time the 2003 season rolled around because he was back with his radar gun–toting guardian angel making $1 million a year.

Ricciardi took great pride in Sturtze, but affection doesn't increase the payroll. So when the pitcher was signed leading up to the '03 campaign, it was because he had served as the Tampa Bay Devil Rays' MVP two seasons before, and Toronto needed a No. 3 starter behind Roy Halladay and Cory Lidle. The reminiscing about Grafton Hill and the rest of Worcester would have to come free of charge.

But, as is the case with any relationship, there are going to be those valleys to complement the peaks, a fact Sturtze, and Tosca, were finding out in the eighth inning of the Blue Jays' July 8 game, the latest must-win meeting with the Red Sox.

There were some misinformed types who believed Ricciardi's pipeline to Tosca extended during the games, that it was truly J.P. who was managing the team. While the phone in the GM's box did ring, it was reserved for moments like the previous night when J.P. was informed that relief pitcher Juan Acevedo had injured his hand punching the ceiling in a fit of frustration. Once the game started the manager was managing, and the general manager was general managing.

Now, as the eighth inning unfolded, the game plan was getting a perfect example of why baseball will always be an imperfect world.

"Tanyon Sturtze, now warming up in the Blue Jays' bullpen."

Mike Shaw of the Jays' media relations staff didn't even get the last syllable out before the GM's box was filled with the voice of Ricciardi. "Why is Tanyon Sturtze warming up in the Blue Jays' bullpen?" If there was a pipeline to the dugout, it would have been used. But there wasn't, and Sturtze was coming into the game to face Boston's Manny Ramirez, a player who had hit six home runs in thirty-four at-bats against the pride of Quinsigamond CC. A fastball right down the middle later and it was seven in thirty-five.

Ricciardi barely closed his eyes after arriving at home from the game epitomizing Major League Baseball agony. Remembering the loss and how it transpired was enough to alter the GM's sleep patterns, but what really cut into J.P.'s slumber-induced escape was looking to a future that awaited just a few hours away. The unpleasant task of jettisoning Major Leaguers was beginning at the crack of 8 A.M.

The day before McCleary carried a stack of transaction forms, the ones used by Major League teams when executing virtually any kind of personnel maneuver. Check here for waivers. Check there for trades. They weren't unlike any form of survey being passed about by door-to-door policy-stumpers. Except the ones held by the assistant general manager of the Blue Jays were dramatically altering the life of at least one person—pitcher Doug Davis, whose form was accompanied by a letter stating he was being sent back to waiver-wire purgatory. It was the second time the pitcher had been assigned elsewhere in the '03 season.

There were others in McCleary's pile bearing the good news of Major League promotions. Toronto's 2002 Rule 5 find, Corey Thurman, was heading back up from Syracuse, as was fellow pitcher Dan Reichert, a player who exemplified the Jays' approach in finding staff-filling arms. Nearly four months before, McCleary was hanging in the hallway outside Tosca's spring training office when Ricciardi came running out. "That was Moorad, he wants us to take a look at Reichert."

Reichert's name wasn't unfamiliar to most in baseball (memories of players with the cache stemming from being picked with the seventh selection in the 1997 draft don't vanquish easily). Neither, of course, was Jeff Moorad's, the agent to seemingly every other player in the majors. The twenty-six-year-old pitcher had been let go by Tampa Bay earlier in the spring when the Devil Rays weren't seeing Reichert's once hammer of a slider make an appearance in St. Petersburg. Now his representative was trying to find him a new home.

"He wants $400,000," continued Ricciardi. "I told him we would get back to him."

This is where McCleary came in. He was the guy who had cracked the code when it came to contracts thanks in part to his most unusual responsibility while with the Yankees: It had been his job in 1987 to transfer all of New York's record keeping from index cards to computers. Even the most mundane rules were becoming understood and a reputation was being built. When another team was confused concerning the intricacies of baseball's legalese, it was the former sports management major from St. John's University they would call.

Now, in the hallway with the horseplay of the Jays' clubhouse just feet away, McCleary was ready to inform Ricciardi of all the merits and potholes of agreeing to Moorad's terms. In a nutshell the message was: Reichert was getting $150,000 in termination so, in actuality, getting the former first-rounder into Jays camp was only going to cost Toronto $250,000.

The exchange between Ricciardi and McCleary was quick, maybe two minutes, but within it were numbers, clauses, and payroll. You just got the feeling the pair had performed this act on stages beyond that of the doorstep to Tosca's office. "OK," J.P. concluded. "I'm going to bring him in."

But it didn't stop there. Moorad went on to tell J.P. about how he was going to spend a night on an aircraft carrier, an experience to be brought on by some local political ties. As it turns out, there are actual people behind the sports agencies' gigantic curtain of coldheartedness. And, in this case, waiting there was a nap on the U.S.S. Surreal.

Reichert was brought in the next day, at 9 A.M., to throw in front of Ricciardi and one of the Jays' chief judges of talent, Bill Livesey. The consensus was the pitcher was a chance worth taking. Low risk, high reward—this was the credo of any architect building a pitching staff on a $53 million payroll. And one of the building blocks was being jammed into place, albeit four months after the original construction began.

But with every new piece of the structure that is inserted, one has to be extracted. In the case of Reichert's promotion, relief pitcher Jeff Tam was the unlucky one to be jettisoned. Tam had shown too many flashes similar to his nightmare of an outing in Boston back in April, and not enough of the pitcher Ricciardi remembered from the days in Oakland. His name hadn't been among those filling McCleary's stack of transaction sheets, but, after another ineffective showing in the Blue Jays' second straight loss to Boston, the line had been drawn.

Letting go is never easy, especially when it's the kind of clubhouse asset the reliever had proven to be. Just days before, a day after Toronto's most monumental loss of the season (every team has at least ten of these "most monumental losses" each season), Tam emerged from the locker room and confronted Tosca. "Here I am," he said, presenting himself to the manager, "your white knight." The picture was priceless for the simple reason that Tam was wearing nothing but a body full of shaving cream. Every team needed a Jeff Tam, but every team also needed someone to consistently get outs in the tail end of a ball game.

Telling the players was tough. Reactions and relationships aren't exactly broached in General Managing 101. Those tasks, however, wouldn't stake claim to the day's pinnacle of persevering. J.P. was about to get news from his sister, Mary, that was much worse than any loss could deliver—his dad had been diagnosed with prostate cancer.

John Ricciardi wasn't unlike his son, preferring to play the game rather than living and dying with the exploits of another. It was natural for a kid from Worcester growing up in the 1940s to at least recognize the presence of Boston's Ted Williams and his teammates. It was just that participating was the preference, not watching.

But if John was going to sit down and actually view somebody else play baseball it was usually going to be the other Boston team, the National League Braves. They ran, and Ricciardi liked to run.

Williams could hit home runs, but he couldn't match the take-the-extra-base style of Braves' outfielders Tommy Holmes, Butch Nieman, and Carden Gillenwater. That's why when it came to taking in a game other than his own, Ricciardi always gave Nickerson Field the nod over the Red Sox's Fenway Park.

Finally, in 1945, a fifteen-year-old Ricciardi succumbed to his more mischievous nature, not so much the love of the hometown team, making it to The Fens for the very first time. The game was against the St. Louis Browns, the team who boasted one-armed left-fielder Pete Gray, and John was skipping school to see what all the hubbub was about. The Red Sox had at least done one thing right, breaking up the monotony that were springtime math classes.

Three years later, John didn't need to ditch school to see the Red Sox because, all of a sudden, he was one of them (albeit of the minor-league variety in nearby Lynn). Fraser Field was just a forty-five-minute drive from Worcester, but it seemed like a world away. Yet it wasn't long before the transition from hometown boy to minor league grinder seemed a whole lot homier. John Ricciardi was getting the call, from Uncle Sam, not Fenway Park. He had been drafted.

John never played professional baseball again thanks to an injury sustained while in the military. The Army had taken away a piece of his ballplaying ability, not because of combat but rather due to an ill-fated, on-base football game. Saluting and throwing a baseball would never be the same again (the former he didn't care for much anyway).

When he returned home, Ricciardi turned to the less demanding game of softball thanks to the semipro Worcester Hawks, and the more-satisfying world of his family. He had grown up with nine brothers and sisters, the same number of siblings boasted by his wife, so when the couple was setting up the lineup for their own family it was decided that three would be enough. John Paul was the oldest, followed by Mary, and then Steven.

John taught his oldest son well, drilling in the mind-set that he should never argue with his coach and try your best on every play.

He knew J.P. loved the game, that was clear from the time the five-year-old rattled off the entire 1965 Red Sox roster to some of the elder Ricciardi's quite amused coworkers.

John never stood in the way of J.P.'s infatuation for the game, letting him stay behind in Worcester with relatives while the rest of the family took its annual midsummer trip to Rhode Island. It was also a two-way street, with the father's joy of watching a son excel as a minor league player and, eventually, the front office of a Major League team going a long way in making up for whatever family misadventures the game had dealt the Ricciardis along the way.

Having John around the games was fun for everyone. It was one of the reasons why the news of the cancer was so tough to fathom. Another being the ordeal that J.P. still remembered from four years before when his mother, Helen, passed away after a seven-year battle with breast cancer.

J.P. had presented the eulogy for his mother, delivering a poetic presentation for the strongest-willed woman he knew. Within the tough-to-swallow speech, the son relayed the memory of how, in those times he did make it to the beach house in Rhode Island, that Helen would always play catcher in the family's Wiffle Ball games. It didn't matter how hard you threw it, she was always going to make the play. She always had home covered, in the playing fields of baseball and life. It was a speech J.P. didn't want to make again.

The only comfort emanating from Mary's phone call was that it appeared as though John's cancer could be treated. Just the same, the uneasiness of July wasn't going anywhere. A few days later, J.P. was trying to come to grips with his baseball team's mortality while serving in the wedding party of Tom Clark, the junior varsity basketball-coaching Oakland scout. From there Ricciardi would wait out the All-Star Break with his family on Cape Cod.

Good news was a much-needed commodity. Thanks to a freckled-face outfielder, it would eventually come Ricciardi's way.

"So, you're the one!"

—Brian Butterfield

BOBBY KIELTY was The One. For the Blue Jays' third base coach, baseball's version of a beefed-up Richie Cunningham had been pegged as the subject of the day thanks to an unaccredited spring training performance. For months Butterfield had been left answerless concerning his most unusual question: Who could possibly let out a burp of gargantuan proportions, so loud and so long that even from the third-base coaching box thirty feet away it had arrived as a most unexpected attention-getter?

Kielty, as Butterfield was now privy to, belched on demand. He was The One. For J.P. Ricciardi, however, the label stuck for an entirely more socially acceptable, easily-explained-to-the-masses reason. Kielty was The One, all right. And as of July 16 The One was property of the Toronto Blue Jays thanks to a trade with the Minnesota Twins.

Ricciardi had been trying to pry Kielty, a twenty-six-year-old with a face that advertised lemonade stands and sandlot baseball games, but a body that screamed "Gold's Gym," from Minnesota for more than one and a half years. As far as the Toronto front office was concerned, this was a guy who was clearly calling the wrong dome his home. Forget Metro, bring on Sky.

Kielty didn't know it, but he had been predestined to play for the 2003 Blue Jays. Why else would his father, Roger, bring the boyhood lessons of watching Ted Williams in Boston clear across the country to Moreno Valley, California, for Bobby to digest from age three and on? Wait for the good pitch, not the most convenient one. That was the Williams way, that was the Kielty way, and, as Bobby had discovered, that was the Blue Jays' way.

The lesson of taking pitches had been nurtured by Roger Kielty by using a handmade cube to define good pitches from bad. Ricciardi didn't need props, he had all too much evidence regarding the merits of a good batting eye. "That's six pitches," he said after watching the first round of Tampa Bay Devil Rays batters in a mid-March spring training game in Dunedin. "That's eleven pitches," he reminded himself after Tampa's first six outs. "That's fifteen pitches after three innings, unbelievable."

Needless to say, Bobby Kielty was not playing for the Devil Rays that March day.

But while Kielty played more like a Blue Jay and less like a member of the swing-at-the-first-pitch Twins, Minnesota knew it had something in the outfielder. This was a player who had been on the fast track to the Rookie of the Year in 2002 while fending off the lineup-card shuffling of Minnesota manager Ron Gardenhire. And even after a 9-for-60, August through September collapse, and the presence of fellow twenty-something outfielders Dustan Mohr, Michael Cuddyer, Torii Hunter, and Jacque Jones, Kielty had his place in the heart of Twins' GM Terry Ryan.

In 1998, a time when Minnesota wasn't winning much of anything, the Twins had defeated the Dodgers, Padres, and Diamondbacks in successfully wooing Kielty after he had gone undrafted in that year's amateur draft. Kielty chose the Twins, and up until Minnesota had hit the All-Star break seven games behind the surprising Kansas City Royals in the American League Central Division, the Twins were still hooked on Kielty.

Most of the infatuation stemmed from Kielty's unmistakable baseball ability, yet no one could blame Minnesota for a hesitancy to let go of one of the franchise's best diamond-in-the-rough finds. After all, this was a kid who had been labeled as a water polo–playing pitcher by his first college, a broken-back unknown at his second school, and nothing more than a fill-in for the prestigious Cape Cod Summer League. And now he was an untouchable who was finally going to be touched by one of the big league's biggest in-season trades.

Kielty was one of the reasons the formula for finding baseball players has never been bottled. Make no doubt about it, if anyone could have figured out the equation it was Bobby, the switch hitting analytical genius. The talent of deciphering could have come from his dad, the Canyon Spring High School math teacher, or his uncle John, an MIT graduate. But, wherever the source, Bobby could figure things out, and when he can't it's the equivalent of popping up a first pitch.

It still drives Kielty mad that he missed a perfect score on the math section of his SATs by one question. Maybe that's why the inability of the scouts to decipher Bobby's ability sooner leaves a maddening impression. Couldn't they see? The answer was there all along.

Kielty's work with his dad as a baseball youth only enhanced his love for hitting. He adored hitting. Unfortunately, USC was more enamored with Kielty's arm. The Trojans adored his pitching. It was a relationship that just wasn't going to work, so he turned to someone who wanted him in the batter's box, not the pitcher's mound—Riverside City College head coach Dennis Rogers.

It was a good thing Rogers and Riverside entered the Kielty story. If it wasn't for the junior college coach the outfielder not only wouldn't be an outfielder, but he also would never have ended up at the University of Mississippi (the coach had connections). And it was at Ole Miss that Bobby's stock began to rise . . . until a fall of gigantic proportions.

Mississippi was a long way from Moreno Valley, California, but not far enough to keep Kielty from coming home during winter break—otherwise known to players like Bobby and the world's greatest snowboarding waiver claim, Brandon Lyon, as the most dangerous time of the year.

It was during this period that Kielty decided to get away from the world of baseball preparation, head to Mountain High Ski Resort and hit the slopes. The fun started, the fun continued and then, with one trip down the snowboarding area while wearing skis, the fun ended . . . for a long, long time. Bobby had gone straight up fifteen feet in the air off a snow-covered half-pipe and come down on his back, a back that was damaged badly enough that his training had become lying in bed for the next six weeks.

Physically, Kielty would return, playing again for the Rebels, although not well enough to get selected in the '98 draft. The mental recovery proved to be a bit more difficult. The tumble never left his mind, especially at night when dreams of the accident continued to serve as an unwelcome reminder to Bobby's biggest setback. If that damn run down the mountain was never made maybe pro ball would be a reality instead of another of a growing list of bad dreams. It was the thought that festered within Kielty, until he finally got a break worth remembering.

Kielty's eligibility was running out at Ole Miss, and so were his hopes of playing professionally. In his mind, it would have been great if he didn't have to head home to California for the summer of '98, but the gateway to pro teams' hearts, the Cape Cod League, wasn't exactly opening its arms for Bobby. That was until another Ole Miss player pulled his name from the Brewster Whitecaps' roster, paving the way for his broken-backed teammate.

Perhaps part of the reason for Kielty's success with the Bobcats was desperation, but another factor just may have been familiarity. Also playing for Brewster was an outfielder named Reed Johnson, the same kid from Fontana who Bobby grew up playing with and against.

It was a great summer. Bobby played well, really well. He led the Cape League in hitting, and earned Most Valuable Player honors. And just to top everything off, Johnson had the equivalent of gold—a car. The four-door red Saturn got the suddenly inseparable friends to their baseball-free destinations, while Kielty's bat suddenly was helping him arrive at a much more out-of-the-way place: the Major Leagues.

Like everybody else who stepped foot on the fields of the Cape in '98, Ricciardi noticed Kielty. And as J.P. nestled into his position in Toronto, that freckled-faced player who took pitch after pitch was becoming a priority. Every time a conversation started with Minnesota and its general manager, Ryan (a former coach of Ricciardi's in the Mets system), the talk always came around to Kielty. Unfortunately for the Jays, the answer was always "no, but thanks for asking . . . again."

But with Minnesota trying to hang on to its contending existence while in a late-June free-fall (eventually losing twenty-two of twenty-eight entering All-Star Weekend), Ryan expressed interest in Stewart. "OK," Ricciardi thought, "it's time to get some pitching." Two hurlers (one in the bigs, one in the minors) were asked for by Toronto. "No and no," was Ryan's answer.

Then, on the Monday after the All-Star Game, along came a shocker. "Do you still have an interest in Kielty?" J.P. was asked by Ryan. Both men knew the answer.

There was no denying Stewart was a good player; the Blue Jays wouldn't have chosen to offer him arbitration instead of fellow outfielder Jose Cruz if he wasn't. But his contract was up after the season, while it was four more years before Kielty could become an outright free agent. Basically, Toronto felt like it was getting a much, much, much more inexpensive clone of its departing .300-hitting left fielder. Potentially equal production plus less money always equaled a much more tolerable $53 million payroll existence.

The next morning after receiving the initial Twins call on Kielty, Ricciardi was enjoying his busman's holiday on the Cape with his family, when his cell phone rang again. It was Ryan.

J.P.'s attention had been on serving up one of his famous "Slippy-doo-slip-slip-eroo" Wiffle Ball pitches to Mariano and Dante, but now the next pitch in the repertoire, the "Susquehanna Side-Winder" would have to wait. The first trade of the deal-happy month of July was about to be consummated.

It was a long road, but the twenty-six-year-old Kielty finally had found his logical, pitch-taking home.

The calls were made, first by Ryan to Kielty, and then by Kielty to his father. Roger had heard the rumors, but he still hesitated in believing his son's message. Pranking his dad was Bobby's specialty, like when an April Fool's Day message coaxed Roger into believing he was about to become a grandfather. "You were traded?" the elder Kielty said, laughing in between each word. But then he heard his son's wife, Meredith, in the background, assuring that this was very real. The 9 A.M. message was no joke.

The next call went to his buddy from the Cape, Johnson, who, as fate would have it, had turned up as an everyday outfielder in Toronto. Johnson saw Kielty's number pop up on his cell phone and thought it curious, not because Bobby was calling, but because they had just talked the day before. Usually the pair only talked once every couple of weeks. "This was strange," Johnson thought. Getting traded always is.

And as the season's second half got under way, and Kielty merged into the Blue Jays' locker room, he continued to soothe the nerves of Toronto's brass. In his first three games with the Jays, playing against his father's hometown team, the Red Sox, Bobby got on base eight times. It was the fourth day at Fenway, however, that ingrained Stewart's replacement in the minds of Blue Jays for life.

On the sunniest of summer Sunday days, Toronto was on its way to a seemingly inevitable loss thanks to the pitching mismatch of Boston's Pedro Martinez against newly acquired (and soon-released) John Wasdin. The final score was 9–4 in favor of the Red Sox, but it was a third-inning defensive masterpiece turned in by Kielty that distinguished the day.

Boston's Trot Nixon's fly ball seemed destined for the Red Sox's right-field bullpen. At Fenway you just usually know if it's going to be a home run or not, and everyone knew this was going to be a home run . . . everyone but Toronto's right fielder, Bobby Kielty. Without breaking stride, Kielty leaped from the middle of the dirt warning track, laid out his body over the five-foot wall (slamming his side into the rock-hard, green padding) and let the ball find his outstretched glove.

The force, alone, would have deterred most fielders. It was ironically reminiscent of his father's experience thirty years before, and less than two miles down the road at Boston University's Nickerson Field. Roger Kielty was presented with the unenviable task of tackling legendary Syracuse running back Ernie Davis on the first-year cornerback's very first collegiate play. Roger was run right over. His son, on the other hand, didn't flinch as he teetered on the wall, trying not to fall into home run territory. The fans didn't know it until the umpires executed the "out" signal, but Kielty made the grab.

Kielty's continuous ski slope–induced dreams of landing on his head continued, but they were nothing compared to the fears of not making a good first impression. Toronto may have left Boston still carrying a nine-game deficit in the wild card standings, but the Blue Jays at least had their catch—a freckled-face, broken-back outfielder named Bobby Kielty.

CHAPTER 8

The Crustacean Creation

*"Our search will be in vain, to find a fairer spot on
earth than Maine! Maine! Maine!"*

—Last three lines of Maine state song

The final refrain in the song describing New England's largest
state wasn't exactly ringing true for three men barreling down the
Maine Turnpike on the night of June 29. The two-lane highway
that ushers visitors in and out of New Hampshire's border ended
with a sign that read: "Leaving Maine, Vacationland." For Theo
Epstein, Bill Lajoie, and Jed Hoyer, it had been anything but.

They didn't even know it yet, but the thrills and spills of Major
League Baseball's trade deadline had taken their place among the
agony of a late June loss and a drive through the darkness and pine
trees of Maine.

It took Hoyer's car approximately an hour to reach the Pisca-
taqua Bridge, where Maine met The Granite State. It was also
about the amount of time it took the man in the passenger seat,
Epstein, to join any kind of conversation with his fellow Boston

Red Sox executives. There were thoughts to be dealt with, and because of it the trip from Hadlock Field in Portland, the home of Boston's Double A affiliate, to Fenway Park might never have seemed longer.

A two-hour ride had turned into a Twilight Zone path to nowhere, all thanks to a Mike Lowell three-run home run. In a season overflowing with irony, this was just the latest mind-blower.

The night before, Boston put such a whooping on the Marlins, scoring twenty-five runs to Florida's eight, that the record books and the teams' interleague apathy had both been revamped. Never before had a team scored ten runs before making an out, as the Red Sox accomplished against Florida pitchers Carl Pavano, Michael Tejera, and Allen Levrault in what was a fifty-minute first inning. The Sox also finished with a team-record twenty-eight hits, leaving the Florida locker room in a state of depression, and its seventy-three-year-old manager Jack McKeon espousing a whirl-wind of venom.

"I didn't realize your pitching was that bad over here at Boston that you would try to add on a sixteen-run lead in the seventh inning," was among the barbs directed at the team McKeon perceived as playing the role of a bully. The clubs might have been virtual strangers throughout their histories, but in 2003, thanks to the Red Sox's acquisition of the Marlins' most notable undrafted, Beaumont wall-banger, Kevin Millar, and now a humiliating whitewashing, familiarity had bred contempt.

Being away from a home game isn't easy for any general manager, but in this case, Epstein and Co. trip to Maine appeared to have more potential for prospect-swapping problem-solving than watching what had become the majors' premier offensive machine take on the Marlins. The Red Sox were comfortably carrying a 46–32 record, were still riding the high of the previous night's blowout, and were getting a right-handed hitting reinforcement in the form of waiver-claim outfielder Gabe Kapler.

Epstein knew what he had at Fenway, but what he wanted to get a better grasp on was what resided two highways and minor league levels away in Portland. And besides, it was Disco Night at Hadlock Field (a little extra incentive in the world of the minor leagues never hurts).

Starting for the Sea Dogs against the Pittsburgh Double A team, Altoona, was one of Boston's leading young lefties, Jorge De La Rosa. Portland's pitching ace could throw ninety-four miles an hour with a look-what-I-found change-up, putting him in the sights of both the Red Sox and any teams that wanted to trade with the Red Sox.

There were others who had made The List (the farm system's cream of the crop): Third baseman Kevin Youkilis, catcher Kelly Shoppach, and right fielder Justin Sherrod. But pitching was the ultimate organization aphrodisiac and Hadlock was going to supply plenty of it on this beautifully clear June night.

The scouting trio knew the task of evaluating should go off without a hitch, thanks in part to one of baseball's preeminent talent assigners, Lajoie. Keeping in touch with how the big club was doing down in Boston wasn't going to be such a walk in the park. It did, however, become a much easier task than anticipated thanks to Sea Dogs' owner Dan Burke.

This was the first year the Portland team was affiliated with the Red Sox after spending its previous existence in (of all teams) the Marlins family. But the proximity to Fenway, along with Burke's familiarity with former Florida and current Boston owner John Henry, made the transition seamless. So when Burke invited Epstein and his crew up into his box to keep an eye on the parent club's game, it was as comfortable as any living room get-together. Burke was a nice guy, plus he had a television set. The only difference between upstairs at Hadlock and back home on a couch of Theo's choosing was the sudden need for superior peripheral vision.

Approximately a hundred yards in front of Epstein resided the Red Sox's future, with De La Rosa showing a few flashes of brilliance, and far too many change-ups. Three feet to the left of the general manager was Burke's thirty-inch TV, where the picture was even rosier. Not only were the Red Sox keeping their foot on the throat of the Marlins via a 9–2 lead after six innings, but they had also been assigned their latest folk hero in the form of Kapler, who had a single, two doubles, and a triple heading into the seventh.

Part of the test each general manager endures throughout the regular season is their ability to fill in the roster's gaps with players like Kapler. This appeared to be one of the easier exams for Epstein. He was just twenty-seven years old, a few seasons removed from carrying the tag of a "can't miss" prospect, and looked the part of a ballplayer perhaps better than anyone in the majors. The outfielder was a rarity—a Jewish Major Leaguer, a bodybuilder, and a player whose potential hadn't worn off but was still released by the Colorado Rockies.

Now he was anything but an aberration, becoming another cult hero among a roster full of them. And he did it in just six innings.

With the sixth inning rolling on through in Portland, Epstein and Hoyer moved down from Burke's box and into the stadium's seats to watch one of the reasons for the trip, Chad Fox. The reliever had been on the disabled list for exactly two months thanks to a strained oblique muscle (knowing the technical names for muscles is mandatory in the world of baseball), and was throwing one and one-third innings as part of his rehabilitation. Fox threw well enough against the Double A hitters, allowing just one hit, but he wasn't the end of the show for the Red Sox evaluators. The guy pitching at the same time for the other team, Altoona's Mike Gonzalez, was also of some interest.

Gonzalez was a hard-throwing left-hander whose value had risen along with his radar gun readings, both in the Pittsburgh organization and around the majors. At 6-foot-2, 217 pounds, the dark-haired Texan always gave the appearance of an intimidating, power reliever. It was just that with a fastball that previously never eclipsed ninety-one miles an hour scouts looked right past the image and settled on his history—thirtieth-round draft pick who had a series of shoulder and knee problems.

But over the last few months, Gonzalez had changed, and so

had the opinions of the people who judged him. First, there was the Arizona Fall League when an out-of-nowhere, ninety-five-mile-an-hour fastball struck out twenty-three batters in just seventeen innings. Then came '03, where he moved from Single A Lynchburg to Altoona in just nine days, a leap he was justifying while showing his stuff for two and one-third innings against the Sea Dogs. Image was now everything.

The Boston trio liked the lefty . . . a lot. While Fox was released a month later, at least the memory of the other guy in Epstein, Lajoie, and Hoyer's crosshairs in Portland, Gonzalez, lasted a lot longer.

By the time the Sea Dogs finished off their 10–6 loss to the Curve, the Boston trio had moved down into the home team's clubhouse to watch the Red Sox's fate back at Fenway. Even before the relocation, bad news came through Epstein's cell phone's scoreboard tracker—Boston gave up four runs in the eighth and was relying on the world's greatest snowboarding waiver claim, Brandon Lyon, to shut the door in the ninth.

Lyon hadn't been nearly as effective as his April and May sprint toward the closer's role, but he also hadn't blown a single save. And this, a three-run bulge, would be stretching the validity of the stat, anyway. So, with the trepidation usually carried behind the Fenway backstop, Epstein, Lajoie, and Hoyer watched the top of the ninth play out in the confines of Portland's coaches' office.

With two outs, Florida still trailed by three but had the tying run at the plate. One Ivan Rodriguez single to center later and the Marlins had the winning run at the plate. Up came Mike Lowell.

The Red Sox had liked the Florida third baseman's game enough to contemplate an off-season deal that would have had the Marlins ship him to Boston, along with Millar, for a package that included Shea Hillenbrand. Now, the Sox brass was hoping they dramatically overestimated Lowell's effectiveness at Fenway. Unfortunately for Epstein and his cohorts, they were right on with their analysis (at least in the ninth inning of June 29).

The right-handed hitting Lowell took a Lyon fastball and sent it sailing to right field. Hoyer's first reaction was that it would never reach the wall, one of the deepest right fields in all of base-ball. The baseball operations assistant had seen the scouting report telling where Lowell routinely hit the ball (known as his "spray chart") and instantly remembered that he virtually never totaled his home runs in that portion of the park.

This time the spray chart had maliciously (in the Red Sox's case, anyway) lied, as the faces in the bowels of Hadlock Field might have suggested.

The three-run-homer-induced melancholy followed Hoyer's car all the way down the Maine Turnpike, through New Hamp-shire, onto Route 128 and straight down Interstate 93 until the buildings of Boston made their appearance. Losing is tough, losing after carrying a seven-run lead into the eighth inning is tougher, and losing in such a monumentally heart-stopping manner while having to watch it on television might be the toughest.

Yet, while the night of June 29 only told the tale of Boston's most disappointing defeat of the season, Epstein, Lajoie, and Hoyer could look back and view it for something else—the day the principals in the Red Sox's trading deadline deals were begun to be put in place.

"The gift of gab is the gift that I have and that girl ain't nothing but the blue plate crab special at Woodman's in Essex, Mass."

—from "Hey Ladies," Beastie Boys

THE LINE OUTSIDE Woodman's would stretch down Route 133, getting longer and longer with each passing summer day. The uniqueness of the smell emanating from the fry-o-laters had piqued the patrons' interest and now they were waiting—waiting for an hour or more.

Those standing single file on the sidewalk every July day were doing so under the premise that their reward might be a taste of the essence of New England seafood. This was, after all, the very same place where Chubby Woodman had invented the fried clam two years before Boston's last World Series win.

There were no promises that the wait for the Essex River's finest was going to pay off, just hope. It was the same formula used thirty miles south at a place called Fenway Park, where people have been taking that same fried-clam leap of faith even before the first heated lard concoction.

It was because of that New England credo—hope for the best, expect the worst—that made the suddenly symbiotic relationship between the Red Sox and a seafood joint in Essex, Massachusetts, perfectly understandable. So when Kyle Woodman and some of Chubby's other relatives decided the Boston front office could use some substantial sustenance as the trading deadline approached, it should have seemed as normal as a *Yankee Magazine* exposé.

The Woodmans' offering to Boston's annual midsummer cause was twelve lobster rolls, complete with napkins, pickles, and potato chips. It was all delivered in an enormous brown box, making the other side of the Fenway Park office (the side that had more to do with scheduling appearances for Wally the Green Monster and less with finding the next Walter Johnson) wonder exactly what Theo Epstein and the boys were doing down there.

Finding the Red Sox's Yawkey Way headquarters was no big thing to Kyle Woodman. Too many times to count the forty-one-year-old eagerly handed over his tens of dollars in order to ride the wave that was a game at Fenway. Up until the trade deadline delivery, his most memorable trip had been as a member of Woodman's clambake crew during the 1999 All-Star Game festivities.

Back in '99 Woodman's was contracted by Major League Baseball to supply its services for the VIPs and the like on the night of the first All-Star Game in Boston since 1960. Kyle and his brother Keith joined everyone within the 617, 508, and 978 area codes in eliciting a feeling of excitement from just being in and around Fenway on such a momentous occasion. But the electricity also prodded their mischievous nature, forcing the brothers away from the group's clambake duties and into the empty park.

It was more than six hours before the festivities and the Woodmans had wriggled their way into the city's most desirable playground—Fenway Park. First they touched the left-field wall, then it was off to use the right-field bullpen, and finally into the dugout. But why stop there? They could boil lobsters any time, but if they just hid in the men's bathroom's stalls for two hours free admission to the All-Star Game could be theirs. So that's exactly what they did.

Now, four years later, the Woodmans were attempting to fashion another yarn regarding their Red Sox summer. In the most crucial of weeks for any big-league front office, the final few days of July, the Boston brain trust was going to be spurred on by the meat of some crustaceans and a bag of bread.

The box of lobster had barely been placed on the desk of Boston assistant general manager Josh Byrnes before lunch began for the Red Sox's decision makers. Epstein took his sandwich and eased back into a plastic chair in front of Byrnes's desk, seemingly gaining a moment or two of escape with each bite.

Byrnes's office, which was also shared by Hoyer, had become the focal point in a hallway of executives. The word was out—there was something other than peanut butter and jelly in the vicinity.

A crowd in the cramped office space, however, was nothing new. It was a room that boasted next to no decorations, just three basically bare white walls. On one side was a bookshelf full of baseball books and media guides, scattered in no particular order, while on the other resided a cutout cardboard figure of the Star Wars character "Yoda," which rested on the window overlooking the Boston Beerworks restaurant across Brookline Avenue.

Luke Skywalker's mentor had been an office-warming gift, perceived by the uninformed as a symbol of Larry Lucchino's reference to the New York Yankees as "The Evil Empire." But to Byrnes and Hoyer the light saber–carrying cutout was nothing more than a decorative change of pace that just happened to strongly resemble the batting stance of former Baltimore Orioles outfielder Albert Belle.

The area was in fact so sparse that Hoyer's desk almost had to be tilted slightly so as to not butt up against Byrnes's space. But despite the lack of creature comforts, the day's meeting place for lunch was more often than not still the place to be. To the right was Epstein's office, an immaculate, two-television-set room, twice the size of the Byrnes/Hoyer place of residence. To the left was farm director Ben Cherington's office, just as well-kept as Epstein yet not quite as large.

Byrnes and Hoyer's think tank was the equivalent of the furnitureless collegiate dorm room everyone met in to talk between afternoon classes or sessions of video games. (The baseball operations' offices were close, and so were their inhabitants.) It just so happened that the decisions that shaped a nation—Red Sox Nation—had been flying around this dressed-up cubicle for the past seven months.

Above where Epstein sat to experience his midday meal was a white message board with the drawn-in image of a dartboard on it. Around the circumference of the image were names. "Wasdin." "Koch." "Sturtze." "Chan Ho!" They were all labels of players who were about as compatible to the Red Sox as a Yankee fan in the Landsdowne Street watering hole The Cask and Flagon. Dreaming up the not-ready-for-Fenway players had helped pass the late-morning minutes in a day whose importance weighed heavily toward the afternoon's hours.

The day before there was a real dartboard with real names of players Boston had its sights on, but that had been temporarily replaced for the benefit of any potential visitors not privy to the Red Sox's impeding roster adjustments. Maintaining information leaks had become a priority for Boston's new regime, and so far the system hadn't broken down.

Formulating the names for the impromptu dartboard helped whittle the morning hours away while the group awaited a call, a call that finally came just minutes after Epstein's last bite of lobster. It was Pittsburgh Pirates general manager Dave Littlefield.

Like the rest of the sea of cell phones in the Red Sox's offices, Epstein's didn't scream with any flashy jingle or deafening ring upon receiving a call. It just buzzed incessantly, making just enough of a vibrating noise as to alert the general manager of the gyration. Upon seeing the phone spring into action, Epstein picked it up, saw the origin of the call and sprung into action. "Hey Dave," he said. Lunch was officially over.

It was now close to 1:30 P.M., just twelve hours since Epstein and Littlefield last spoke. The subject of their conversations revolved around a trade, one which the Pittsburgh GM hoped would somehow send Boston's Brandon Lyon to the Pirates and while also, Epstein hoped, put lefty relief pitcher Scott Sauerbeck in a Red Sox uniform.

Littlefield was a man boasting the youth of the growing group of new guard that was infiltrating baseball front offices. His athleticism allowed for a three-and-one-half-year stay in the Philadelphia Phillies' farm system, and then a return to the world of football thanks to a spot on the University of Massachusetts Minutemen, where he earned a roster spot as a linebacker. But it wasn't until a blown-out knee and subsequent walk into the UMass baseball offices to inquire about getting back into baseball as a coach that Littlefield started his path to player transactions.

Now the Pirates were blowing up a good portion of their roster, already having traded starters Kenny Lofton and Aramis Ramirez to the Chicago Cubs, and closer Mike Williams to Philadelphia. They wanted to get younger, they wanted to get more cost-effective, and Littlefield was now hoping Lyon was going to help the process along.

Epstein bolted out of the office of Byrnes and Hoyer, adjourning to the solitude of his own surroundings. The assistant GM knew what was going on in the other room (the Red Sox had been talking with Littlefield for more than three weeks about variations of the deal) and didn't appear wracked with any sort of nerves or anxiety. Byrnes's attention, in fact, seemed fixed on the prospects of getting a sampling of whatever everyone was drooling over in that big, brown box three feet away from his laptop computer.

For Byrnes, the impending deal with the Pirates wasn't the only trade-off staring him in the face. He had just returned from the dentist complete with a mouth full of novocaine, forcing a decision to be made—Were the prospects of biting his tongue worth the hint of lobster on whatever active taste buds he currently possessed? The answer, as it turned out, symbolized what was to transpire moments later.

"Why not?!"

As he was prone to do, Byrnes used the instance to conjure up a sampling of the television sitcom *Seinfeld.* This time the reference was to that of the show's "Jimmy" episode in Season 6, when the Kramer character struggles with finishing his day after being slowed by a novocaine shot to the mouth. The mentions of pop culture were understandable considering the youth that prevailed in the Red Sox offices. *Seinfeld* and the like were easy icebreakers.

For the thirty-three-year-old Byrnes, however, the reaction was even more instinctive considering the actress who played the character "Elaine" in the show, Julia Louis-Dreyfuss, had served as his babysitter while growing up near Washington, D.C. Epstein's grandfather may have brought the family an Academy Award, but in realm of the new-age Red Sox, any connection to *Seinfeld* really made the admiration-endorphins start churning.

Seinfeld babysitter or not, Byrnes had a good sense of humor and an easy way about him. The former baseball captain at Haverford University was the first among the new Sox decision makers to experience the increasingly familiar meteoric rise. At just the age of twenty-six he became the scouting director of the Cleveland Indians, and by twenty-nine he had followed former Indians' employee Dan O'Dowd to Colorado to become the National League's youngest-ever assistant general manager.

It was an ascension that was easily understood, for Byrnes not only had the pedigree (second-most career home runs of any Haverford player), but he also had a gift that stretched beyond physical ability. Josh could always see the big picture.

The almost–Toronto Blue Jays general manager Paul DePodesta saw Byrnes's gift for sorting out a situation's priorities in the winter of 1996. Depo, a newcomer to the Cleveland organization, had been assigned the duty of figuring out the market analysis for that off-season's crop of free agents and arbitration cases. It was a duty Byrnes had attended to the previous year.

DePodesta's first order of business was to talk to Byrnes about how the process was done. There wasn't much talking. "This is how I did, find a better way to do it," said the mentor to the protégé, dropping a binder full of facts and figures on Depo's desk. The challenge had been made to continue the task's metamorphosis. This was seeing the big picture—an improved product meant a better team. The next season the Cleveland Indians went to the World Series.

In his time with Cleveland, Depo kept seeing Byrnes's subtle gifts. Sit at a game with Josh and you'd get much more than analysis of the here and the now. You would get a vision of whatever that scenario had in store for the players' moments down the road.

In the eyes of the Oakland A's assistant general manager, and now the youthfully uncontaminated Boston front office, Byrnes was the most valuable of assets—a logician magician.

Now, just days before the trading deadline, Byrnes was going to be called upon to see the logic in the Red Sox's next big move.

Pittsburgh would do a deal with the Sox if it included a kid by the name of Anastacio.

Anastacio was a right-handed pitcher named Anastacio Martinez, and the fact that Littlefield wanted him was no surprise to the Red Sox. He was just twenty-four years old, threw hard (ninety-three miles per hour) and had excelled in his new role as closer for Boston's Double A affiliate in Portland, Maine. But there was another reason the Sox weren't shocked to hear Martinez's name thrown into the trade winds—minor league game-enders tend to have a way of separating themselves from the pack.

Martinez (another participant in the Epstein-watched June 29 Portland game) took up the role of closer at the beginning of the season and had run with it. Room for error is in abundance as a starter, but as Anastacio and the Sox were finding out, sometimes the intense shortness of a relief role can be just the trick. Now the pitcher was closing any uncertainty revolving around Boston's ability to obtain Sauerbeck.

It was going to be Martinez and Lyon for Gonzalez and Sauer-beck.

Martinez. Gonzalez. The trip to Portland was proving to be worthwhile. And just for good measure, the field at which the minor leaguers showed their wares to Epstein, Hoyer, and Lajoie was three blocks from where Littlefield grew up, and named after one of the Pittsburgh GM's former coaches, Edson Hadlock. If there was ever a trade that was destined to be made it was this one—the Crustacean Creation.

The Sox wanted to get this thing done because, as always, the Yankees were lurking.

What Epstein didn't realize was that the Yankees had given up their pursuit of Sauerbeck four days earlier. New York general manager Brian Cashman had used the Major League grapevine to understand the path Littlefield might be going. Cash heard from one of his players, who heard from a Red Sox player that a deal for the lefty might be a done deal. That was enough to point Cash-man in another direction by the time Boston's lobster rolls were being delivered. (Later that day the Yankees settled for the man who nailed down the Red Sox's World Series's heartbreak seventeen years before, lefty Jesse Orosco.)

The Red Sox need not worry, just celebrate. Time for the handshakes.

In baseball, handshakes are perceived as the successful culmination of three hours of so of pitching, hitting, and everything else that goes along with claiming victory inside the foul lines. But in the front office back rooms there were often bouts with success that had nothing to do with pine tar or rosin bags. And as far as Epstein was concerned, a trade like this one was worthy of the ceremonial congratulatory greeting, even if it was executed among the two desks, three plain white walls, and an cardboard image of Luke Skywalker's little green mentor.

The feel-good flurry of events wasn't done yet. Calling the phone on Byrnes's desk was Jerry DiPoto, the relief-pitcher-turned-scout whom Epstein had sent to Birmingham, Alabama, to watch Gonzalez. The very same Gonzalez Theo had seen in Vacationland. Now it was time to get the viewpoint of someone who had been on those same mounds and thrown those same baseballs.

The news was good. Gonzalez pitched just one inning in DiPoto's presence, but during his unsuspecting audition he struck out two former Major Leaguers, Jason Hart and Mike Lamb, on just seven pitches. The scouts' radar guns touched ninety-six while consistently staying in the midnineties throughout the five-strikeout performance.

Words like "awesome," phrases such as "I could see him as a closer," and statements preaching "he was great," all came out of the black phone and into the ears of the group huddled around Byrnes and his desk.

"What's his deception like?" would be the only question asked of DiPoto by Epstein, or anyone for that matter. Gonzalez was, after all, a lefty and the more deceiving a left-hander is to a batter of the same description the better.

"His deception is his stuff," DiPoto answered, allowing for another springboard of resounding positive reviews for Gonzalez. It was all information the scout had relayed via his written report late the night before, but exclamation points and italics can only go so far. The enthusiasm in DiPoto's voice was the ultimate punctuation.

The report on Gonzalez was a good sign, because the Red Sox had just traded for him. Epstein finally informed DiPoto, who had seemingly run out of adjectives in trying to relay his affection for Gonzalez's talent. "Lyon and Martinez for Sauerbeck and Gonzalez."

"That's great. That's a great trade," DiPoto beamed, exuding the relief of a teenager who had just gotten into the college of choice.

"You must be good luck because every time we send you somewhere we end up making a trade," said Epstein, harkening back to DiPoto's contributions to the Byung-Hyun Kim trade. "OK Jerry, we'll see you later."

Epstein was now immersed in a sea of adrenaline. The usually controlled air about him had been displaced by a feeling of accomplishment that can only be attained after hours of laborious execution. This wasn't a task the magnitude of the Hoover Dam, the Panama Canal, or perhaps even the new seats atop the Green Monster. But the look that engulfed Epstein's demeanor was probably not so different from any of the workers who toiled on such projects until their absolute completion.

Pure satisfaction.

The tasks that accompanied the deal, however, were far from done. It was now the general manager's job to inform Red Sox manager Grady Little that he lost his former closer, but picked up something much more valuable to Boston's ever-evolving bullpen—a dirt-digging, left-handed, curveball-flippin' freak.

"I do not think much of a man who is not wiser today than he was yesterday."

—Abraham Lincoln

SCOTT SAUERBECK was like the rest of the kids growing up on the Cincinnati sandlots in the 1970s—he would constantly pray to hit that perfect just-beat-the-throw triple.

As is the case with most pitchers who are branded with their better-than-the-rest reputation in the days of Little League and high school, the blond-haired kid did it all on a baseball field. Sauerbeck could hit, he could run, he could throw, and, as was required by the unwritten law of playing in Pete Rose's neighborhood, he could slide without his feet leading the way.

On the first day of every baseball season, Sauerbeck's coaches would set up the tumbling mats approximately fifty feet from a line of baseball players just waiting to be turned into human torpedoes. The drill was set up in order to make certain that every boy knew the proper way to slide, otherwise known as the Pete Rose way—headfirst, with as much air between your belly and the ground as each player's courage would allow.

Catching the air was the key. The image of Rose hurtling his fire hydrant body and mop of brown hair through space, heading toward the third base bag that rested between the legs of Boston Red Sox third baseman Rico Petrocelli, was more than a memory for kids from Cincy, it was a manual.

Sauerbeck's left arm was gold to any team he played on, a fact that would be later defined when he was drafted by the New York Mets in the twenty-third round of the 1994 draft after four years at Miami University in Ohio. But if he didn't risk life and limb (at least limb) while trying to emulate his Cincinnati neighbor than there was no use putting on the uniform. Scott knew that the scars from the generation's preferred acrobatic slide would usually always heal, but fighting through the wounds of baseball ridicule was downright paralyzing.

Sauerbeck and his golden left arm survived those feats of aviation, and now they were the property of the Boston Red Sox.

It was one of the most unexplainable, yet universally accepted, bits of science that could be found on a baseball diamond—hitters who batted left-handed had a difficult time getting a bead on a baseball thrown by a left-handed pitcher. And nobody in baseball had taken advantage of the sixty-feet, six-inch bit of bafflement in 2002 better than Sauerbeck. It was a season in which lefty hitters carried a .198 on-base percentage against the easygoing southpaw, the lowest ratio among all pitchers in the National League.

His method of torture consisted of curveball after curveball. Sauerbeck didn't quite know why it curved like it did—relying on a twist of his wrist rather than the certain grip of the ball—but he wasn't complaining nearly as much as his opposition. Scott had taken the mound 158 times in the previous two years, was making more than $2 million, and now found himself in the middle of his first pennant race.

Once a headfirst-sliding fiend, Sauerbeck had understandably become a self-described "curveball-flippin' freak."

With his ability to make a two-laced white ball dance and dart while hurtling through the air, it was fitting that science had always intrigued Sauerbeck. But it wasn't the usual brotherhood of baseball and physics that he had locked in on. Scott wondered more about what was going on in the earth rather than anything that was taking place above it.

Geology was Sauerbeck's thing, and he had gone back to school in the off-season, starting in 2000 to prove it. His logical reintroduction into Miami University would have been to attend some classes and write a paper on why a ball appeared to abruptly change its path somewhere between the hand and home. But Scott didn't care that a Brooklyn man by the name of Candy Cummings had started the curveball craze in 1867 in a game against Harvard after practicing with a bucket of clamshells. He was more concerned with the place those clamshells came from.

Like the nickname affixed to many of his new Boston teammates, Sauerbeck was a "Dirtdog," and thankfully for the student, there just happened to be a Red Sox fan by the name of John Hughes who was more than willing to help Scott embrace his curious nature.

Hughes was a former catcher (albeit not good enough of one to play beyond high school) who struck up residency in Red Sox Nation while attending Dartmouth College, a school that resided no more than three hours from Fenway Park in Hanover, New Hampshire. He had first loved the Yankees, then the Mets, but had now given his heart to Boston, with an obvious tip of the hat to anything involving baseball.

By the time Sauerbeck returned to Miami, Hughes was Dr. Hughes, associate dean of the College of Arts and Sciences at the college. The dirt doctor remembered Scott as a pretty decent starting pitcher in college who hadn't necessarily been entrenched in awe-inspiring status in the classroom or between the foul lines.

But this was a different student . . . a different story. Sauerbeck was going to help Hughes live out a somewhat detoured dream, bringing the backstop with the bad ankles back into the world of baseball, of the professional variety no less.

As part of the pitcher's course load Scott would stealthily take samples from every pitcher's mound he visited throughout the 2000 season and carry those containers back to the college for analysis. The pitching hills may have been mandated to be a standard ten inches high by Major League Baseball since 1969, but just how different was the stuff that made those mounds?

Nobody had any idea that Sauerbeck was pilfering National League dirt with each visit to the mound. Maybe it was better the project was kept a secret. Groundskeepers had their insecurities and ballplayers weren't known for their unabashed open-mindedness. So it remained a lefty pitcher's dirty little guilty pleasure.

Hughes's respect for his student quickly grew beyond the awe of big-league hero-worshipping. Sauerbeck was a hard working, diligent student of the science of geology, who just happened to make more money than any professor could dream of. When they were in the laboratory, however, there was no lifestyle separation between the pitcher and his teacher.

The professor's confidence and admiration in Sauerbeck became undeniable upon receiving the labeled vials of National League dirt. The department's first Major Leaguer was becoming also the inaugural student to be trusted with a $300,000 machine called the X-ray diffractometer. In the world of geology, the machine was like the Taj Mahal of microscopes. It was also the key element in deciphering just how different the compositions of the pitching mounds were.

The study proved worthy of its effort, showing subtle differences between each city's mounds. Cincinnati carried the most hematite (rust), San Francisco was heavy on quartz, and all of the domed stadiums had a substance called smectite. Smectite? The others ballparks' samples were making sense, usually being differentiated by the area's natural geology. But smectite, the substance that was throwing Hughes an 0-and-2 curveball, was distinguished by its presence in, of all things, kitty litter. The confusion continued when realizing that the particles in question immediately turned to mush upon coming in contact with any kind of moisture. It was the kind of query that started to make the whole project seem worthwhile.

Domed stadiums had mounds made up of kitty litter–carrying element because it never rained in a domed stadium. Eureka!

Sauerbeck would never toe the pitching rubber the same way again.

Sauerbeck's journey to his May 2001 graduation still had another road to go down, one leading to the desert of Arizona. It was on that dive into fieldwork, starting two days after Christmas, that the pitcher entered a world about as far away from the luxury of the Major Leagues as he had been since entering the big leagues two years before.

The portion of Arizona Sauerbeck's group staked camp just miles from the Mexican border. It was a notion that didn't distinguish the location from the rest of the state's wasteland until he started to see the abandoned trucks. The broken-down pickups were, as Miami's hardest-throwing geology student was told, the result of illegal immigrants choosing to hoof it on foot after crossing into the United States.

Sauerbeck thought it was a good story to tell upon returning to civilization . . . until he came upon a better one.

The twenty-eight-year-old owner of a Major League arm and Major League contract was spending the late-December night sleeping outside in a sleeping bag when he heard the noises. All of a sudden, what was once audible now was physical. A dazed and confused Sauerbeck sprung up to realize what was going on—his camp was in the path of a legion of Mexicans who were racing to become Americans.

Sauerbeck may never make the Hall of Fame, but, then again, Roger Clemens would never be stampeded by illegal immigrants, either.

Now, just moments after the Boston-Pittsburgh trade had been consummated, Littlefield was calling Sauerbeck into Pirates' manager Lloyd McClendon's office to inform him of his next adventure—the effects of putting a curveball-flippin' freak into the middle of a pennant race.

THE CRUSTACEAN CREATION

"It happens."

—Brandon Lyon

AS THE MEDIA FILTERED into Fenway Park's fifth-floor press box, the word started trickling in—press conference, 3:30 P.M., in the closetlike, first-floor interview room. The press would have to wait thirty minutes to find out what was going on. In the Red Sox clubhouse Lyon already knew.

As impersonal as a newspaper's transaction log might make a trade appear, the look on Lyon's face as he scrambled to secure moving boxes for his stuff certainly suggested otherwise. Fittingly wearing a Burton Snowboards T-shirt, the world's greatest snowboarding waiver claim had accepted the news from Epstein with a handshake and begun the process of cleaning out his locker. The actions were logical, the feeling he had was anything but.

A locker usually contains about two cardboard boxes full of stuff—cleats, workout clothes, photographs, vitamins . . . the works. Lyon's haul was no different, except that it had never been loaded up in the middle of a season. Then there were the dealings with the apartment, the leased furniture and everything else that made moving the second-most mind-numbing part of being traded. And to make matters worse, the process was being bumped up exponentially. The Pirates heard the rumblings that Lyon's elbow was sore, and they wanted the pitcher in Pittsburgh the next morning for a physical.

Explaining the mogul-induced protruding bone in his pitching shoulder was easy, so were the scars from the teenage rollerblading incident. What the Pittsburgh doctors wanted to take an up close and personal look at was Lyon's right elbow, which had seemingly wore down as his most intensely scrutinized season played out. For the better part of the day after the trade, the pitcher toiled through one of life's annoyances—sitting in a doctor's office.

221

They left, they came back, they left again and then came back once more. Along with the final visit came two words—Arthrogram MRI—that Lyon wasn't truly familiar with, but still represented more seeds of uncertainty in the newcomer to this world of player-swapping. He simply thought this was procedure, shooting blue dye into the body so that the magnetic resonance image could pick up every nook and cranny of doubt that resided in the subject's arm. What he didn't know was that this was far from the norm.

Once the blue dye is inserted, activities such as pitching aren't an option for at least a couple of weeks. A trip to the disabled list, and a player-exchange battle between two clubs, were officially in the offing.

Pittsburgh claimed it was dealt damaged goods in Lyon. The Pirates' doctors insisted the MRI showed wear and tear more than the norm in the pitcher's most valuable of body parts—his right elbow. The Red Sox medical men, on the other hand, also knew how to read the image and what they saw wasn't what was being described by their Pittsburgh counterparts. Boston had a different take. In its estimation, almost every pitcher who has thrown a ball long enough to make it to the Majors will have some wear and tear, and that's exactly what was distinguishing itself in Lyon's arm.

Lyon found himself in a no-man's land. With the Pittsburgh roster purging, empty lockers were easy to find in the Pirates' clubhouse, a reality that made Lyon's act of unpacking appreciably easier. But in terms of familiarizing himself with his new neighbors, it wasn't ideal. He casually knew pitcher Josh Fogg from the minors, and catcher Jason Kendall introduced himself from a few lockers away, but that was pretty much it in terms of get-to-know-yous for the pitcher known now as the world's greatest medical mystery/snowboarding waiver claim.

Exactly a week after the first wave of the Crustacean Creation was born, the Red Sox took a break from debating MRI images to strike another deal. This one was with the Cincinnati Reds, who were joining Pittsburgh in the "sellers" side of the trade deadline ledger. The Reds were sending Scott Williamson, the ghost-viewing reliever, for minor leaguer Phil Dumatrait.

It wasn't the first time the Sox had been teetering on the edge of dealing for Williamson, having attempted to include the reliever in a package including Reds pitcher Chris Reitsma in exchange for Lyon. But now, Boston was basically receiving two for the price of one. And it just so happened that those two, the curveball-flippin' freak and the ghost-viewing reliever, lived two houses down from one another in Cincinnati. Add in that the Yankees had been cut off at the pass in both transactions, and it sure felt like some good karma was starting to filter on down through the offices of the boys from baseball operations. (It was a feeling enhanced later that night when Bill Mueller became the first major leaguer to hit grand slams from both sides of the plate in a 14–7 win over Texas.)

Two days later, on the final day of July, the capper arrived. Epstein and Littlefield had put the magnetic resonance image differences aside and reworked the Crustacean Creation. Lyon headed back to Boston, as did Martinez, while Gonzalez rejoined the Pirates. The Red Sox kept Sauerbeck, but surrendered highly coveted minor league infielder Freddy Sanchez in exchange for starting pitcher Jeff Suppan. In the end, the Sox were getting the best lefty reliever available and one of the premier starters on the market for an unproven middle infielder. On the streets of Boston, the man now simply known as "Theo" had reached hero status (there are few things more important to Bostonians in the heart of the summer than the Red Sox making a good trading-deadline deal).

Back in Pittsburgh, Lyon, his head still spinning (albeit while wearing his new Pirates hat), heard he was heading back to Boston while watching ESPN on the clubhouse television. By this time, this kind of surprise couldn't dent the numbness that had encrusted itself around the world's greatest snowboarding waiver claim's psyche. The dizziness just continued when he got back to the apartment he had left behind just more than a week before and found out that both the landlord and the furniture company wanted him to sign on for brand-new year leases. New ninety-three-mile-an-hour fastball or not, nothing was going to come easy for Lyon this time around.

The same could be said for his first former team, the Boston Red Sox.

C H A P T E R 9

And Now for His Musical Interlude

"Glory days, well they'll pass you by."

—Bruce Springsteen

Diane Ricciardi, a woman who gives the appearance that she has relished every moment of her previous forty-one years while opening her arms to embrace the next quarter century, is a spiritual lady. Her life's lineup card isn't flexible—there's her family hitting third and God in the cleanup spot. It was, after all, the latter whom Diane joined her husband, J.P. in praying to the night before deciding to relocate their lives to Toronto.

But as with any good lineup there has to be a table setter, and in Diane's case that person just happened to be the "Boss" (the one not named Steinbrenner)—Bruce Springsteen.

Springsteen's music has never controlled Diane's life, but it has made a significant dent in it. The initial impression made by the emotion-exhausting singer came in 1975 when Diane's brother bought the album, "Born to Run." As a thirteen-year-old, she was hypnotized by the source of whatever yelling emanated from her sibling's room. Then came the concert. Fourth row. Providence Civic Center. Four hours. It was, as she coined the evening, a sixteen-year-old's first spiritual experience.

The Springsteen concerts kept flying through New England as Diane merged with her adult years, and along with the shows usually came the girl from Worcester's Belmont Hill. Even in the early years of the couple's marriage, a time that had landed the Ricciardis and their two black Labrador Retrievers in a four-room apartment on Shrewsbury Street, Diane found a way to see her musical hero.

An example of the infatuation came during the artist's Tunnel of Love tour. The 1988 nationwide, hard-charging Springsteen-a-thon included sixty-seven shows, one of which Diane was going to make sure she was at. Not only was Bruce playing right down the street in the Worcester Centrum, but the three appearances actually were the tour's starting blocks. So on February 25 Diane called J.P. and told him she was going straight from her job at the bank to The Centrum with whatever money was at her disposal and she was going to buy a scalper's ticket.

Diane had never questioned J.P.'s unsolicited excursions to out-of-the-way sandlots in a quest to find the perfect ballplayer, so how was he going to stand in the way of his wife's quest? Baseball and Bruce—the Ricciardi's passions were easily understood.

Now, on the first day of August 2003, Springsteen was serving as the gap between chaos and sanity once again. J.P. was taking his wife, along with eighteen friends, to Gillette Stadium in Foxboro to see the Boss.

For Diane, braving the forty-five-minute ride down Route 495 in a downpour was as easily justified as any of the twenty-three Bruce shows she had been to before. For J.P., the trip served two purposes, neither having to do with "Thunder Road." First, it was a chance to finally see the year-old home of the New England Patriots. Secondly, and dramatically more important, the evening out allowed for a much-welcome diversion from trades that were made, and not made, just prior to the 4 P.M., waiver-free dealing deadline of the day before. Flat-out, it was a frustration-filled final few days of July.

By the time the 31st wound down, J.P. knew he would be sitting on the sidelines during one of Major League Baseball's most exciting days. He had let it be known what it would take to secure one of his players and, in his mind, the completion of any deal would be initiated within the memory dialing of the other general managers' cell phones. The Blue Jays were knee deep in what the corporate world deems "credible commitment" (showing a firm resolve to stand by an original philosophy) and they weren't backing down.

Kelvim Escobar was available, but on Toronto's terms only.

Escobar was maddeningly inconsistent, didn't have the track record befitting an upper-echelon ball thrower, and hadn't been able to distinguish himself as a top tier closer or starter. But, boy, did he have an arm. As the Boss once echoed, the solidly built Venezuelan "could throw that speed ball by you, make you look like a fool." Jon Lalonde, the man usually responsible for documenting Toronto's radar gun readings behind home plate, saw only two pitchers touch "99" throughout the season's first four months—Baltimore's Jorge Julio and Escobar.

It was just that teams didn't know what to make of Escobar. His six-year career mirrored his performance's uncertainty, relieving some years, starting others. This season the plan was for the closer role to cement the righty pitcher's value, except the problem came when he spent more time in April continuing games than finishing them out. By May, the heart-stopping/perplexing dilemma that was Escobar had unnerved the Blue Jays in more ways than one. Nobody wanted to trade for a reliever who offered little or no relief.

So, in early May, Ricciardi started to talk with his fellow decision makers—Law, Tosca, McCleary, the whole gang. The consensus was that Escobar always got stronger any time he ventured into a second inning, a sure sign that maybe starting might be a better fit for all parties involved. A week later, the decision was jump-started—the pitcher wanted out of the bullpen and into the rotation. The fastball-throwing enigma's value was about to go vertical.

The calls regarding Escobar started as early as mid-May, as Theo Epstein discovered while sitting in Fenway Park's home team's dugout. Ricciardi had called Epstein earlier in the damp spring day concerning the Red Sox's potential interest of one of Toronto's relievers. It wasn't as if the Blue Jays' bullpen was overflowing with good fortune, it was just in the world of baseball circa May 2003, all available relief pitchers were going to be offered up to the unsolved puzzle that was Boston's relief corps.

"Hey J.P., yeah, I think we're going to have to pass," Epstein told his not-surprised counterpart. "We really need guys who are going to throw strikes."

But Ricciardi had more on his mind. He knew Boston was a team that could potentially be in the market for the free agent-to-be, Escobar, once the race for good pitchers (starters or relievers) began. It was never too early to lay a little groundwork.

"We certainly like his arm," said Epstein after a minute or two of taking in Ricciardi's preemptive sales pitch.

An inquiry was set in motion.

By the time Boston reemerged on the scene regarding Escobar, it wasn't alone. The pitcher took to his new role of starter, allowing the rest of the league to take a major liking to the back end of what had become one of baseball's best one-two starting punches (with Roy Halladay leading the way). Ricciardi's cell phone was ringing, and most of the callers were flush with the thought of adding the new-and-improved Kelvim Escobar into their push for the pennant.

The frequency that J.P.'s blue, portable phone was signaling incoming calls was almost comical. The season before Tim McCleary figured Ricciardi's bill eclipsed more than $9,000 for the season. This time around, with the help of one of the Major's most sought after fastball-throwing commodities, the minutes had piled up at an even loftier rate.

Ricciardi was just coming to grips with the whole idea of living life at the mercy of a cell phone. Technology usually wasn't his thing. But ever since Diane bought him that first, enormously cumbersome portable telephone (cell phones weren't in the A's budget), J.P. latched on and didn't let go . . . except in Baltimore. After a 2002 game against the Orioles he executed a general manager's ultimate oopsy–daisy, losing his link to the outside world in a cab. (As far as anyone knew, there were no transactions emanating from the Checker Taxi Company.)

This time around, the days leading to the trade deadline saw Ricciardi's cell phone firmly in hand, and usually on ear. There were only two other general managers programmed into the instrument's phone book (Billy Beane and Theo Epstein), but that was of little consequence considering it was J.P. who people were calling, not the other way around.

San Francisco, Boston, New York, St. Louis, Cincinnati, and Atlanta. They all wanted to know what it was going to take to get Escobar. They were all told the cost: Players named Foppert, De La Rosa, Fossum, Drew, Wainwright. These were the price tags, and there was not going to be any last-minute, going out of business sales.

The Blue Jays were knee deep in credible commitment . . . right to the very end.

There were a few consolations when it came to Escobar's presence on the Blue Jays' roster come August 1. The first was that the date hadn't marked the be-all and end-all when it came to reaping the benefits of the pitcher's departure. Toronto could still trade its No. 2 starter; it was just that his name was going to have to be placed on Major League Baseball's computer-generated waiver wire. Then, if no team staked a claim to the pitcher, Ricciardi would be free to cut a deal. As much as the rules clouded the simplicity that was following the game, they did add a healthy dose of intrigue.

The dilemma for teams wanting to block potential player swaps was that if a claim was made, then it was at the discretion of the team jettisoning the player whether or not to allow the subject to be set free. It was one tricky forty-eight-hour window.

McCleary, for one, had witnessed firsthand perhaps the supreme example of the kind of pitfall that could be awaiting the claiming club—the day the era of making thirty blankets came to a screeching halt.

It was August 6, 1998, and the Blue Jays were sending their closer, Randy Myers, out into the world of waivers. The left-handed reliever was still pretty good—leading the American League in saves the year before with Baltimore, and notching twenty-eight saves in the first half of the initial season of a three-year deal with Toronto. It was just that then-Toronto general manager Gord Ash and McCleary had determined that it was time to go in another direction, and the remaining $13.2 million on Myers's contract wasn't going to come along for the ride.

Anybody who wanted Myers could have him for the nominal fee of a $20,000 waiver claim (or the most modest of trade proposals).

At the time, San Diego was jostling for position with Atlanta for National League supremacy. Word had gotten out (thanks to the folks in Toronto) that the Braves were interested in Myers and a trade could be imminent. It was a deal that the Padres couldn't let happen, so, even though they already had their game-ender in Trevor Hoffman, they swooped in with the claim on the closer. Then came the phone call—much to the surprise of San Diego general manager Kevin Towers, the Jays were not going to be pulling Myers back. It was, by far, the most expensive present of the '98 season.

Instead of paying the $20,000, San Diego shipped a pair of minor leaguers to the Blue Jays for the Padres' very expensive set-up man. The news only got worse for the claiming team the following season, when with two years still left on Myers's contract, he was subjected to rotator cuff surgery. For the martial arts expert/lefty reliever, it was the end of a career. For the rest of baseball, it was the end of the casual waiver-wire plucking.

Now, waiver claims are done with a fingertip tentativeness instead of the previously accepted all-arms-out hoarding nature. That's why there was hope when it came to Escobar.

But in the end, the waiver wire would be unkind to the Blue Jays. Not only was Escobar plucked by Minnesota, but outfielder Frank Catalanotto, a player whose value had jumped by leaps and bounds since signing with the Jays in the off-season, ran into a Red Sox roadblock. The sequences weren't the end of the world, but in the realm of rebuilding, it was always nice to have those August options.

It wasn't all that bad. The Blue Jays were going to still be able to enjoy the good days of ninety-nine-mile-an-hour heat Escobar would bring to the final two months. And if he did choose to leave town after the season, there would at least be one or two doses of Toronto's lifeblood waiting for the Jays in the form of draft picks (this was compensation for the loss of top tier free agents). In baseball, rarely a move is made without Plan B hiding somewhere around the corner.

The Escobar scenario might have been utterly unpredictable, but at least the Springsteen deal at Gillette Stadium was right on the mark—a perfect 3-plus-hour set. But then that blue cell phone started kicking up again.

The beacon of hope for the Blue Jays' season, Halladay, had finally lost a game after winning fifteen straight decisions.

The Boss was prophetic (on this rainy first day of August, anyway)—glory days were passing the Blue Jays by. But, even with the memories of trade deadlines and win streaks gone by, there was one refrain from Springsteen that took root more than any other:

These are better days baby, these are better days it's true; These are better days, there's better days shining through.

THE STANDINGS MIGHT have shown that the Blue Jays had just dropped to one game below .500 for the first time since the

momentous run through May, but Ricciardi hadn't lost his optimism. J.P. knew there might not be any playoffs, but there were
going to be plenty of better days before the season was out . . . he
was right.

* * *

*"Saw things clearer once you were in my . . .
rearview mirror."*

—Pearl Jam

MEGAN KAISER knew what she was doing.

The gregarious twenty-six-year-old had been put in charge of
the Fenway Park musical selections in an odd sort of happen-
stance. Dr. Charles Steinberg, the Red Sox's vice president of public affairs, needed someone with the musical background to deliver
the park's patrons with the timeliest and most tasteful of musical
selections. Kaiser, a Fenway Park ambassador, knew music. Steinberg knew she knew music. So a simple question was asked: Name
a song from a musical that incorporates an American League city
in it.

Easy—"Everything is up to date in Kansas City." The job was
hers.

Now, in the late-afternoon of August 21, she was using the
center-field speakers to send a message to Boston's visitors, Oakland. The A's might have sent The Nation into its dark corner of
summer worries with two straight wins over the Red Sox. And
maybe Billy Beane's team was two games in front of the hosts in
the race for the playoff's wild-card berth. So what! Kaiser wanted
to let the enemy know, through the angst-driven words of Pearl
Jam lead singer Eddie Vedder, the Red Sox wanted the A's in their
rearview mirror in the standings and, as far as the park's disc
jockey was concerned, that's where they were going to be.

The musical memo was, if nothing else, well thought out. Not
only would a reversal in win-loss position ease the pain of a

waiting-to-exhale Red Sox fandom, but the song also allowed for some much-needed smile-inducing memories for the front office. Epstein was as big a Pearl Jam fan as there was in baseball. It was an admiration that only grew as he became an avid participant in guitar playing, although he hadn't taken up the discipline until a few years before. His skill level approached above average—the same level as the story behind his impetus to begin playing the beast.

Night after night the same dream reoccurred, that of Led Zeppelin calling him up on stage to bang out a riff. But too many times to count, the same problem presented itself—he didn't know how to play. So, with the presentation of a guitar from his sister, Anya, the fears were squelched, a cover band was formed (Trauser) and a new dream began.

Thanks to Kaiser, the Red Sox were looking toward the grunge band from Seattle for guidance once again. This time, it was firmly in the realm of a world that had been anything but entertainment—baseball. But while the words "rearview mirror" were being screamed from above the Fenway diamond, the reality of the situation couldn't be soothed with any song. With an Oakland win on this perfect Boston summer's Thursday night, the Red Sox would be in an increasingly inescapable three-game hole.

The Red Sox hadn't been the only ones turning to music for a slice of sanity. Beane was in town with a big reason for his back-turning on the Boston job—his thirteen-year-old daughter, Casey. The father and daughter spent the night before playing baseball hooky to attend a Dropkick Murphy's concert on the Boston waterfront, watching Wednesday's A's win at Fenway on a television in the back room of Boston's Fleet Pavilion. It was safely assumed that by the time Pearl Jam uttered its first Fenway Park word on Thursday afternoon, everything was going Oakland's way. Then something changed.

A turn of good fortune wasn't exactly what the Red Sox had in mind on Thursday afternoon. Not only was an Oakland sweep staring them in the mug, but word had been called into the front office that Pedro Martinez was not going to be able to pitch as must-win a game as Boston had all season. The pitcher was in bed with the eleven most dreaded letters in the new edition of the Sox fans' handbook for misery—p-h-a-r-y-n-g-i-t-i-s. A severe inflammation of Martinez's throat was leaving his team gasping for pennant race oxygen.

But at 1:30 P.M., just about the time Martinez departed St. Elizabeth's Medical Center, Casey Fossum became the first person subjected to the winds of change. Grady Little called just to say hi . . . and also that the slight lefty was going to pitch for the first time in ten days. Fortunes were about to be altered.

There might have been other elements that assisted Boston's day of music and mirth. The Saugus Little Leaguers were on the field as a reward for reaching the North American final of the organization's World Series, which could have brought some good fortune. (A standing ovation in the media dining room must be good for something.) It was also the night the Red Sox broke out their "Rally Karaoke Guy" video, showing an eighteen-year-old Beaumont Basher, Kevin Millar, lip sync The Boss' "Born in the USA." Most people, in fact, predictably pointed to the strangely marketable home movie as the reason for Boston's change of luck.

But whatever, or however it happened, it couldn't have been a reality if not for Fossum—the pitcher who looked like he had liposuction and forgot to say when.

In a season of unpredictable twist and turns, Fossum was Boston's most unpredictable bump in the road. For an entire off-season Epstein was forced to work every conceivable angle just not to trade the lefty. Besides Atlanta's "we'll give you Kevin Millwood" proposal before the Nicaragua experience, there were the calls to Montreal.

Bartolo Colon. Bartolo Colon. That's all Red Sox fans heard. That's all Casey Fossum heard. Boston is going to get Bartolo Colon, and it is going to give up its best young starter to get the stocky fireballer. But Red Sox fans, and Fossum, weren't hearing right. Colon wasn't the object of Epstein's inquiries. It was another Expos pitcher, a younger one who didn't present as many

physical risks as the contract-expiring, scale-denting Colon—
Javier Vazquez.

The problem was that as much as the Sox desired Vazquez,
Montreal general manager Omar Minaya lusted after Fossum, a
commodity the Red Sox weren't ready to give up on. Sure, Boston
had money, but not enough to disregard a talented, cheap, third-
year starter. Moves like that, in Epstein's mind, made whatever
money was available run out appreciably faster.

So, a deal was made that would send Vazquez to Boston without touching Fossum. It was done . . . until Minaya came back
with word that Montreal manager Frank Robinson wasn't on
board. So, another deal was made that would send Vazquez to
Boston without touching Fossum. It was done . . . until Minaya
came back . . . (you get the idea). There was no Vaszquez, but at
least the Red Sox still had Fossum.

Fossum's presence in the must-have category among Major
League Baseball baffled the general baseball-following public. He
just didn't look the part, but he sure acted it. The war against perception had started as an eight-year-old and hadn't let up a bit. It
was back in his first year of playing Little League that this tiny kid
from Cherry Hill, New Jersey, unleashed an arm seemingly not
belonging to the frail frame it was attached to.

Most fledgling ballplayers can't throw hard enough to break a
pane of glass. Fossum went one step further, breaking the ankle
of his eight-year-old opponent with one misplaced heater. A local
legend was born. Fossum's body might not have been growing at
an expediential rate, but his reputation was. There were issues with
control (a scary proposition for potential owners of more potential broken body parts), but they weren't serious enough to keep
Fossum from entering his first big ring—the Little League Northeast championship.

Fossum was getting the call to pitch against Trumbull, Connecticut, and its star hurler, future National Hockey League player
Chris Drury. But four Cherry Hill errors in the first inning had
helped the skinny little lefty meet a most unfamiliar foe—
adversity. Drury went to Williamsport, while, soon thereafter,

Fossum and his family relocated to Waco, Texas. His dad, Jim, was an FBI agent and his business was taking the family to the southern Texas town.

Casey's war against perception would have to be waged in amongst the unfamiliar Lone Star lifestyle.

His arm predictably made its mark on his new team and teammates, but the scouts weren't so quick to start filing Fossum away. So Casey took it into his own hands. Pat Rigby, a scout with the Texas Rangers, had joined a group of talent evaluators in watching another Waco hurler. While the Midway High team took its infield and outfield pregame practice, the scouts had hunkered down along the right-field fence to dissect their subject's bullpen session when a voice bellowed toward the group of middle-aged men. It was coming from a little, skinny, obviously very young, right fielder.

"You guys will be back in two years to see me," said the high-pitched declaration. Fossum was only partly right—the scouts would come back, but sooner than he expected.

There were five no-hitters. There was the game in which he struck out nineteen batters (including Grady Little's nephew). And, of course, there was that arm. By the time the Arizona Diamondbacks selected Fossum in the seventh round of the 1996 draft, it appeared as though the war on perception had been won. He was being offered $300,000 to play professional baseball, a destination he had set his sights on every time he joined his brother, Clancy, in throwing off that mound they built in the family's backyard. But Casey wasn't satisfied, so the war waged on.

He continued to pitch for and against the best. Along with a Midway team that came within a game of the Texas state championship, Fossum also suited up for a trip to the Connie Mack World Series in Farmington, New Mexico, with the prestigious AAU Dallas Mustangs (along with Vernon Wells). Then came college, where one and one-half hours from his home he continued to fight the good fight at Texas A&M University. Perception was being whittled away, but until that first-round call came it was, in Fossum's mind, still lingering.

On the night before the 1999 draft, Fossum thought he had his victory. Red Sox area scout Jim Robinson had called, executing the procedural "is everything all right?" kind of inquiry. Bring on that first-round call. But the first wave of picks went by, and there was no mention of the skinny kid from Waco. Finally, in the sandwich round (between the first and second), "Fossum" was assigned his team. The almost-first-round status might not have been a clear-cut victory, but it was close enough. The war on perception was to be waged on a new battlefield—pro ball.

By the time the winter months before the 2003 season arrived, Fossum had kicked perception's ass. That's why teams like Montreal were waving the white flag, yearning to show the twenty-four-year-old hurler just how much it respected the unconventional pitching package. It was supposed to be the best of times for Casey, but it wasn't. Not knowing where you are going to call home is never a soothing proposition. And, to make matters worse, Fossum had committed to attending January's Boston Baseball Writer's Dinner, an event where plenty of "are you going to be traded?" questions were on the docket. The night of tuxedos and black ties wasn't panning out as the pitcher's winter wonderland.

Despite the uneasiness, Fossum boarded the plane bound for Boston. When he got off all of his fears were a thing of the past. As soon as the Federal Aviation Administration would allow, Casey turned on his cell phone. He had a message. It was a friend of his letting him know that Colon had been traded to the Chicago White Sox. In the matter of a four-hour plane ride, peace of mind was put back in the fold—or so Fossum thought.

Adversity may have introduced itself against the Trumbull Little Leaguers, but it wasn't until the 2003 spring training that the feeling fully festered in Fossum's psyche. The war on perception had shifted. No longer was it Casey's goal to prove he was simply good enough. Now it was all about showing everyone that he was good enough to be perceived better than the subjects he was supposed to be traded for. Suddenly, Bartolo Colon's spring training box scores were becoming a must-read in Boston.

Fossum had never needed to try too hard to win his battles, but something had changed. The ordained No. 3 starter in the Boston rotation was bowing before the enemy—perception—and had a 1–3 record with a 16.05 spring training ERA to show for it. It was foreign territory for a pitcher who might have had three less-than-sterling performances in an entire collegiate season, never mind a couple of sun-soaked Florida weeks. Advice was coming from everywhere—parents, friends, but most importantly, pitching coach Tony Cloninger.

Standing by his side throughout the entire spring training from hell was Cloninger, whose support finally yielded a comfortable minor league workout in the exhibition season's final week. It was enough of a building block to show regular season flashes of the darling of the off-season trade talks, the original Casey Fossum— five starts, two wins, and a 3.94 ERA in the month of April. But in May the troubles returned in the form of a hard-to-fathom 7.85 ERA. Then the woes got serious, shifting from performance to a physical ailment. Fossum had battled perception (on a variety of fronts), but now his enemy was coming in the most foreign of forms—shoulder stiffness. The body that many predicted would eventually break down finally had . . . albeit for the very first time.

Before the All-Star Game Fossum started twelve games, but since the break, leading up to Kaiser's rearview mirror exhortation, the lefty had opened a game just once. His moments since April had usually been uninspiring, although there was that one inning of relief against the New York Yankees on July 27th that stood out.

That Sunday night showdown would be remembered by many for multiple reasons—for the Boston front office guys it was the day they played pickup basketball in the morning before watching their team play from atop the Green Monster seats (ESPN had taken their usual behind-home-plate vantage points); for many of the other fans on top of the wall it was the night two guys became the first to climb up the structure from the Lansdowne Street sidewalk; for Yankees' general manager Brian Cashman it was the morning he got to take his five-year-old daughter on Boston's

Duck Boat Tour; and everybody else, the evening was simply when Jason Varitek and Johnny Damon hit huge home runs to beat New York in front of a playoff-like frenzied crowd.

Fossum, however, saw it differently. It might have been just one scoreless inning, but it was a feeling of accomplishment that had been missing for much of the season. Now, almost a month later, he was getting a chance to relive that sensation thanks to Pedro Martinez's sore throat. The numbers weren't eye-popping— five and one-third innings, eight hits, five runs—but the pitcher's aura was. Considering he had been given six hours' notice that he was going to pitch for the first time in ten days, the ability to hold the fort against the A's while his offense scored fourteen runs was much more than a footnote in Fossum's 2003 saga.

He had stared down the perception—this time that he couldn't hide Martinez's absence—and come out on top once again.

Boston took the win against Oakland, fed off its momentum, and went on to sweep its subsequent four-game series with another wild-card contender, Seattle. Fossum would only pitch one more inning the rest of the season (succumbing to more shoulder ailments) but, if nothing else, he had the memory of playing the part of Pedro for at least one late-August night.

---

*"Mister I ain't a boy, no I'm a man, and I believe
in a promised land."*

—Bruce Springsteen

DANTE RICCIARDI stared into the catcher, got the sign, and wound up ready to deliver his best "slippy-doo-slip-slip-eroo" to the waiting batter. It would have been the idealistic setting for any seven-year-old with aspirations of living out big-league dreams, except for one problem . . . there was no catcher, there was no sign, there was no ball, and there was no batter.

J.P.'s eldest son was in the zone of imagination, while his father and his dad's coworker, Law, were occupied with the ribs. Dante wanted no part of the offerings of "The Gator Pit," a barbecue area set up for patrons of the Lowell Spinners' games. Forget the corn on the cob, bring on the next imaginary hitter. It was twenty-nine days into the month of August and baseball was coursing through the Ricciardi boys' blood with a vengeance.

The last invisible batter was retired thirty minutes before the beginning of the impetus behind Ricciardi's forty-five-minute trip from West Boylston to LeLacheur Stadium—a game between Toronto's short-season Single A team Auburn and Boston's Lowell club. J.P. had already been on and off the phone more than a few times with Toronto traveling secretary Bart Given, his source for in-game information when it came to the Blue Jays. The body might have been four full levels of pro ball and thousands of miles away from the action, but a general manager's mind never leaves his team.

Given's message was that storm clouds were brewing in Cleveland. That was good news. J.P. was in Lowell to catch a glimpse for the first time of the players he drafted, not go through the once-a-week Escobar roller coaster via sporadic cell phone messages. For this one day, the less baseball the better, except, of course, if it entailed Dante striking out the mythical side sometime between a sip of lemonade and a bite of cotton candy.

By the time Ricciardi took his seat with Dante and Law directly behind home plate at the always-sold-out five-thousand-seat stadium, a rare sense of game-day relaxation came over J.P. Before Ricciardi was an Auburn team that had been running away with the New York–Penn League, built almost entirely by the efforts of Toronto's draft board almost three months earlier. For both Ricciardi and Law, this was like unwrapping a three-month-old, unidentifiable present. They were finally going to see the reason why Cashman insisted Toronto was "building the perfect beast."

But before the game began, fate decided to unleash its ironic sense of humor on the banks of the Merrimack River.

Thanks to the patron sitting directly in front of the Ricciardis,

Dante couldn't see pitch one. The obstructed view wasn't necessarily because of the youngster's height disadvantage, but more due to the blonde-streaked afro bulging out of the tilted hat just feet away.

Abe Alvarez, the vision-impaired, war-painted, crooked-hat, soft-throwing lefty that Boston beat Toronto to by one pick was charting pitches. Upon learning who the obstruction was, Ricciardi and Law just laughed. "Almost a Jay," J.P. said with a smile. They had come to see what was going to be, and been struck with an unexpected dose of what-could-have-been.

Ricciardi didn't know it, but the Blue Jays had returned the favor seven rounds later after Alvarez's number was echoed. With Jamie Vermilyea's card pulled and ready to be called in Boston's nice fat suite of a draft room, Toronto made the lanky righty pitcher their property. Draft disappointment happened, it was just that most general managers weren't confronted with staring at the one-that-got-away's head for nine innings so soon after he slipped away.

Even with the presence of Alvarez, regrets weren't anywhere to be found among the Blue Jays' brass. Josh Banks, a player that was neck-and-neck with Abe in the eyes of Toronto, was making a case for his second-round existence. And now he was minutes away from giving Ricciardi a firsthand look at what the draft's fiftieth pick was bringing the Jays.

But before Banks even took the mound, Auburn was ready to give Ricciardi, Law, and Dante a big ol' dose of Blue Jay baseball.

The Doubledays' offense was to the New York-Penn League what the Red Sox's bats were to the American League. Statistically speaking, there was Auburn and then everybody else. Batting average, home runs, RBI, and walks. You name it, Toronto's professional novices were leading the way, and doing it in the fashion befitting the big club. Wait for the right pitch, and only the right pitch, and then rip it.

Exhibit A: Leadoff man, Juan Peralta. First offering from Lowell pitcher Angel Santos—ball. Second pitch—ball. That was all it took. "He's our kind of guy," Ricciardi said to Law with a smirk.

Three offerings later and Peralta was on first base with a base hit. It was the first of five hits for the night.

Exhibit B: Jayce Tingler. "He looks like me in a uniform," said Law in amazement. At 5-foot-8, 155 pounds, the Jays' executive wasn't far off in his analysis. But not only was the outfielder a reality, he was a tenth-round reality. Tingler was drafted for his baseball instincts, but would be remembered inside the Jays' chain of command for simply being drafted.

Just about the time Toronto was set to pull the card of the University of Missouri product, Jays' president Paul Godfrey walked into the cramped space of a draft room. "Why don't you make the pick," a bystander said to the big boss. And so it was, Godfrey's only utterance into the speakerphone was to tell the baseball world Toronto was securing the unique talents of Tingler.

Ricciardi and Law would pass the word to Godfrey—don't bother looking at the player, just his numbers. And against Lowell the box score told the story of a No. 2 hitter who scored twice in just three plate appearances.

Exhibit C: Vito Chiaravalloti. What Tingler was to Godfrey, Chiaravalloti was to Law.

It was the fifteenth round, where the scouting reports meet the statistical analysis with more force than ever before. Anyone drafted on the tail end of the first day's twenty rounds more than likely never got a look-see from the Ricciardis of the world. That wouldn't come until days when short-season Single A teams like Auburn would make late-August trips to play in front of the organization's general manager.

It was why few, if any, in the Toronto draft room would have distinguished Chiaravalloti in their draft-day memory banks if not for his name. Nobody knew how to pronounce it . . . except the Blue Jays' master of statistical analysis.

Law's intelligence had never been bound by the parameters of statistics, a notion that wasn't out of the ordinary for any Harvard University graduates. While many people whittled away their time in front of the nothingness of television and the like, Keith took the time to learn one of the languages a branch from his family tree had once been immersed in—Italian. Just like analyzing baseball, it seemed like an interesting thing to do.

Now, in the fifteenth round of the 2003 draft, the Blue Jays needed someone to step up. As he had since the day's first minute, Law answered the call.

"Vito Chee-ra-va-lloti, first baseman, University of Richmond." Law had nailed it, and, judging by Vito's first three months, so had the Blue Jays.

By the time Chiaravalloti stepped to the plate in what was becoming a thirteen-run, first-inning introduction for Ricciardi to his first-place Doubledays, he had already started to make a name for himself outside of the walls of SkyDome. Vito wasn't just having a good season, he was having a historic season.

The son of two native Italians (both of whom came to the United States in 1956 yet didn't know each other for five more years) was on the cusp of a feat not accomplished in the New York–Penn League since 1972. The 6-foot-2 rock of a young man was leading the league in batting average, home runs, and RBI, known in baseball circles the most elusive of statistical prizes—the Triple Crown.

One look at Chiaravalloti and the riddle begins. How could this player, with a body that appeared born to torture opposing pitchers, slip into the part of the draft where the term "prospects" ends, and "project" begins? It wasn't as if he was hidden, not with the eventual No. 4 pick in the draft, pitcher Tim Stauffer, playing on the same Richmond team.

Adding to the mystery was Vito's statistical history, one which included shattering Richmond's marks for home runs, RBI, runs, and total bases. He even took a ton of pitches, feeding into some teams' appetite for a bevy of bases on balls. There were surely concerns, but what were they?

As the draft progressed, the potential answers flew through Chiaravalloti's mind.

Maybe it was all that time in the pool. If Chiaravalloti hadn't adjusted his schedule to become a national champion in the 100-meter backstroke, then he could have used those extra hours to perfect baseball skills that blossomed only after his mother made him play Little League.

And what if Vito ignored those Little League officials who made him drop the security blanket that was his thirty-two-ounce, Gary Carter model wooden bat when he was twelve years old? Perhaps all those whispers that he was nothing more than a product of the aluminum bat environment of college baseball would have gone away.

Then there was his speed, or lack of it. Unfortunately, teams had witnessed Chiaravalloti's lack of agility from his days of circling the bases in New York's outfield fence–free Parade Grounds. If only there was a wall, something to turn those inside-the-parkers into walk-in-the-park no-doubters, then running might simply never become an issue.

But with each round that went by, the questions became unanswerable. For the first time in his life, Chiaravalloti wasn't in control. Picking a college? Being a big fish in the small pond of Richmond was a lot easier than trying find the lead pack at Stanford. Cutting his jet-black hair? It was always Bergen Point Hair Styling if for no other reason that Vito Sr. was the owner and Vito Jr.'s pictures and awards were the wallpaper of choice. Now, however, the choice wasn't his to make.

Coming to grips with the reality of a Chiaravalloti-free first day of the draft was becoming a bit easier for Vito to digest as time passed. He decided that seeing a movie, *Bruce Almighty,* with his girlfriend would be a good way to ease the pain. That was until, while sitting in the Loews Theatres' parking lot, his mother called. She wasn't handling the rejection so well, as the sobbing on the other end of the line suggested.

Then came the beep. "Mom, hold on a second," Chiaravalloti said. On the other line was his friend, Tim O'Leary. The word was out—Keith Law had told the baseball world the Blue Jays were making the first baseman their own, and he was doing it without mispronouncing a single syllable of Vito's last name. The movie tickets were never bought, the tears transformed from agony to joy and all was right with the world in the best barbershop in Bayonne, New Jersey.

So why did it take fifteen rounds for Chiaravalloti to be claimed by a Major League team? It was eighty-five days since the question was last asked, and it still hadn't been definitively answered. Vito had hit a home run in his third at-bat as a pro and never looked back, dominating his first foray into the world of pro ball. Maybe, because of his unfathomable success, no one dared tried to define the predraft doubts.

As Ricciardi watched Chiaravalloti for the first time—a three-hit, two home run, six RBI performance—only one answer could be acceptable: Nobody knew how to pronounce his name. Toronto had laid down the Law, and Keith made it pay off in the form of a Triple Crown–winning enigma.

By the time J.P. got in his car to drive his exhausted seven-year-old back down Route 495, his quest for comfort regarding his most recent draft class had been soothed.

Alvarez might not have given up an earned run in his first nineteen professional innings, but Banks wasn't bad either. In front of J.P. he was dominant, pitching five hitless innings, striking out ten and walking just one. Maybe having pick No. 50 wasn't so bad after all.

The night's good vibes not only exuded from Auburn's starting pitcher, but its entire team. The Doubledays knew the Toronto general manager was going to be in attendance (a fact dominating pregame dugout chatter), and they were going to make the most of it.

Final score: Auburn 25, Lowell 4.

The Spinners' offices had a picture of its organization's chief, Epstein, hung above a "use only for emergencies" red phone. This night, however, it was the visitors who relayed the message to the man upstairs—congratulations on a successful 2003 draft.

"It ain't nothin' like the real thing."

—U2

FIVE DAYS LATER after Dante's night out with his dad, success had yet to be determined in the offices of the Red Sox.

Boston was a game behind Seattle in the wild card race and three in back of the inexplicably red-hot A's. The loss of Mulder obviously hadn't derailed Oakland's annual run through September, as its lot in the standings might suggest.

"They've won ten games in a row," said Epstein of the A's, soaking in the newspaper's standings while eating the second of his two-roast-beef-sandwich lunch. "How is that possible?" The reasoning really wasn't that important, the result was.

It could have been worse. Boston had been on the verge of calling the other end of the momentum-pendulum home. But its ship was seemingly steadied. The night before the Red Sox rode a classic John Burkett, six innings of one-run ball past the Chicago White Sox and the man who was never meant to wear the red and white of Boston, Bartolo Colon. It was a victory two days before the two-sandwich sit-down, however, that perhaps cemented the momentum into Boston's corner.

In Philadelphia's Veterans Stadium, the site of one of the Red Sox's most painful losses earlier in the season (a Jim Thome thirteenth-inning home run will often inflict agony), Boston battled back from a two-run deficit in the ninth, scoring six times to sweep the one-game series against the Phillies. Keying the comeback was a game-tying squibber by utility man Lou Merloni and Trot Nixon's majestic grand slam, perhaps the most emotionally charged hit of the season. The first day of the regular season's last month was becoming the wave that the Red Sox were attempting to ride all the way into the postseason.

Making the previous two days' events even more gratifying for Epstein was that the Red Sox overcame the odds . . . and the odd. Enigmatic slugger Manny Ramirez hadn't played in the previous

five games because of the combination of Martinez-induced pharyngitis and the unwillingness to properly treat the treatable ailment. The superstar now wasn't getting another treatment, that
befitting a star. He had been benched.

Epstein tried not to read the papers, although his parents now
were subscribers of both Boston dailies, as well as the *New York
Times*. But, with the roast beef wrappers still in front of him, he
wanted to get a feel for the media's take on Manny-gate, and look
at the box score showing another Oakland win. In the midst of
the newsprint, there was some good news—the transaction log was
reminding Theo he was the proud owner of a steak dinner courtesy of his old friend in San Diego, Padres' general manager Kevin
Towers.

Epstein and Towers, one of the game's best talent evaluators,
loved to test each other. Who was better, that player or that
player? Or was it that guy who was going to make it, or this guy?
The Padres' GM had gotten the head start on breaking down the
intricacies of a prospect, having come up through the ranks of the
organization as a scout. But Theo was closing fast, as was exemplified by the September 3 list of baseball transactions: San Diego had
called up pitcher Mike Bynum.

Bynum was a guy who battled knee problems since being
selected in the first round of the 1999 draft. He had seemingly lost
his slider, and status as a top prospect in the Padres' system. But
he hadn't lost an ally in Epstein. But when it came time for "who
we're keeping, who we're leaving behind" types of decisions,
Towers preferred an athletic outfielder named Darren Blakely. The
two players were spawning a San Diego front office ritual—the
reliance on a steak dinner to identify the premier talent evaluator.
Whoever had their allotted minor leaguer make it to the majors
first, then the other was on the hook for the tab at Outback Steak
House.

The smile on Epstein's face announced the results: Bynum had
become a big leaguer for the second time in two years, while
Blakely was getting ready to suit up for the Independent League
Brockton Rox thirty miles down Interstate 95. In a time of the sea-

son where doubt resides around every corner, it was, if nothing else, a nice bit of reaffirmation.

Despite all the wins, the residence in the race for the postseason and the Bynum-enhanced sense of accomplishment, the feeling in the baseball operations corridor was unlike anything the new regime had experienced. The last day of August took with it the final chance for teams to improve their rosters with playoff-eligible players. It also left Epstein with a certain feeling of helplessness. These were the players that were going to have to get it done.

Was the roster positioned just as Epstein had imagined? Not quite. The particulars from the Crustacean Creation, pitchers Jeff Suppan and Scott Sauerbeck, had been unnervingly ineffective. So while the players their fans morphed with the saying, "Cowboy Up," thanks to the everyday vocabulary of Nixon and the T-shirt design of reliever Mike Timlin, the front office circled its wagons around another slogan: "We don't know shit!"

The organizational philosophy had taken a turn toward self-effacing reality. If there was one thing the season taught the Red Sox decision makers it was that you never really have it all figured out. And just at the precise moment that you do believe the truth has been nailed, it does a 180-degree turn. They didn't know shit, but neither did anyone else in baseball.

In the eyes of the suddenly enlightened Red Sox, they could do the exact opposite of what they thought to be correct and it would probably work out 50 percent of the time. The T-shirts were in the works: "We don't know shit!" on the front hovering over a picture of the ultimate head-scratcher, the $32 million Cuban, Jose Contreras.

So while The Nation frowned and fretted in the opening days of September (third-grade classrooms were abuzz with the talk of pharyngitis), the front office escaped from the "what could have beens" and "what might bes" over to nearby Clemente Field. Contrary to the perception of the always-nervous Red Sox fan base, the only afternoon worry the front office had on the second day of September was whether or not Epstein and Hoyer were going to be able to out-duel Carr's team in their three-on-three, touch football clash.

The day after the big games (on Clemente, and in Chicago), with Boston's baseball operations' personnel walking appreciably more gingerly than normal, Theo continued to read about Manny, the A's winning streak, and the New England Patriots releasing their starting safety, Lawyer Milloy. The final news was perhaps even more perplexing than any of the other items. "Why would they do that right before their first game?" he asked, along with the rest of New England. He, of all people, knew general managers (regardless of the sport) had their reasons.

But the move did present a problem—what was Epstein going to do with his No. 36, blue-and-white Milloy game jersey? It was in that shirt, after all, that he had kicked a fifty-three-yard field goal in front of fellow Padres employee Jason MacLeod at a San Diego area high school. Acquiring utility infielders was nice, but fifty-yarders were the stuff of legends.

Finally, the newspaper had been dissected to Epstein's satisfaction and the oddly helpless September existence continued. This season, which had passed with remarkable speed, was now being slowed by pennant race speed bumps known as the hours before game time. The paper was read, check. The sandwiches had been devoured, check. Next on the list was preparing for that night's interoffice fantasy football draft, a task made appreciably easier thanks to the help of Epstein's assistant, Brian O'Halloran.

In the sea of out of the ordinary stories regarding how the Red Sox baseball operations staff came to be, nobody could quite match O'Halloran. He was one of the department's elder statesmen (thirty-two), but looked younger than any of his coworkers. His was a journey that began just south of Boston in Weymouth, ventured through the Soviet Republic of Georgia, stopped for a while in Los Angeles, then San Diego, before settling down in an unsettling existence back in his home state.

Like Epstein, the diminutive O'Halloran's baseball career peaked out in Little League, where he earned All-Star status for three years before playing just one junior varsity season at Weymouth South High. His path from high school took him to Colby College in Maine, where academia included a double-major in political science and Russian studies. The seeds being planted in O'Halloran's future weren't exactly looking like they were going to reap the bounty of baseball.

O'Halloran got even further away from his favorite game, and hometown, when he spent his entire junior year living in a very different Georgia than the one claiming Atlanta as its capital. He arrived in the country in September 1991 and three months later there was no more country. O'Halloran saw tanks, demonstrations, and, just for good measure, a few civil wars. The U.S. State Department had advised all Americans to depart the country, but O'Halloran stayed put in his electricity- and running water-free place in the capital city of Tbilisi (for a while anyway). Suddenly, the twenty-year-old Weymouth Little Leaguer's claim to fame was that he was the only American left in a collapsing country.

O'Halloran finished out his senior year at Colby, but returned to Tbilisi after graduation after being awarded a fellowship to study ethnic conflict. Dreams of interviewing ballplayers with names only a diehard fan could pronounce had unexpectedly morphed into seeking out foreign presidents with monikers only a diehard political science major could utter stutter-free (somehow "Shevardnadze" just rolled off the tongue).

His ability to speak fluently in both Russian and Georgian (two totally separate dialects) finally paid off in the professional world when a Washington, D.C., international logistics company sent him to Russia for three years. But baseball had planted itself in O'Halloran's mind, and at twenty-seven years old he was starting to see the dream of baseball-induced income passing by with each mind-numbingly cold Russian day. Rubles or no rubles, he was coming home to take his best shot at entering the back door of his dream.

The gateway to the big leagues started forming with letters and e-mails to anyone associated with the game—executives, agents, Colby graduates, anybody. The success was moderate, with O'Halloran taking up shop in the Pawtucket Red Sox's group sales department for a summer, while also dabbling with the sports agency service, Woolf Associates. Still not satisfied with his direction, he journeyed to Los Angeles to start his quest for an MBA while attending UCLA. The miles were piling up, and so were the contacts.

Finally, in January 2002 it all paid off. After meeting the Padres' people, Epstein and Towers, at the baseball Winter Meetings in Boston, O'Halloran joined up with San Diego as a baseball operations intern. He scouted, delved into contracts, and flirted with statistical analysis, all the while convincing his fiancee, Jean, this wasn't a hollow promise. The internship was encouraging, but still not enough to keep him from pulling up shop and moving back to Boston so that his wife-to-be could begin her own quest—garnering a master's degree in language and literacy at Harvard.

By this time Epstein had already carved out the course toward the East Coast, making his mark at Fenway. O'Halloran knew that even with his connection, a job with the Red Sox wasn't a realistic possibility. What Theo could, and did, do, however, was open the Sox offices' door for middle-of-the-night and weekend volunteer work (there wasn't enough computers or cubicles for an unpaid assistant to be hanging around during the daylight hours). Money was running out, but O'Halloran's experience was flowing over. Finally, persistence paid off.

The businesslike baseball wannabe need not want to anymore. He was. In January 2003, the Red Sox hired O'Halloran as Epstein's administrative assistant, doing everything from manning the radar gun to sorting out the department's budget. There was no need for Russian translations, and experience with revolutions wasn't a must. But there was an opening for someone who desperately wanted to mix up a whole lot of smarts with just as much passion for a pennant, and that description fit Brian O'Halloran like a well-measured Cossack.

Now, with a month to play in O'Halloran's first full-time season, the task was simple: hand over a manila folder full of football playing identities that had enough potential to earn a spot on Epstein's Fighting Fish Tacos.

If it weren't for O'Halloran, Theo would be left helpless drafting in the eighth spot of the twelve-team league. (After all, he was running a Major League Baseball team.) But at least the GM looked the part, exuding the casual nature of the post-trade deadline days with a black-and-white sweat suit.

"Who are you, Al Davis?" asked a voice from the hallway, referring to Epstein's wardrobe's similarity to that of the no-hold's-barred owner of the NFL's Oakland Raiders.

"That's right . . . 'Just win baby!'" boasted the Boston GM.

A slogan for the stretch drive had been set.

CHAPTER 10

Somewhat Happy Trails

"There isn't a better place to play baseball."

—Tim Wakefield

It was like comparing a Picasso to a Warhol—one picture not even reminiscent of the other.

The scene being portrayed in St. Petersburg just two hours before Boston's third to last game of the season couldn't have been any different than what the Red Sox left behind at Fenway Park the night before. Gone were the images of crazed fans and champagne-doused players from a playoff-clinching, postgame party. It had been a celebration built from a season-long trek through uncertainty, culminating with a win in the final regular-season home game over the Baltimore Orioles.

The lockers were plastered with plastic, "Wild Card Champions" T-shirts and hats were strewn everywhere, and players had even run down Yawkey Way in nearly full uniforms to enjoy the fruits of their labor with a barroom full of delirium. The Red Sox were headed to the playoffs, but first they were going to take a three day Florida vacation. Peace, quiet, and hangovers—all symbolized by the chirping of a cricket.

Just 120 minutes from the first pitch and Tropicana Field was deathly quiet, so silent that the only obstruction on the path to Zen was a single cricket's sporadic chirp at the far end of the visitors' dugout. In Boston, a blow horn had no guarantee of being heard in the hubbub of pregame anticipation, never mind the exultation of an insect.

But this wasn't Fenway Park, it was the home of the striving-for-a-better-life Devil Rays. As predicted, Tampa Bay's opening day celebration against the Red Sox had peaked out the noise meter—a notion that was more than welcome to a Boston team that was in dire need of a break from commotion. The last series of the weekend didn't mean anything, and for that the Sox could thank the pinnacle all run-producing lineups.

By the time the schedule's final Fenway games came around, the Red Sox already had their spot in the history books. September 17 saw Boston take claim to the Major League record for most extra-base hits in a season (608), while the mark for best slugging percentage (held by baseball's credo when it came to offensive symbolism, the 1927 New York Yankees), was waiting at season's end. The Boston front office had put together a run-scoring concoction that was now just a few wins, or Seattle losses, away from showing its stuff in the postseason. But, evidently, the Baltimore Orioles weren't impressed enough to roll out the playoff welcome mat.

The Orioles, a team that had been the Red Sox's bed of nails throughout the season, were giving the Fenway patrons those all-too-familiar chills. They were feelings not lost on Theo Epstein. On the night of September 23, it was hard enough to swallow the reality that was a 5–2 Baltimore lead heading in the bottom of the ninth, but he was also dealing with an obstacle course of emotions along the way. Perched in his usual behind-home-plate seat, Epstein was being showered with a Budweiser-laced tirade from a fan hoping to garner the kind of attention his parents evidently never gave him.

Theo knew his visibility in amongst the cramped spaces of Fenway would always be a catch-22. Kevin Towers, his San Diego mentor, had helped Epstein learn the value of seeing the game from behind the plate. You learn—from the pitchers, from the batters, and from the scouts sitting to the left, right, front, and back. In his seven years at the helm of the Padres, Towers hadn't once watched a road game from anywhere but the stands, and, if at all possible, it was a practice Epstein was going to take up in Boston.

There was also the distraction of the cell phone, although that was of Theo's choosing. The season had become, as Jed Hoyer described it, "The Summer of the Cell Phone." Epstein used it for everything—transactions, a method to allow for some often-needed personal space, and, more and more frequently, the source for in-game, out-of-town scores. What was Seattle doing? In between watching the Baltimore-induced bad news and trying to ignore the drunken insults from just below Section 21, the Mariners-Anaheim score was a top priority. The Red Sox lineup was good (maybe even great), but until Seattle lost too many, or Boston won just enough, it wasn't going to meet The Nation's requirements.

So with the Mariners' game just getting under way in Anaheim, and Epstein's heckler feeling the effects of the seventh-inning beer tap shut-off, Todd Walker stepped to the plate. Two runners, Nomar Garciaparra and Jason Varitek, were on base, but the chances of the laid-back Louisianan second baseman making up the three-run deficit with a two-out home run off of the league's hardest thrower, Jorge Julio, seemed remote at best.

The moment wasn't without some hope for the Sox, for, if nothing else, Walker could flat-out hit (always could). His smooth left-handed swing had hit at Louisiana State University, and in a world he hadn't even visited as a fan before breaking in with Minnesota in 1996—the Major Leagues. This is why he was in Boston, because the Red Sox needed a second baseman who could hit.

The thirty-year-old did have his drawbacks, most revolving around fielding range that resulted in more failed dives into the dirt than any infielder in baseball. But there were so many other positives, which was the reason why Boston started talking with Cincinnati general manager Jim Bowden in the early days of December. Bowden was one of the few GMs who negotiated deals via e-mail, a fact Epstein found out when delving into Walker's availability. First came the talk of Boston getting relievers Gabe White and Scott Sullivan, along with Walker, for some minor leaguers. Then it was just White and Walker for a few youngsters. Then a deal was struck through the art of the e-mail—Walker for two prospects. The Red Sox had their second baseman, while Epstein claimed his first Internet-consummated trade.

Now the Red Sox were counting on Walker—not the unsure-of-himself player who hit below .216 through the dog days of July and August, but rather the September juggernaut who would finish the month at a .347 clip. The Louisiana lefty would have to bring Boston further away from the edge of postseason uncertainty. He delivered.

With the count 3-and-2, Walker turned around a ninety-eight-mile-an-hour Julio heater, lofting it just high and long enough to reach the safety of the Boston bullpen. Most of the Red Sox front office types sitting around Epstein stood in anticipation, not fully believing the ball had enough legs to eclipse the right-field boundary. Epstein, however, didn't stand. Instead, he just stared into the back of the fan in front of him and waited for the sellout crowd's reaction. The back jumped up and down, the air became thick with euphoria, and the Red Sox lived to play another inning.

By the time the Red Sox came up in the tenth inning, Baltimore had a new pitcher, Kurt Ainsworth, but the karma around Fenway Park hadn't changed a bit. Walker's three-run home run had added a most unexpected dose of elation to a season already chock-full of titillating surprises. Now it was David Ortiz's turn.

Ortiz was the mountain of a man nobody ever seemed too thrilled to fully discover. His four seasons with Minnesota never resulted in more than 130 games played, which sadly seemed about right. He did hit a career-high twenty home runs in 2002, but even those totals didn't appear to do his 6-foot-4, 230-plus-pound frame justice. Still, after the '02 campaign the twenty-seven-year-old Dominican became a free agent, and that was good enough for the Red Sox to put him on their list.

While wading through the off-season, the Boston front office knew its team needed two or three more bats, preferably coming from players manning the first base/designated hitter positions. The available subjects were targeted—Kevin Millar, Jeremy Giambi, Travis Lee, Greg Colbrunn, Brad Fullmer, and Ortiz. The Millar saga was just taking root, while Giambi would be traded for in the middle of December. The finalists for the third spot came down to Ortiz, a player the Sox tried to deal for during the previous season's trading deadline, and the powerfully built Fullmer.

Two scouts were sent to Los Angeles to work out Fullmer, while another, Dave Jauss, was dispatched to the Dominican Republic to give Ortiz a look-see. The Sox's biggest concern regarding Ortiz was his ability to field even the most stagnant of stations—first base. Jauss sent the report: The jovial, far-from-chiseled Ortiz looked good . . . good enough to sign.

As it turned out, Ortiz's glove was good enough, although he wouldn't need it. Millar eventually became the everyday guy at the not-so-hot corner, allowing Ortiz to flourish in his natural position, designated hitter. By the time Ainsworth delivered his first pitch, the player known for his choice of hugs over handshakes was leading the Red Sox in go-ahead and two-out RBI. One 2-and-1 change-up later, and Ortiz's totals had been added to.

Epstein immediately turned to find his heckler, but he was conveniently lost in the commotion of Fenway's disappearing skepticism. Regardless, Fenway disc jockey Megan Kaiser had popped in Boston's victory march, the Standells' "I Love That Dirty Water," and life was good. It would take another Seattle loss and one more Red Sox win to make it official, but Ortiz's homer was what really allowed everyone to soak in the inevitable—Boston was heading to St. Petersburg with a date to play in the postseason.

Forty-three hours after Ortiz executed his 360-foot victory lap around the bases, the cricket's chirp subsided, the Tropicana Field lights eventually were brought to full power, and a crowd of what seemed like 21,000 Red Sox fans and 240 Devil Rays boosters piled in to watch Pedro Martinez pitch three meaningless innings.

For a team that was clothed by home run heroics, apathy never fit better.

"Experience is the accumulation of your mistakes."

—Carlos Tosca's father, Carlos Enrique Tosca

THE SEASON-ENDING weekend 1,097 miles north of Tropicana Field was exactly that for the Blue Jays—the end of their season. There would be no playoffs, no Wild Card Champion hangovers and no postseason roster decisions. Unfortunately for the Jays, the only common thread they shared with the Red Sox's Florida sojourn was an overriding "who cares" from the baseball-attending public. But those in Toronto should have cared; they were watching a pivotal step in the Blue Jays' ever-accelerating building process.

The paths taken by the two teams to get to their respective three-game series weren't as different as the attendance figures and spot in the standings, might have suggested. Just as Boston had erupted into a ball of uncontrollable elation following Thursday's clincher, a similar sample-size celebration took its place in the box of the Blue Jays' general manager. With the usual crew in attendance—J.P. Ricciardi, Tim McCleary, Keith Law, Ron Sandelli—Carlos Delgado, the $18-million-a-year exception to the Jays' rule of frugality, was kicking off the campaign's feel-good final four days.

Delgado was a player who was doing everything in his power to justify his exorbitant paychecks. He worked hard, got along with his teammates, and most importantly, made pitchers feel like wetting their pants. Carlos could hit home runs, and with just over thirteen thousand fans in the stands and four pieces of the front office in the GM's bunker, he decided to hit four of them against Tampa Bay. The 1,646 feet worth of Delgado-driven rockets had left Ricciardi and his guys aglow (and it had nothing to do with the suffocating heat given off from the sign just below the box's first row of seats).

Two days later, it was the turn of Harry Leroy Halladay III to lead the Blue Jays' charge into the off-season.

By the time Roy (Harry never stuck, from first grade and on) Halladay stared down at Cleveland Indians batter Johnny Peralta, the notion that the 6-foot-6, red-bearded Colorado native was about to earn his team-record twenty-second win of the season had been more than digested by the Jays' followers. He did, after all, win fifteen straight decisions before succumbing on the first day of August. (His propensity to overstride on his delivery had finally gotten the better of him.) In the past two seasons, Halladay grabbed forty of his fifty-eight career victories, and in the last month of the '03 season the twenty-six-year-old was giving up less than one and a half runs per every nine innings.

Baseball had been witnessing Halladay's best, which was now the Major League's best.

The sight of the Toronto's ace keenly setting up hitters with his ninety-five-mile-an-hour fastball before sending their buckled knees back to the dugout courtesy of a well-hidden, tumbling knuckle-curveball was a source of comfort for the entire Blue Jays' family. But the No. 1 starter kind of security Toronto had come to count on from Halladay wasn't always a way of life, even in the '03 season.

Just five months before, Paul Godfrey sat in his Fenway Park box seat hoping for the best from his staff ace, but witnessing the worst.

"C'mon Doc," Godfrey yelled to the pitcher carrying the nickname derived from the Old West character, Doc Holliday. "I think this is the game Doc really gets it going," the Jays' president then said to whoever might be within earshot. It was Easter Sunday and Godfrey's entire family had made the trip to Boston. The only thing that would make the moment better was if this game was, indeed, the day Halladay really got it going.

It wasn't fair, but Halladay's low points were always looked upon with the memory of two years before not far behind . . . memories that were pigeon-holing a career's rough spots.

Roy was the can't-miss kid from Arvada West High—striking out 105 batters in sixty-three innings in his senior season with the Wildcats, while also finishing third in the Colorado High School Cross Country Championships for good measure. He was the kid who had learned the pitching rights and wrongs from Roger Clemens' two-year stay at SkyDome and was going to be Blue Jays' next "Rocket." He was the kid who came one out away from throwing a no-hitter in just his second start in the Majors. But by the beginning of the 2001 season, he was also the kid who had fallen all the way back down to Dunedin. It was an existence even the pies at Iris's Restaurant couldn't make an optimistic dent in.

Maybe it was the pressure that came with signing a three-year, $3.7 million contract well before anyone anticipated such a deal would be broached. Maybe it was simply the entire package of expectations. But whatever the reason, Halladay knew careers and future multimillion dollar contracts are never built by the kind of ERA that he constructed in 2000 (10.64). It was a fact nobody had to tell him, but was reinforced by the Jays anyway when the organization left him behind in Dunedin upon the start of the '01 season.

Roy's mentor was his dad (a pilot by the same name as his son). Next came nearby pitching guru Bus Campbell, who was handed the reigns to Halladay's development by the aspiring hurler's twelfth birthday. But by the time a pen swooped "Roy Halladay" onto that first contract in 1995 (instantly making Roy an eight-hundred-and-ninety-five-thousandaire) the lanky righty was more on his own than ever.

It was a scenario that appeared to be working fine, with Campbell watching the games on the satellite dish the Halladays gave him for Christmas in '98, and Dad keeping in constant touch. But this unexpected trip back to the minors called for some new interference. That's where one jack-of-all-trades pitching coach and one purveyor of the athletic mind came in.

Mel Queen, the Blue Jays' no-nonsense, organizational pitcher-fixer, first got Halladay's physical peccadilloes in order. The arm angle was dropped, and a curveball was rediscovered. Instead of the straight-as-an-arrow balls Roy had been becoming all too familiar with, the pitcher was now making his pitches predictably unpredictable. Then came the second phase of Halladay's reconstruction—controlling his mind with the adeptness he had displayed in harnessing his heater.

Harvey Dorfman, a sports psychologist who had ingrained himself into the fabric of more than a few baseball teams, was going to convince Halladay to hold himself accountable. Gone was the feeling of what might go wrong, and in its place was a knowledge of what was going to go right. There was a reason he had fought back the thin air of his 5,380-feet-above-sea level hometown to become Colorado's best prep pitcher of all time. Roy just had to remember what that reason was.

By the time the season of transformation ended, and '02 began, Halladay was ready to burst with the anticipation of achievement. The result was unbelievably heartening (to both the pitcher and his bosses)—an American League-best 239$^1/_3$ innings, nineteen wins, a 2.93 ERA, and twenty-four games in which he went seven innings or longer. The kid from Arvada was back.

"That's the Doc I'm used to seeing," continued Godfrey after a strikeout of Boston batter Kevin Millar. The team's president had seen enough of Halladay to know the good from the bad, and the new from the old. Roy wouldn't win that day, still working out the kinks that staff aces from around the league always encounter at some point. But, as Godfrey observed, dominance wasn't far away.

More than three exclusively victorious months later, Halladay finally lost a game. Almost two months after that, he was making his final start of the season fully immersed in the supremacy Godfrey had foreseen on the chilly, sun-soaked April day.

The pitcher who documents his game plan on paper before

each game, handing it out to his catcher and Toronto pitching coach Gil Patterson, was just finishing off his latest script. "Peralta, 4–3." The Blue Jays won their eighteenth game of the month and the 21,154 SkyDome fans rose in appreciation—of a pitcher and his team's season.

A day later Toronto won again, giving it eighty-six for the season. Handshakes from Ricciardi were once again in order—to the boys in the box, the players, coaches, and even the group of field caretakers dubbed "The World's Fastest Grounds Crew." It seemed like just the other day that the general manager sat on an exercise bike in the heat of spring training yearning to build around an eighty-five-win season. As far as he was concerned, the Blue Jays were one game ahead of the curve.

As the good feelings of Toronto's second straight nineteen-win September slowly left the clubhouse, heading for the anticipation of the next season, Ricciardi took up residence with Brian Butterfield in SkyDome's coaches' room. Forget reminiscing and pats on the back; in the eyes of Butter there was only one way to celebrate—watching a New England Patriots game against the Washington Redskins. There wasn't any "Do Not Disturb" sign on the door, but the third base coach sure wished there was. There was a baseball season to remember and a football team to follow.

Butter and J.P. weren't alone in their attention shifts. In the Tropicana Field visitors' clubhouse Lou Merloni, the Boston Red Sox utility infielder from Framingham, Massachusetts, was also transfixed on his Patriots. Most of Framingham Lou's teammates had already hit the road, leaving him standing in the middle of the spacious room gazing at two of the four television sets hanging from the ceiling. It would be one of the last bits of solitude before the insanity of the playoffs began.

It was getting to be about that time—where a football season's birth meets the death of all but eight baseball teams. The Red Sox were one of those teams still living.

"If you don't want Billy to play for you, don't watch him play."

—William Mueller Sr.

MERLONI FINALLY LEFT the spacious Tropicana Field visitors' locker room, disgusted with the Patriots' inability to mount a game-winning drive. One person, however, still remained. Bill Mueller sat in his corner locker, still not even approaching the finality of a shower and clean set of street clothes. The third baseman wasn't quite ready to let the 162-game schedule drift off.

Mueller—the player whose "highlight" reel had given the Red Sox front office a dose of the second-thought chills—was balancing his checkbook as the proud owner of the American League batting title.

Mueller's former San Francisco Giants manager, Dusty Baker, had told the unassuming third baseman's parents, Bill Sr. and Barbara, at a 1998 charity function, that someday their son was going to win a batting championship. Either Baker was being nice to the folks, or he had correctly executed one of baseball's most unrealistic prophecies.

The 5-foot-9, 175-pound Mueller played hard, could man a mean third base, and did hit .300 or above in each of his four minor league seasons. But possessing the supreme batting average in all of either the American or National Leagues after 162 games wasn't part of the plan. Yet, neither was making it to the Majors.

Bill Sr. knew by the time his only son reached eleven years old that Billy wasn't going to be a big kid. Big Bill was sold on the Little Leaguer's talent—thanks in part to the duo's four-day-a-week games of hit and catch behind their Maryland Heights, Missouri, condominium. But he knew that doing what you can with what you have was just as big a priority as extracting the talent (a lesson that allowed Bill Sr. to serve as the goalie for the two-time NCAA national champion St. Louis University men's soccer team). Billy needed an edge. He needed to switch-hit.

263

So during Billy's eleventh summer, his father started trying something different. The kid could already shoot a basketball with his left hand, and adeptly kick a soccer ball lefty as well. So the segue to hitting from the other side of the plate only seemed natural. Billy couldn't try the feat competitively, but that didn't mean the bucket of thirty to thirty-five tennis balls weren't going to be fired back from both a right-handed and left-handed batter. Bill Sr. knew the time would come when the talent would reap dividends; his son was just going to have to trust him.

Finally, in the last game as a twelve-year-old Little Leaguer, Billy was allowed to give it a try. Six hits later and the hesitation was nothing more than a memory.

The hits didn't stop coming, and neither did 101 reasons why Billy was a ballplayer's ballplayer. There was that big tournament game against Crestwood High when, with two outs, the bases loaded and the score knotted up, Mueller worked a full count before finally drawing a walk to bring in the winning run for his DeSmet High team. Or the instance while at Southwest Missouri State that saw the then-senior shortstop execute a perfect slide home in front of the sea of scouts there to see Wichita State pitcher Darren Dreifort. The run won the game for SMSU and earned Billy a whole new wave of respect.

"We'll see you in the big leagues someday," the strapping Dreifort said while patting the much-shorter Mueller on the head following the game-winning sprint home. The pitcher had been subjected to the obvious—look past the height and weight, watch Billy play, and become a believer.

Someone saw something in Mueller. That's why with the 414th pick in the 1993 draft, San Francisco took the undersized switch-hitter. And just because Billy was getting paid, that didn't mean anything was going to change. Year after year, starting in Single A Everett, then moving through San Jose, Shreveport, and Phoenix before finally settling in San Francisco, Billy kept on swinging that unmistakable swing. Big Bill's tennis ball soft-tosses were being replaced by top-shelf fastballs, but that didn't alter an ambidextrous cut that took shape more than fourteen years before the Giants called in 1996.

Sit back . . . weight on back foot . . . bat held high . . . let the hips lead the way . . . explode toward the ball not leaving any bit of energy behind. This was Billy's swing behind the family's Maryland Heights condo, and this was Billy's swing when the Red Sox came calling with a two-year contract. Like it or not, there was usually no arguing with the results.

But by the time a deal was signed with Boston, the swing had been getting rusty. Two years in Chicago with the Cubs yielded two extended trips to the disabled list due to a problem with a left knee that was mangled by the brick Wrigley Field wall. Mueller paid the price going after a foul pop, sliding into the grandstand's barrier, leaving him out of action for most of the 2001 season, and out of the Cubs' plans for much of the following campaign.

For a kid who was born on St. Patrick's Day, good luck wasn't exactly setting up shop in Billy's corner.

The run on misfortune didn't seem to stop upon his exit from the Windy City, as was displayed by Mueller's spring training with his new team. The uncertainties of unfamiliar surroundings and old knees contributed to a .188 batting average for Boston's entire preseason. Not helping Billy's faith in his role with the Red Sox was that the player the Sox figured they would have traded by the time the regular season arrived, Shea Hillenbrand, entered the real games carrying a .448 spring average.

But, just like always, Mueller might not have been given a spot on the inside lane, but when it mattered the most, he was the one leading the pack. Hillenbrand left town, Billy was given the every-day third base job and Big Bill and Barbara were left revolving their evenings around whatever pictures their satellite dish could deliver. Fortunately for the Mueller family, the season provided crystal clear images of a most familiar sight—Billy getting hits.

By the time Boston's three-day vacation in St. Petersburg came around Mueller had gotten enough hits to join the company of New York's Derek Jeter and teammate Manny Ramirez in the race for a batting championship. It was the night before the final game of the regular season and Billy, the kid responsible for more than a litter of stray tennis balls in Maryland Heights was carrying a .327 batting average, one point better than Jeter.

Earlier that day, Epstein had approached Mueller with the organization's plan. Manny wasn't playing and Jeter was still chasing, so it was suggested that Billy not be penciled in the starting lineup while the powers that be kept an eye on the Yankees game. But no matter what the approach, Mueller wasn't about to get his hopes up. Winning ball games, staying healthy, and being ready for the playoffs were the priorities; monitoring the Yankees' shortstop wasn't.

Most didn't realize it, but the seemingly innocuous third baseman had already drowned in the emotional waves of postseason awards. Three years before, Mueller led the entire National League in fielding percentage, making one less error than Philadelphia's Scott Rolen in the exact same number of chances. Yet, when the prestigious Gold Gloves were handed out to the perceived best fielders at each position, Mueller was left empty-handed. It was a memory that helped Billy brace himself for disappointment.

The night before the league's statistical judgment day, Mueller hung out with teammates Bill Haselman and Doug Mirabelli back at the team's haunted hotel, The Vinoy. Unlike when Scott Williamson made his not-of-this-world sighting earlier in the season, there were no ghosts lurking around the hotel bar. There were, however, some things potentially more frightening—Red Sox fans on vacation. The sign out front asked visitors not to take pictures with the famous guests, but it said nothing about good luck embraces, and "I'm not a lunatic" messages of congratulations. They couldn't help themselves, these were the adopted sons of New England.

And along with the stream of brazen, open-ended conversations came mentions of the batting title. For one day, Mueller was going to the preeminent priority for The Nation.

As the day of the game unfolded, Big Bill was putting his satellite dish to the test. For most of the season the task had been to simply pick up the voices of Red Sox announcers Don Orsillo and

Jerry Remy. This Sunday afternoon there was going to be some serious multitasking. The Yankees game, and every Derek Jeter at-bat that went with it, had become priority 1A.

By day's end Jeter had gone 0-for-3, while Mueller executed one token appearance after the Yankees shortstop's first two fruitless at-bats. Big Bill and Barbara had nothing to worry about. The champagne was put in their son's locker and Billy had his batting title.

"This moment is exactly as it should be."
—the sign over Red Sox outfielder Gabe Kapler's locker

FOR SEVEN YEARS Ricciardi resisted the temptation, first with Dante and then Mariano. He was not going to take them to Fenway Park until it was certain that they would remember what they experienced. J.P. still remembered walking out early on his first trip to the expanse of green concrete and red plastic seats, hearing Ray Fosse's home run upon hitting the sidewalk, and he wasn't going to deprive his kids of a similar piece of nostalgia.

On a crystal clear Sunday afternoon in early October Ricciardi finally gave in. The kids were going to Fenway.

If there was ever going to be a game that embedded itself in the minds of fledgling baseball fans it was going to be the fourth game of Boston's best-of-five playoff series with the Oakland A's (or at least, that was the premise J.P. was going with). So, along with Diane and some other family members, Dante and Mariano were dressed in matching green-and-white polo shirts and handed one baseball cap apiece, one a blue Red Sox hat and the other symbolizing the green and gold of the A's.

Sure, Dante's A's hat elicited a few cross-eyed looks from the Red Sox fans whose season was one loss away from ending. But J.P. and Diane didn't care. For mom, the support for Oakland seemed only right since it was the organization that helped the

Ricciardis pay for their house and 401K plan. Dad's acceptance of the headgear was simple: he still had a legion of friends on the visitors side, including his best buddy, A's general manager Billy Beane.

Two nights before Billy and J.P. had gotten the chance to execute an increasingly uncommon occurrence—catching up over some drinks and a couple plates of food.

There was a lot to talk about at the dinner for two at Boston's Capital Grille. Beane's A's had played two, tough-to-figure games against Boston, winning both. For Billy, pinpointing what had happened and how it might effect the immediate future was a priority. Deciphering the week's goings-on was a dilemma that was heavily on the mind of not only Billy, but also his Red Sox counterpart, Epstein. Simply put, the playoffs were making everyone dizzy.

The Game 1 frustration for Epstein had started early, with the inexplicable sight of an A's coach walking in the Red Sox locker room forty-five minutes before the game to get an autograph from Boston shortstop Nomar Garciaparra. Epstein knew the postseason setting was going to be somewhat surreal (having experienced San Diego's run to the World Series in 1998), but having the opposition cross enemy lines to enhance a lithograph just minutes before a postseason's beginning was, in Theo's eyes, too much.

The vibe causing Epstein's sinking feeling officially culminated four hours and thirty-seven minutes after the first pitch was thrown. At 2:45 A.M. Eastern Standard Time, The Nation was shocked when Oakland catcher Ramon Hernandez executed a perfect two-out, bases-loaded bunt to score Eric Chavez with the game-winning run. While the result might have been shocking to the Red Sox, the manner in which its final scene had been set wasn't. They had the reports—Hernandez had a propensity to bunt in such situations—but Boston didn't have the correct execution.

It was also the last time Boston's sidewinding Korean, Byung-Hyun Kim, would pitch in the playoffs. After a September in which he hadn't given up an earned run, Kim opened the door for

Oakland by issuing a walk and hitting a batter to begin the ninth inning. Then, in a cruel twist of fate, the player the Red Sox had originally thought they were getting back for Shea Hillenbrand (before Kim), Erubiel Durazo, sent the game into extra innings with a two-out, opposite field single off Alan Embree. Meanwhile, the A's bullpen was in the midst of shutting out the historically embedded Sox lineup for five and one-third innings. That left room for the Hernandez heroics.

One hundred years before, to the day, Boston faced off with the Pittsburgh Pirates in the first World Series game ever played. Judging by the problems emanating from Game 1, and the subsequent 5–1 loss the next afternoon, it didn't appear as though a centennial reunion with the Series was shaping up for the Sox. Epstein and the boys were heading back to Boston one loss away from entering a place Toronto and twenty-one other Major League teams were all too familiar with—the off-season.

Chuck Millar had watched his son, Kevin, struggle with the rest of his history-making lineup mates against Oakland pitchers Tim Hudson and Barry Zito. He knew the pain Kevin must have been going through. But then, well into the night, hours after the Red Sox Game 2 loss, Chuck got a call. The Beaumont Basher sure didn't sound like a guy who was teetering on the edge of elimination.

"Hey dad," a still wide-awake Kevin said. "You'll never believe what we're doing. I'm in the trainer's room getting my head shaved." The mullet was being transformed, and so was a mindset. Gone was the hair of more than half the roster (eventually including Epstein and the rest of baseball operations thanks to the handiwork of Galen Carr) and with it went the memory of what happened in Oakland.

The night after Ricciardi and Beane's Capital Grille get-together, Boston stared down Game 3 and all the misery it potentially carried. Some of the Oakland players, who had already been bombarded with the questions of losing a two-game lead for the second straight season, knew in warm-ups that something was already awry. The A's were throwing the ball all over the place, a trend that eventually led to four Oakland errors (three in one inning). Then came a sign. Forget the haircuts. Forget all the statistics. Forget the cowboy hat–infested crowd. When two base runners get thrown out at the plate in the same inning—as was the case with the A's in the sixth—momentum might be picking up a new address.

First, Oakland's Eric Byrnes missed the plate, getting blocked by Jason Varitek after racing home on a Miguel Tejada dribbler. But because the base runner's knee had been damaged from the Boston catcher's extended tree trunk of a leg, Byrnes was left grimacing in pain well beyond home plate instead of retagging his originally intended target. It would have given the A's a tie; instead it allowed for just another absurdly unique memory for The Nation.

The second sign came in the form of Rule 7.06 in the Major League Baseball thicker-than-thick rulebook. The passage stated that it is the umpire's judgment whether to award an extra base to an obstructed runner. So, Bill Welke used his best judgment. Ramon Hernandez's single to left field would tie the game, scoring Durazo, but when Tejada bumped into Mueller rounding third the ump ruled the play obstruction. The problem for Oakland was that a confused Tejada stopped running and jogged slowly home, allowing for an easy tag from Varitek. Confusing? Yes. Surprising for this Red Sox team? Hardly.

The game went on, with the lone symbol of consistency for the Sox's 2003 bullpen, thirty-seven-year-old, Texas born and bred Mike Timlin, joining Williamson in pitching four perfect innings of relief. There was to be no Kim sighting. Before the game he had given the Fenway crowd a middle-finger salute, joining a sore shoulder in sealing his farewell to the '03 season. It was to be Timlin, Williamson, and the hard-throwing Embree the rest of the way . . . however long that may be.

Thanks to Trot Nixon, the insanity wouldn't stop on the frigid, Saturday night.

Nixon was a player Boston fans had always wanted to love, and really had no reason not to. He was billed as the franchise's next great homegrown hope to man the fields of Fenway after being tabbed as the team's first-round pick in 1993. The North Carolina native could have gone to play quarterback at his state university, but chose the much more drawn out, yet potentially more financially rewarding, path to the Majors, instead.

By the time '03 came around Nixon seemed to nestle his way into the life of a Red Sox regular. He was their right fielder. But when the first day of spring training arrived, the once run-like-the-wind outfielder didn't look the part. He had gained nearly thirty pounds in the off-season—some stemming from added muscle, others from the anxiety that came with attempting to quit chewing tobacco. Hitting lefties had always been Nixon's nemesis, but that was nothing compared to looking the other way in a sea of snuff cans that was a big-league clubhouse.

By the time Nixon came to the plate in the eleventh inning of what was looming as his team's final game, he still didn't look the part of a superstar-to-be (but then again, neither did most of the Red Sox). His thick six-foot frame was hobbled by a calf injury, which had forced the lefty hitter out of the lineup for the regular season's final five games, unhinging his swing in the process. But now the pain was being numbed by a combination of the cold and the scenario—pinch-hitting in a tie game against Oakland's rookie phenom Rich Harden.

Three pitches in and the pain was completely gone, for Nixon, his teammates, and the red-and-white sea of hope-seekers around them. A ninety-eight-mile-an-hour fastball had been placed into the first row of the center field bleachers, allowing for the resuscitation of a season, and a chance for Dante and Mariano Ricciardi to finally see their dad's forbidden baseball palace—Fenway Park.

The kids were having a great time at Game 4—J.P.'s kids, Leslie Epstein's kids, and the kids calling themselves Boston big leaguers. Oakland A's ace Tim Hudson had left after just one inning because of a hip injury (later diagnosed by some of the media the remnants of a Friday night barroom brawl), leaving the game in the hands of Steve Sparks. And even though the knuckleballer was performing admirably, the Red Sox still carried a 2–1 lead heading in the sixth. With thirty-eight-year-old, soft-tossing John Burkett on the mound, the consensus throughout the stands was peppered with the thoughts of inevitability. Surely Burkett, the pitcher who had performed well enough to claim the rotation's No. 4 spot over trade deadline acquisition Jeff Suppan, could fend off the weak-hitting A's until Sparks eventually was doubled and homered into submission.

But just as Wally the Green Monster (Fenway's roving, furry, green mascot) visited Dante and Mariano in Section 18, everything changed. Burkett was wearing down, first allowing a game-tying triple to Adam Melhuse and then serving up a "please hit me" offering to Jermaine Dye. The pitch would be the pitcher's final one of the day, as Dye hit the ball about as hard as physics would allow, finding the Green Monster seats and a 4–2 advantage for Oakland. Suddenly the Ricciardi boys were the only ones having a good time.

Red Sox manager Grady Little clearly had left Burkett in too long, a notion that hadn't escaped the fans around the Ricciardi's seats, which were adjacent with Boston's on-deck batting circle. Some let their displeasure of Little's disregard for the starter's pitch-count known through internal stewing. (Head-shaking was always popular among the Red Sox fans.) Others, such as part-time season-ticket holder, and full-time horror novelist, Stephen King, chose not to let Little off the hook with nary a peep.

"You left him in there too long, you cracker!" yelled King at the top of his lungs, standing as if he was in the privacy of his own living room. He didn't care. In his profession, one of the first rules is that if you're going to kill something (such as a Red Sox season) at least do it creatively—not with the dagger of an overextended, junk-balling fourth starter.

Despite the fears of King and Boston brethren, there was still hope. Walker, the smooth-swinging Louisianan, dented the doldrums in the home half of the sixth, hitting his third home run of the series to cut the deficit to one. But it was two innings later when Ortiz sealed the home team's fate.

The bear-hugging Dominican hadn't gotten a hit in his previous sixteen at-bats, and Oakland closer Keith Foulke didn't appear to be the kind of pitcher to serve as a slump-breaker. Foulke could throw ninety miles an hour or better, but it was his seemingly similarly delivered pitches that clocked in at seventy-five that had left Boston baffled in the two A's wins. The choice was whether to sit on a high school fastball or a big leaguer heater; choosing both wasn't an option. And with the October shadows taunting each hitter with an unnerving visual path to the pitcher's mound, it looked like the chance of Ortiz bringing Manny Ramirez and Nomar Garciaparra home with two outs in the eighth were nothing more than another hollow Fenway dream.

But, for some reason, Foulke wasn't throwing his best pitch, the change-up. Epstein, like most who knew the closer, waited and waited and waited, but the previously unhittable slow stuff just never came. Finally, thanks to yet another Foulke fastball, Ortiz got his first hit of the series—a rocket of a double over the head of Dye in right field, giving Boston the lead, the momentum, and a healthy dose of euphoria, which it would carry back to Oakland for the decisive Game 5.

The Red Sox and their families boarded the Brush Hill Bus Company's vehicles as hundreds of well-wishers serenaded the entourage with chant after chant. Meanwhile, Mariano and Dante joined their family in driving back down the Mass Pike, ready for a lifetime more of trips to Boston's ball yard. The missions were accomplished—memories had been made for everyone involved.

By the time the ninth inning of Game 5 arrived, Epstein had his haircut telling the tale of playoff hope (thanks to the No. 1 attachment on Tim Wakefield's clippers) and a season of anxiousness (uncovering new gray hairs). Both Theo and his new 'do were riding out the series' finale in the Boston clubhouse.

The Boston GM had come down toward the field in the fifth inning to check on center fielder Johnny Damon, whose collision with second baseman Damian Jackson elicited a ten-minute delay and an ambulance ride off the field. Damon was in rough shape (suffering a concussion), but his team wasn't—carrying a three-run lead into the sixth with one of baseball's best, Pedro Martinez, on the mound.

The clubhouse, and the company of traveling secretary Jack McCormick and Tony Cloninger (the pitching coach who had battled from cancer to be with the team), was Epstein's safe haven. He had been standing in the runway leading from the Oakland dugout to the locker room entrance's stairs. But, as the players had learned throughout the series, that pathway was the equivalent of a holding tank for which the Oakland fans used to spray their venom. Epstein was not immune to the ritual, usually getting sprayed with the "try doing it on our payroll" line of insults.

But the narrow, green-carpeted room hardly seemed comforting as the trio witnessed the game's final moments unfold. Oakland had cut the lead to 4–3, and Williamson (Boston's final answer to the season-long closing debate) was high with everything, walking Scott Hatteberg and Jose Guillen to lead off the ninth. Little then turned to Derek Lowe, the pitcher whose early season hat-tugging and dirt-kicking had morphed into a vision of reliability. Lowe took the mound in relief in Game 1, returning three days later to start Game 3. And now, after a sacrifice bunt, he was faced with runners on second and third and just one out with the weight of a season on his shoulders. As loud as the frenzied Oakland crowd had become, an equal amount of silence enveloped the space around the Boston lockers.

Then came his pitch. It wasn't a pitch, it was his pitch—a pitch perhaps only Derek Lowe can throw. It was a sinking fastball that started right at the hip of pinch-hitter Adam Melhuse only to weave its way into the strike zone for a third strike. Two outs.

After an intentional walk to load the bases, the pitch made a second appearance, once again, making a beeline for Terrence Long's right leg before dipping out over the plate for another strike three. Three outs. Game over. Series over.

Hatteberg, the former Red Sox catcher who started his former team's ninth-inning nervousness with a walk, couldn't help but remember catching Lowe back in the day. He remembered his stuff was always filthy, but he never recalled those two pitches making an appearance. Lowe was always a four-seam fastball guy, head-shakingly afraid to burrow that sinker in on left-handed hitters. But obviously Lowe had changed, as had his pitch. And because of it Boston was heading to New York to play the Yankees in the American League Championship Series.

Damon would stay behind for a night in the hospital, but everyone else was hitting the road. Problems were few, although Epstein did have one—in the champagne-soaked clubhouse his dress shirt had been rendered unwearable. So, with the Boston owners and their wives looking at the GM with a confused eye, Theo boarded the plane toward the championship series wearing the mandatory sports jacket over a Pearl Jam Green Disease T-shirt. (Where the plane's older generation saw youthful exuberance, Epstein simply viewed necessity.)

In the end, wardrobes didn't matter. As far as the entire group was concerned, winning was the only thing that was a priority and that fit just fine.

"The gods of baseball wanted to see this happen."

—Kevin Millar

IN A SEASON OF firsts at Fenway, this was perhaps the most outrageous—the general manager of a Major League team sitting in the last row of Section 3. As distant as the memory of the Blue Jays' season had become, it couldn't have been any further away than their GM's residence for Game 5 of the ALCS.

Ricciardi didn't mind his sight line from one of the park's worst seats. A rainout two days before had resulted in a ticket snafu, and besides, his main focus was making sure his dad, two uncles, and cousin were going to have a good time. They were going to get to see the Red Sox and Yankees break their two games to two series deadlock, but SkyDome rules applied—Blue Jays gear would have to be worn.

The game wasn't much to look at, anyway. Yankees' pitcher David Wells befuddled the Boston hitters long enough for Ricciardi (and the rest of the park) to exclaim, "Here comes the Sandman. Game's over." It didn't take a baseball pedigree to understand that the sight of closer Mariano Rivera usually meant a Yankees' win, which in this case it was resulting in the Red Sox residing one loss away from elimination.

As the final outs loomed, the fans started to begin their journey up the stairs between Section 3 and 4, past the row of Blue Jays sweatshirts and hats. Every once in a while one of those dismayed patrons would turn to their left just before reaching the top step and yell, "Hey, Jay!" Ricciardi had been recognized, but not in the usual baseball general manager kind of way. While a lot of people knew of J.P., it seemed as though almost as many actually knew J.P.

First was a few of Ricciardi's former basketball players from Holy Name. (The sight of them holding legally bought beers offered J.P. his own depressing age identification.) "You'll be here in five years," one of the former players yelled. Ricciardi just smiled. They all meant well, but the folks back home still didn't get it. He was happy in Toronto.

Then came Swifty. "Jay!" This time it was Michael Swift, the brother of a former fellow coach at Holy Name. But a quick wave and a smile wasn't going to do. The jovially rotund Swifty wanted a hug. The Red Sox may have been on the verge of being one-upped by the dreaded Yankees, but, to some, the presence of Ricciardi was offering some solace. In the world of Worcester, Major League Baseball was presented in two forms—the Red Sox and J.P.

Swifty and the former hoop players were consoled by the presence of Ricciardi. And boy did they need some sort of consolation. The optimism of the day's beginning—cowboy hat ice sculptures, parades of red and white down Brookline Avenue. . . . the works—was gone. It had been a series without great games, but with superior excitement, and now the giddiness was firmly in the land of George Steinbrenner and his very expensive team.

With Game 6 and 7 slated for Yankee Stadium, the security of

Fenway was gone and so was any kind of comfort level that the Red Sox's season had built up. The lineup wasn't hitting (again), the next game's starter, soft-tossing John Burkett, would have to bridge the gap to a decisive winner-take-all affair, and even then, the usually irrefutable talent of Pedro Martinez was in question.

A Game 3 showdown between Martinez and Clemens had yielded a bench-clearing, midfield meeting that culminated in seventy-two-year-old Yankees bench coach Don Zimmer making a beeline for Pedro. In full stride (albeit, very short strides), the grandfatherly Zimmer raised his right arm to take a swing at the Boston pitcher before being side-stepped and guided to the ground by Martinez. Zimmer eventually got up, but the Red Sox never did.

The game's calling card was further enhanced in the ninth when Paul Williams, a member of Fenway's grounds crew, got into baseball's first bullpen wrestling match with Yankees reliever Jeff Nelson. The 6-foot-4 Williams emerged from the fray with bruises and cleat marks, some from a similarly disheveled Nelson, and others as a result from Yankees outfielder Karim Garcia jumping into the fray from his position in right field. The Yankees and Red Sox were never about the ordinary.

The particulars of the fight might have been a mystery game game's end, but the fallout from the evening's scoreboard totals weren't hard to decipher. The Yankees not only had won, 4–3, but had done so against a very mortal Martinez. The question would linger—even if Pedro got to Game 7, would his presence mean more than it did five days before? The Red Sox were hoping to get a chance to find out.

The homemade sign above Boston's Game 6 starter's Fenway locker read: Red Sox Rules, 1. Hit home runs; 2. Get outs; 3; Throw strikes; 4. Get all the pop flies; 5. Throw good pitches— Max Burkett. A seven-year old's wish was his father's team's command. For the first time in the playoffs, the Red Sox scored more than five runs, thanks in part to home runs by Varitek and Nixon that knifed through Yankee Stadium's twenty-five-mile-an-hour winds.

In the end, it all added up to a 9–6 Boston victory and the Bronx's first Game 7 since Lou Burdette and his Milwaukee Braves came to town and tortured the Yanks and their fans. Forty-six years later, the Red Sox were getting their turn.

"Can I have your autograph?"

—Jeremy Zoll, Yankees fan

JEREMY ZOLL was on a roll.

The thirteen-year-old from Ridgewood, New Jersey, not only had scored tickets for The Game, the twenty-sixth meeting of the season between his New York Yankees and the Boston Red Sox, but was also hauling in the autographs. He had all the Yankees, and now the signatures of Boston's Johnny Damon, Kevin Millar, and Gabe Kapler were in his possession. Then came the roadblock—Theo Epstein.

"Mr. Epstein, Mr. Epstein," said the kid, Zoll, from behind the Boston dugout. Theo turned. "Can I have your autograph?"

It was two hours before what Epstein had deemed "The Enchilada Game" (for the whole enchilada), and the GM was in a good mood. His team was hitting again, Pedro was pitching again and momentum appeared to be back in Boston's corner . . . again. There was no reason not to be optimistic.

"You're kidding me, right," Epstein answered Zoll. "I'm not going to give you an autograph with you wearing *that*." "*That*" was a sore sight for any Red Sox follower's eyes—a Yankees hat and game jersey. "I'll tell you what, take *that* off and I'll sign," Theo continued, knowing he had the thirteen-year-old in a Boston's fan's dream predicament. Even if it was for a few minutes, the kid was going to be making baseball's most commonly discussed decision—Yankees or Red Sox.

Ten months before it was Cuban pitching ace Jose Contreras who was taking sides, now it was Jeremy Zoll.

Before Epstein got out his last word, Zoll was tearing off every bit of clothing with a hint of Yankees on it. Jeremy wasn't being timed, but his haste to strip the white pinstriped shirt off his back gave the appearance of desperation. The ball was thrown down, Zoll had his autograph, and Theo had his first victory of the day. For approximately five minutes, the Red Sox had won the battle for the youth of New York. (If only Contreras was as accommodating as the kid behind the dugout.)

The smile stayed on Epstein's face well after Zoll's merged back into the crowd. (It was no surprise that the thirteen-year-old stealthily switched his allegiance back to New York in the process.) The day was already a great one for Theo, having had a chance to have lunch with his sister, Anya, while warding off occasional New Yorker verbal jabs with big grins of optimism. By the time his cell phone rang moments after the Zoll signing, Epstein was able to confidently tell the caller—the team's psychologist—that everything was under control. (He was just making the rounds.)

For Leslie Epstein, the early evening pregame preparation wasn't going quite as smoothly. He and his wife, Ilene, had been victimized by a city-stopping water main break, forcing the couple to abandon their subway car well before the Yankee Stadium stop. A stroll through the Bronx wasn't exactly the ideal method of soothing nerves before the big game, as the Epsteins found out. But with their son Paul as protection, Clemens's opening pitch was witnessed firsthand and an unforgettable night had begun.

Back in Boston, in the unassuming confines of Brookline's Holiday Inn, sat The World's Greatest Snowboarding Waiver Claim, Brandon Lyon. The former Red Sox closer (and Pirate for just more than a day) hadn't been put on Boston's playoff roster. The team had sent him to Fort Myers in an effort to stay sharp for any impending World Series action, but as the series' finale approached Lyon had returned north. He could have been any Red Sox fan in the dark hotel restaurant, and thanks in part to the identity protection of the bartender, he was.

For all involved, the scene had been set.

What the Epsteins, Lyon, and the rest of the baseball world were witnessing was what appeared to be the birth of a blowout. Nixon, perhaps the one American League hitter that read Clemens best, started the scoring with a two-run homer to right in the second. Boston added another run before the frame was out when Varitek scored on an error by Yankees' third baseman Enrique Wilson.

Wilson's presence was the product of New York manager Joe Torre's roll-of-the-dice lineup. The usually light-hitting Wilson (who inexplicably tortured Martinez) would replace Aaron Boone, the Yankees' big trade deadline pickup who had been miserably ineffective since arriving from Cincinnati. Another change was moving the struggling Jason Giambi to the seventh spot in the lineup, three spots down from his usual cleanup residence. Desperate times called for desperate measures, a notion Torre wasn't afraid to admit.

In the fourth, it was Millar who got to Clemens, depositing a fastball into the left-field stands. Nixon followed with a walk, Mueller singled, and out came Torre. The Hall of Fame-to-be pitcher whose entrance had come nineteen years earlier with Boston was now being shown the exit by the Red Sox. The Rocket was leaving a game (and maybe a season and career) with runners on first and third, nobody out, and his team losing by four runs. As far as New Yorkers were concerned, Clemens's storybook ending was in the process of being authored by the wrong team.

Nobody thought much of Mike Mussina's first Major League relief appearance. Throughout his stay in New York, Red Sox fans looked upon the introspective righty from Stanford with some disdain considering he had turned down Boston's free agent offer two years before. But by the time Torre raised his right arm to signal for Clemens's replacement, The Nation didn't care much that it was "Moose." And even when Varitek struck out and Damon grounded into a inning-ending double play, the appearance was nothing more than a road bump on the way to The Series.

The apathy regarding Mussina's accomplishment stemmed from Martinez's dominance. Pedro had shaken off the extra dose of Yankee Stadium hoots and hollers stemming from his Game 3 run-in with Zimmer. As the doubts subsided, the pitcher's velocity increased, rising up from first-inning readings of eighty-eight to his fifth-inning ninety-four-mile-an-hour dominance. Even after a Giambi solo home run in the fifth, there wasn't one Martinez naysayer among the panic-stricken hosts. Pedro was pitching like Pedro. There was a reason his agent Fernando Cuza had asked for a pile of money back on the morning of Opening Day—at times like this Martinez was worth it.

The end-of-the-world approach the Yankees felt heading into the seventh with a three-run deficit was in large part due to a premature view of the off-season. There was also, however, a strong desire to escape the shadow of uncertainty George Steinbrenner was casting on his team. Thirty years before, the Cleveland shipping magnate had become the owner of the then-seventy-year-old New York franchise. The boisterous, turtleneck-wearing seventy-three-year-old had employed eighteen managers while sitting out three years' worth of suspensions from Major League Baseball. In short, he did not take losing lightly, which was sure to be exemplified once again if there wasn't a dramatic change in the final hours of October 16.

Cashman, Torre, the coaches, and a roster full of players had all perched themselves on the edge of baseball's most structurally unsound check-signing formation—Mount Steinbrenner.

Steinbrenner's poster boy for his don't-tell-me-what-to-do spending philosophy, Giambi, was doing his part. After Martinez retired the first two batters, baseball's highest-paid No. 7 hitter found the bleachers in right-center field for the second time, cutting Boston's lead to two runs. But even that home run was tempered by the determination of the Red Sox, as Ortiz greeted another starter-turned-reliever, David Wells, with a blast over the right-field wall. The score was 5–2, and Boston had found itself six outs away from the World Series. After a Nick Johnson popup, it was five.

Martinez had thrown more than 100 pitches—usually the number that snuffed out his baseball immortality—but was still in the game. He ended the seventh by striking out Alfonso Soriano on a ninety-four-mile-an-hour high-riser and Johnson didn't look all that comfortable before issuing out No. 1 in the eighth. But the same couldn't be said for Derek Jeter.

The Yankees' shortstop, and one of the game's preeminent clutch hitters, got enough behind an inside-out swing to place a line-drive over the head of Nixon in right field. The double was subsequently followed by a Bernie Williams smash over the head of shortstop Nomar Garciaparra, plating Jeter and making it a two-run game. That was Martinez's 115th pitch, a statistic not hidden to the Red Sox bullpen, where two of October's best relievers, Mike Timlin and Alan Embree, were watching from in between warm-up tosses. Little knew it too, that's why he emerged from the dugout.

From Little's first step onto the dirt of The Stadium's playing field, the thought throughout the world (those of which who cared about such things) was that Pedro had thrown his last pitch of the night. The left-handed hitting Hideki Matsui, the Japanese import whose recent history against Martinez included doubles in Game 3 and four innings earlier, was up next and Embree seemed a natural fit for the situation.

But when Little left the mound, Martinez remained. He was leaving him in. "He is leaving him in?!" yelled the gathering at The Cask and Flagon. "He is leaving him in?!" screamed the living rooms of New England. "He is leaving him in?!" echoed through the media room in the bowels of The Stadium.

As one coach entrenched in the world of big-league baseball summed up the situation, "At the time I was thinking I might have left him in, too. But then again, I was on my third pitcher of Miller Lite." Boston was still ahead by two runs, but still its fans were drunk with anger. They had seen it all before. Bucky Dent's home run in '78. Bob Stanley jogging in from the bullpen in '86. Grady Little walking off the mound having done nothing more than give Pedro Martinez a pat on the back. It was the beginning of the end.

Martinez got two quick strikes on Matsui before the Japanese slugger unfolded his coiled batting stance, sending an inside fastball screaming down the right-field line. Now there were runners on second and third with Pedro's pitch count now at 118. Timlin and Embree remained watching from their right-field perch, but Little didn't budge. The ace was going to face Jorge Posada with the tying run at second base.

Two balls and two strikes. That was the count when Little's decision was sealed in the annals of all the reasons Boston hadn't won a World Series in eighty-five years. Posada swung as hard as he could, but the Martinez fastball had burrowed itself in on the switch-hitter's hands. Red Sox second baseman Todd Walker joined Garciaparra in sprinting back toward shallow center field, hoping somehow the pop-up would hang in the air longer than Sir Isaac Newton intended. Gravity suddenly became the enemy of the Red Sox. Posada's ball dropped, two runs scored, Little finally replaced Pedro, and Boston eventually got out of the inning carrying a tie into the ninth.

Exit momentum . . . enter The Sandman.

Mariano Rivera hadn't pitched as many as three innings in seven seasons, but that was exactly what he was going to do against Boston. Torre's initial decision to take out his star pitcher (Clemens) had paid off. Now the Yankees' manager was choosing to pull a Little and ignore pitch counts. But just like virtually every single move made by Torre on the mid-October night, the decision was the correct one. Three innings had gone up, three innings went down, and still the game remained tied at 5–5.

Back in California, Chuck Millar sat back and just shook his head. Sure, the game was unbelievable in itself. But what had struck Kevin's dad was the prediction made by the younger Millar to Chuck just before the Yankees series began—it was not only going to go seven games, but the seventh game was going to last eleven innings. Unfortunately for the Red Sox, their first baseman was right on the money.

By the time Boone—a late-innings replacement for Wilson—stepped to the plate to lead off the eleventh, the whispers were starting—maybe the Red Sox had weathered the storm. Rivera was done for the night, and Boston's pitcher, Tim Wakefield, could baffle Yankees hitters for innings to come. He had done it as a starter in Game 4 and there didn't appear to be a reason why his knuckleball couldn't do it again in the still breezy early morning hours of October 17.

But before the words of hope could exit the lips around New England—at 12:16 A.M.—Boone swung as hard as he could, interrupting a Nation's worth of sentences in the process. Time had run out on the Red Sox season. It was dead.

***

"He's a good kid."

—Bobby Mattick referring to Grady Little

LITTLE WAS A good kid. He excelled in being a good kid. And when he needed to be a bad kid he let his eyes do the talking, choosing to shoot a look through his somewhat squinted eyelids before having to accelerate his slow, southern drawl in anger. It was because of his affably down-to-earth nature that players liked playing for him and baseball people enjoyed his company. It was also why it was sometimes painful to watch the Red Sox manager trudge through the 2003 season.

The fifty-year-old had been hired by the Red Sox during the '02 spring training, walking into a standing ovation in the Boston clubhouse upon being introduced to his new team. Some of the players knew Little from his time as the team's bench coach under then-manager Jimy Williams, while team president Larry Lucchino had been familiarized with his style during a one-year stint in San Diego. And after Boston won ninety-three games in his first season as a Major League manager, the choice seemed logical enough. But uncertainty remained. One year was left on Little's two-year contract, and it was staying that way.

Despite the wins, Little wasn't blind to the contractural cliff that waited at season's end. But what could he do?

"Do you know when the last time someone was executed

using the guillotine?" came the out-of-nowhere question from Little in front of a virtually empty batting cage entourage in early July. Then came a pause, from both the questioner and those being questioned.

Little just stared off onto SkyDome's field and continued his stream of consciousness, "I'm going to be all right no matter what happens to me. I'll just go back to my farm and play in golf tournaments. I'll be perfectly happy playing golf tournaments seven days a week. That's what I'll do." The message (however off the beaten track) was clear: guillotine and golf carts meant only one thing to Little—unemployment.

A few weeks later, back at Fenway Park, Mattick, the eighty-five-year-old Blue Jays institution, was sitting in the visitors' dugout when he spied Little. Mattick was enjoying his conversation with John Ricciardi, whom had served as his golf host earlier in the day, but the sight of Grady was an opportunity too good to pass up.

There was some hesitation since Mattick had let Little go from his Single A managing job back in 1985. But at the very least Johnny Pesky, the eighty-one-year-old Red Sox coach, could act as a potential buffer. Back in the '30s Pesky had actually been the clubhouse kid for one of Mattick's first minor league teams in Portland. Even after seventy years, baseball ties are nearly impossible to break.

Mattick's fears were quickly put to rest. (It isn't Little's way to make someone uncomfortable.) "You know, you're the only person that has ever fired me," the Red Sox manager informed his Blue Jays' counterpart. Of course the surprising news came with the typical pat on the shoulder, broad smile, and gleam in the eye. The termination was a claim to fame that Mattick wasn't especially proud of, but it did stand out in the annals of baseball triviality.

Twelve days after the Red Sox's last game of the season, Little still hadn't been professionally guillotined by anyone but Mattick. But the news still wasn't good. Boston was giving its manager the hook—not firing, just not rehiring.

The Yankees' season had also been killed after dropping out of the world championship race thanks to a six-game World Series defeat at the hands of the Florida Marlins. As Red Sox managerial critic Stephen King once wrote in his book Shawshank Redemption: "Get busy living, or get busy dying."

All teams involved were ready for the birth of a new season.

"It was quite a ride."

—J.P. Ricciardi

THE GRAYNESS had taken over Boston on the morning of Ricciardi's exit out of town. The destination was New Orleans, the site of the Major League Baseball Winter Meetings, where everyone in the profession congregated to make small talk, trades, and peace of mind. Joining Ricciardi in the Delta terminal was a large contingent of the Boston brain trust. They were also leaving the cold of December 12 behind, along with the first leg of what was becoming an increasingly wild race to become king of the hill in the American League East.

Ricciardi's maneuvering revolved around the reconstruction of a pitching staff. Gone was the freckled-faced, broken-back outfielder Bobby Kielty, who headed to Oakland in exchange for lefty starting pitcher Ted Lilly. Also jumping in the Blue Jays' starting rotation were Miguel Batista and Pat Hentgen, undeniable upgrades from those who lived the life in the 2003 starting rotation.

There was also the re-signing of Dante Ricciardi's favorite player, Frank Catalanotto, and catcher Greg Myers, along with the addition of relief pitchers Kerry Lightenberg and Justin Speier. Ricciardi had even dipped into the Asian market, a place previously untouched by the current Blue Jays' regime, being let in the back door to sign eighteen-year-old Taiwan hurler Chi-Hung Cheng. Toronto's director of Far East scouting (J.P. Ricciardi) couldn't make it across the Pacific, but since Cheng just happened to be in Dunedin the same time as J.P., Tony LaCava, and Tim McCleary, it worked out just fine.

Epstein had also been busy, well beyond the uncomfortable few days that encompassed the Little decision. The memory of Nicaragua was put in the "who cares" category thanks to a Thanksgiving dinner at pitcher Curt Schilling's house.

Theo had brokered a deal that sent The World's Greatest Snowboarding Waiver Claim (Brandon Lyon), the 160-pound, ankle-breaking lefty (Casey Fossum), the starting pitcher for the Portland Sea Dogs on Disco Night (Jorge De La Rosa), and a record-setting kick returner from Jackson State (Michael Goss) to Arizona for Schilling. Now it was up to the thirty-seven-year-old epitome of power-pitching to agree to come to Boston.

Schilling had a no-trade clause that he would have to waive, and restructuring his current contract, along with getting a hard sales pitch from Epstein, was the only way such a scenario could unfold. So the night before Thanksgiving Theo called his parents and told them he wasn't going to be home for Thanksgiving dinner. There was a No. 1A starter to be reeled in.

Epstein eventually got Schilling, a new manager (Terry Francona), and even the closer who didn't want to throw David Ortiz a change-up, Keith Foulke. Of course, by the time the planes were boarded for the Big Easy, the Yankees had also upped the ante with deals for pitchers Javier Vazquez, Kevin Brown, Paul Quantrill, and Tom Gordon. Nobody said Steinbrenner was going to make it easy.

So, finally, after warding off the threat of an impending snowstorm Ricciardi joined his Boston compatriots in beginning their trip to the Winter Meetings. J.P. was happy. Roy Halladay was happy (winning the Cy Young will do that). Theo was happy. Their families were happy. Their teams were happy. They had all survived the latest in what would be a long line of "the longest season ever."

Leslie Epstein's brother was right, if there is no life there is no death. And what a life the 2003 season was.

287

EPILOGUE

"Isn't that Gretzky?"

—J.P. Ricciardi

There was a game going on at Joker Marchant Stadium in Lakeland, Florida, but few within shouting distance of the dugouts chose to make it a priority. Hockey God Wayne Gretzky was doing a poor job of blending in (jeans and Detroit Tigers baseball hat be damned), and because of it his presence had dominated everything after the fifth inning.

Whatever sport, whichever venue, when it came to the followers of the Canadian sporting world there was Gretzky and then everybody else. That much hadn't changed. It would never change. There were, however, plenty of particulars in the cloudless spring training atmosphere that reeked of unfamiliarity.

New players, new uniforms, and a new lot in life. These were the snapshots that made a brief sighting of Gretzky nothing more than a hiccup in Ricciardi's day of evaluation. The Blue Jays were moving on, and so was their general manager.

As Ricciardi sat just to the right of his team's dugout, and within earshot of the row of Toronto coaches who were executing their spring training right to watch the game from folding chairs, the foundation was feeling stronger. Two years of rebuilding were officially in the books, and the Blue Jays were walking and talking like a group ready to write a much more palatable chapter for their fans.

The days of piecing together a "hope for the best" kind of roster seemed like a distant memory. In fact, perhaps the only connection the Blue Jays' front office hung on to regarding the past was the unfulfilled promise made by its leader. Ricciardi had told his group of decision makers that he would foot the bill for a dinner at a different restaurant for each victory the Blue Jays notched from No. 81 onward. The culinary expeditions started at McDonald's and, five wins later, left J.P. saving up for one of Toronto's five-star eateries.

Fifty-million-dollar payroll or not, winning was getting expensive. But once the Blue Jays got that taste of success, an addiction for the stuff took root.

Third baseman Eric Hinske had slimmed down and was fully healed. Center fielder Vernon Wells was also appreciably lighter (twenty pounds to be exact) and appeared primed for superstar status. Roy Halladay was signed for a long time, and this time he was entering the season with legitimate running mates in newcomers Miguel Batista, Ted Lilly, and Pat Hentgen. Heck, even third base coach Brian Butterfield was more enthusiastic than ever, partly because of second baseman Orlando Hudson's maturation into the fielder Butter always thought he could become, and also due to another Super Bowl trophy for his New England Patriots. (The Pats never did lose again after that loss on baseball's final day of the regular season.)

The Blue Jays had virtually everything in place to be good, very good. Perhaps ninety wins and beyond kind of good. But just like Gretzky had drawn away the attention off the Jays' new black-and-blue playing garb during Toronto's early March game with Detroit, there were forces residing in Tampa and Fort Myers blinding the rest of baseball.

George Steinbrenner had fanned the flames with his favorite kind of kindling—dollar bills, and a lot of them.

"Manny says this is Game 8. He says if we don't win today, it's over."

—Kevin Millar

Two days before Gretzky's presence allowed for a slight ripple in the otherwise serene setting of Lakeland, the circus came to town on the outskirts of Route 41 in Fort Myers.

It was, as a *Boston Globe* columnist succinctly described, "the most anticipated meaningless sporting event in New England history." It was George's $200 million sea of pinstripes against the Red Sox. It was the memories of Aaron Boone's Game 7 home run against the Red Sox. It was Alex Rodriguez against the Red Sox. It was the New York Yankees against the Boston Red Sox in the most-watched spring training game in the history of baseball.

The Fort Myers fire marshal had turned a blind eye toward City of Palms Park for the Sunday extravaganza, which totaled an announced audience of 7,304 (314 more than the park officially held). Some of the patrons had paid as much as $500 on eBay for the right to attend a workout of meaningless proportion, while others camped out in the grassy parking lot for a shot at standing-room-only tickets. Boston's director of media relations Glenn Geffner was left having to dust off his "maybe next game" response for media members a little late on the credential request take, already allowing more press (268) to enter the tiny, two-row press box than many divisional playoff series would warrant.

This was coming to Iowa to see a baseball field cut from a cornfield. They might have had an idea why it was so important to be there, but, realistically, it was more about the afternoon's calling. As far as the baseball-following community was concerned the Major Leagues had contracted into: Yankees, Red Sox, and everybody else, and everybody else was taking a day off.

Three weeks before, the scene was slated to be entirely different. The Red Sox had seemed to expel all traces of Boone from their system, building the league's best pitching rotation with the addition of Curt Schilling, while applying the bullpen exclamation point they lacked a season ago. For the first time since caring became so in vogue at Fenway Park, Boston had become the pursued instead of the pursuers. But back came Boone.

The Yankees third baseman, who served as a constant reminder for the Red Sox front office of its three-way trade proposal that would have sent Boone to Seattle instead of burrowing him in the minds of Boston, had decided to play pick-up basketball. His knee also made a decision—that it was going to fold on a hinge it didn't have. The result was a torn anterior cruciate ligament and the Yankees' search for a new position player to the right of shortstop Derek Jeter.

Few in Boston seemed to register New York's newest positional chasm, instead focusing on the Red Sox's inability to close a deal that would have elicited a litany of designs regarding the impending World Championship rings. Alex Rodriguez, the best shortstop in the game and the previous season's Most Valuable Player, was headed to the Red Sox in exchange for Manny Ramirez. To make room, shortstop Nomar Garciaparra and the one remaining year on his contract was to be shipped to the Chicago White Sox with reliever Scott Williamson, with All-Star outfielder Magglio Ordonez taking Ramirez's spot in left.

It was done. All that was left was for the Major League Baseball Player's Union to approve the restructuring of the $179 million left on the remaining seven years of Rodriguez's contract. But feathers were ruffled—through words in the press and at the negotiating table—and the deal that would have irreversably impaled Yankees fans never came to be.

So while Red Sox fans contented themselves with the solace of knowing their team at least was attempting pennant-clinching moves, the door was swinging open for the Yankees. And, as any baseball person will tell you, when the door swings open for New York, George's checkbook isn't too far behind. In less than a week—the week leading up to the first days of the spring season—the Yanks had grabbed the title as the team to beat. Thanks to Steinbrenner's willingness to pay the piper, and deal second baseman Alfonso Soriano to the Texas Rangers, A-Rod was Boston's newest Yankee-third-baseman nemesis.

The chase was continuing, with the very unapathetic surroundings of a spring training game serving as the starting line. One of 162 was right around the corner, and so was another year in the life of the Boston Red Sox and Toronto Blue Jays.

BIBLIOGRAPHY

Baker, Geoff. "A Tale of Two Hinskes." *Toronto Star*, 20 August 2002.

Berardino, Mike. "Millar Saga Miffs Marlins." *South Florida Sun-Sentinel*, 17 February 2003.

Dvorchak, Robert. "Sauerbeck Digs His New Degree." *Pittsburgh Post-Gazette*, 6 May 2001.

Krentzman, Jackie. "The Ballplayer Next Door." *Giants Magazine*, June 1998.

Marvis, Barbara J. *Famous People of Hispanic Heritage, Volume V.* Hockessin, Del.: Mitchell Lane Publishers, 1997.

Taylor, Letta. "New York Yankees Cuban Baseball Pitcher Jose Contreras' Price of Defection." *Newsday*, 29 July 2003.

Tomase, John. "New Kid on the Block." *Lawrence (Mass.) Eagle-Tribune*, 26 November 2002.

Topkin, Marc. "Rays MVP Flourishes After His Long Journey." *St. Petersburg (Fla.) Times*, 24 March 2002.

THE AUTHOR

Rob Bradford works the Red Sox and Boston Celtics beat for the *Lowell Sun.* His baseball playing career ended after college thanks to four pulled hamstrings, three active children, two slow feet, and one mediocre throwing arm.